C0-ATQ-001

THE REAGAN PRESIDENCY

The Reagan Presidency

An Incomplete Revolution?

Edited by
Dilys M. Hill
Reader in Politics
University of Southampton

Raymond A. Moore
Professor of Government and International Relations
University of South Carolina

Phil Williams
Professor in International Security
University of Pittsburgh

St. Martin's Press   New York

0268444

~~124934~~

© Dilys M. Hill, Raymond A. Moore and Phil Williams, 1990

All rights reserved. For information, write:
Scholarly and Reference Division,
St. Martin's Press, Inc., 175 Fifth Avenue,
New York, N.Y. 10010

First published in the United States of America in 1990

Printed in Hong Kong

ISBN 0–312–03646–9

Library of Congress Cataloging-in-Publication Data
The Reagan presidency/[edited by Dilys M. Hill, Raymond A. Moore,
Phil Williams]; in association with the Centre for International
Policy Studies, University of Southampton.
p. cm.
ISBN 0–312–03646–9
1. United States—Politics and government—1981–1989. 2. United
States—Foreign relations—1981–1989. 3. Conservatism—United
States—History—20th century. 4. Reagan, Ronald. I. Hill, Dilys
M. II. Moore, Raymond A. III. Williams, Phil, 1948– .
IV. University of Southampton. Centre for International Policy
Studies.
E876.R4116 1990
973.927′092—dc20   89–36458
                                                                    CIP

Contents

0268444   v   1 24034

PART IV   THE LEGACY

Notes on the Contributors

Charles W. Dunn is Professor and Head of Department of Political Science, Clemson University, Clemson, South Carolina. He is the author/editor of eight books, including *The Future of the American Presidency* (1975) and *Constitutional Democracy in America* (1987). He is co-author with J. David Woodard of the forthcoming book *The Future of American Conservatism*.

Louis Fisher works for the Congressional Research Service, Library of Congress, and has written extensively on the separation of powers and is the author of *Constitutional Dialogues* and *Constitutional Conflicts between Congress and the President*.

Dilys M. Hill is Reader in Politics in the Department of Politics, University of Southampton. She has written extensively on urban and domestic policy in Britain and the United States and is co-editor (with Glenn Abernathy and Phil Williams) of *The Carter Years: The President and Policy Making* (1984) and editor of *Human Rights and Foreign Policy* (1989).

Joseph J. Hogan is Professor and head of the Department of Management in the Birmingham Business School, City of Birmingham Polytechnic. He has published widely on American politics and economics, has been Visiting Professor at the Roosevelt Center for Public Policy Studies, Washington, DC, and is editor of *The Reagan Years* (1987).

Raymond A. Moore is Professor of Government and International Studies, University of South Carolina, Columbia, South Carolina, and has written extensively on American foreign policy and international affairs and is co-author of *The Constitution Under Pressure: A Time For Change* (1987), *When Presidents Are Great* (1988) and *Making America Competitive: Policies For A Global Future* (1988).

Gillian Peele is Fellow and Tutor in Politics, Lady Margaret Hall, University of Oxford, and has published widely on American and British politics. She is co-author of *The Government of the UK* (2nd edition 1985) and author of *Revival and Reaction: The Right in Contemporary America* (1984).

Marcia Lynn Whicker is Professor in the Department of Public Administration, Virginia Commonwealth University, Richmond, Virginia, and has written extensively in the field of presidential studies and international affairs. She is the co-author of *The Constitution Under Pressure: A Time For Change* (1987), *When Presidents Are Great* (1988) and *Making America Competitive: Policies for a Global Future* (1988).

Phil Williams is Professor in International Security, University of Pittsburgh, and was formerly Senior Lecturer in Politics, University of Southampton. He is the author of a large body of work on defence policy and international affairs. His works include *Crisis Management* (1975), *The Senate and US Troops in Europe* (1985) and *Superpower Detente: A Reappraisal* (1988).

J. David Woodard is Associate Professor in the Department of Political Science, Clemson University, Clemson, South Carolina, and has written on the mass media, religion, urban politics and school desegregation and is the co-author of *The Burden of Busing* (1988). He is co-author with Charles W. Dunn of the forthcoming book *The Future of American Conservatism*.

Tinsley E. Yarbrough is Professor in the Department of Political Science, East Carolina University, Greenville, North Carolina, and is a leading expert on the judiciary and on civil rights. He is the editor of *The Reagan Administration and Human Rights* (1985).

Part I

Introduction

1 The Reagan Presidency: Style and Substance

Dilys M. Hill and Phil Williams

Ronald Reagan's Farewell Address to the Republican Party in August 1988 ended with the words: 'We did all that could be done. Never less'. Their importance, however, lies not just in the judgement of history on their validity, but in the fact that they echo Reagan's famous 'A Time for Choosing' television speech of 1964, given as co-chairman of Californian Citizens for Goldwater:

> You and I have a rendezvous with destiny. We can preserve for our children this, the last best hope of man on earth, or we can sentence them to take the first step into a thousand years of darkness. If we fail, at least let our children say of us, we justified our brief moment here. We did all that could be done.[1]

History may go a long way to endorse this picture of a 'can-do' presidency, although it is also likely to point to important omissions and shortcomings in the overall performance of the Reagan administration. The two-term Reagan presidency marked a significant change of direction in both the domestic and foreign policy spheres. In large part this change was grounded in Reagan's ideological stance: the strands of neoliberal and neoconservative thinking which have been labelled the 'New Right' with its stress on the minimalist state and the free market.

New right thinking influenced domestic policy primarily through supply-side 'Reaganomics' and the cutbacks in the growth of domestic expenditure which affected both the major welfare programmes of Aid for Families with Dependent Children (AFDC) and Medicaid, and federal grant aid to states and local governments. In the new right canon, the minimalist state is also the strong state: in foreign policy, Reagan's principled stance was, therefore, that of a resolute and proud nation which would reverse the dangerous weaknesses and unpreparedness of the Carter administration.

3

America would again walk tall in the world. This was a favourite Reagan theme in the presidential campaign of 1980. In part, it was an attempt to exploit the frustrations and resentments at a decade in which the United States had lost a war, in which the presidency had been discredited and in which there was a general sense of malaise and decline. The Carter administration had defined its foreign policy task in terms of coping with complexity in an interdependent world. The Reagan administration, in contrast saw the world in much simpler terms. Not only did it define the foreign policy challenge as the military threat posed by the Soviet Union and its proxies, but it also emphasised that this challenge could be overcome by actions designed to regenerate American power and purpose (see Chapter 9, Raymond A. Moore, 'The Reagan Presidency and Foreign Policy').

The context for the new approach, then, was an agenda which would overcome the malaise and decline afflicting America, both domestically and in foreign affairs. A more ideologically driven agenda, with its repudiation of the incrementalist growth of post-war policy and its associated federal bureaucratic juggernaut, was not the only factor which distinguished the Reagan presidency however. The personality and political style of the President were formidable weapons not only in winning the White House but also in sustaining the populist appeal of the administration.

THE AGENDA AND THE MAN: PRESIDENTIAL STYLE

It is a truism that a president's style is a key element in the achievements – and the shortcomings – of his administration. This is so because the American system places the incumbent in a position where his choice of key personnel and his handling of the policy system from the White House inevitably highlight his individual priorities and the way he approaches them. In James Barber's definition, 'Style is the President's habitual way of performing his three political roles: rhetoric, personal relations, and homework'.[2] Ronald Reagan's presidential style became at times the dominant element in the debate on the working of the administration: his communication skills; his relaxed approach to decision making and the emphasis on delegation; his determined optimism even in the face of setbacks; his adherence to a few key issues; his relations with his close advisers and the role which the First Lady played in these relationships. The irony is that the presidential style was simultaneously one of the main strengths and one of the major weaknesses of the Reagan administration.

Much has been written about Ronald Reagan's personality and political style and its outcomes. This has included assertions of his laziness, disengagement from daily decision making, his use of anecdotes at meetings with his advisers, and his reliance on cue cards for all meetings and engagements.[3] If Reagan was inattentive to what Joseph Nye has called the prime ministerial aspects of the Presidency, however, he exploited its monarchical potential to the full.[4] Not only did this go a long way towards restoring the prestige of an office that had been badly tarnished during the 1970s, but it also contributed to the renewed sense of faith in the United States itself. Some of the gloss was taken off by Irangate, but the general standing of the office of the presidency was higher when Reagan left the White House than when he arrived. The simple fact that Reagan served two full terms in office – and was the first president since Eisenhower to do so – added elements of stability, continuity, and predictability to American politics that transcended the particular actions and policies of the administration.

If his re-election in 1984 provided Reagan with additional opportunities to imprint his personality and style on American politics and policies, it also revealed the considerable appeal that this personality and style had for much of the American public. Indeed, there are several key aspects of Reagan's personality and style which help to explain not only the direction of the administration's policies but also the successes and failures.

The first element is the attitudes, beliefs and policy preferences that Reagan brought to the White House. Although Reagan was often dismissed, especially in Western Europe, as a figurehead who had little understanding of complex policy issues, he was also a man of deep conviction, committed to implementing certain programmes that he believed were essential to American prosperity and security. If the President's belief system revolved around some fundamental axioms rather than a high degree of intellectual sophistication it was none the less important for that. Indeed, a major key to the Reagan presidency was the evolution of his thinking and action over a long period. Initially a supporter of Franklin Roosevelt and the new Deal, Reagan's period as president of the Screen Actors' Guild saw him become a major figure in the campaign against communist subversives in the motion picture industry. Although a hard-line anti-communist stance was not incompatible with economic and social liberalism Reagan's crusade against communists in Hollywood began the political reappraisal that would lead through the proselytizing for General Electric, to the 1964 support for Goldwater and his two-term Governorship of the largest state in the Union, California.

This long political apprenticeship established Reagan's enduring commitment to certain objectives, notably reduced government and taxes, individual freedom, and vigorous anti-communist action. It also established his method of working, with its reliance on key personnel who were expected to provide the programme details of the dominant ideas which he was known to hold. As Lou Cannon put it, 'He is never dragged down by details because he is never involved in them. He is not held accountable for his personal disasters because he is disengaged from the people who work for him'.[5] To his critics this meant a president who reigned but seldom ruled or, as David Broder expressed it, 'those who work with Mr Reagan quickly come to understand how little his policy views rest on information or facts, and how much they rely on his instincts and long-cherished beliefs'.[6] The result was a White House organisation which made great efforts to highlight the president's strengths while avoiding settings, like press conferences, where his ambiguous relation to facts might be exposed (see Chapter 3, Marcia Lynn Whicker, 'Managing and Organizing the Reagan White House'). Some analysts, including the historian Garry Wills, drew attention to Reagan's projection of myths, not as a result of conscious distortions of the truth (Reagan's claim that he had filmed Nazi death camps just after the war when he had never been to Germany for example) but as believed reinforcers of moral points.[7]

The second important distinguishing mark of the Reagan style was the combination of an engaging and outward-going disposition with the skills learned from long experience of the communications world (see Chapter 6, Charles W. Dunn and J. David Woodard, 'Ideological Images for a Television Age: Ronald Reagan as Party Leader'). Consequently Reagan commanded a broad and unshakeable degree of popular affection based on his 'nice guy' image rather than on policy action or outcomes. The result was important: people 'felt good' in the Reagan years and confidence in Reagan the leader meant re-established confidence in the office of the presidency. No longer was the debate focused on the impossibility of the modern presidency, marked by popular distrust of government and riven by crises of overload, stalemate, and lobby dominance of policy. The presidency became revalued as exemplifying America's confident role in the world; even the looming shadow of the trade and budget deficits could not completely overcome the 'can do' mood set in the early Reagan years. In that sense, Reagan overcame the crisis view of the presidency which dominated much of the Nixon, Ford and Carter years, and re-established its cogency and primacy in the policy process.

Although the restoration of faith in both the presidency and the United States was a considerable achievement, it is sometimes explained simply in terms of Reagan's skills in television appearances. If Reagan was a master of what has been described as the 'rhetorical presidency', however, this was partly because of the substance of the rhetoric.[8] The President's speeches were evocative of cherished ideals that were deeply embedded in the American tradition and spirit: pride in country, in self and family, 'home-town' values and a resolute face to the world. The homespun wisdom that was often woven into his speeches by the president himself, was central to his appeal and popularity. Although Reagan was a critic of the direction of American domestic policies in the 1960s and American security policies in the 1970s, in both cases he harked back to periods in American history when circumstances were more in accord with his own thinking. In domestic politics, it was to the nineteenth century and the tough individualism that had opened up the frontier, that he looked. Indeed, Reagan's assault on big government, was fully consistent with the ideals of individualism and self-help that were central themes in American political culture. In security policy the President harked back partly to the nineteenth century when immediate threats to American security were virtually non-existent and partly to the 1950s when the United States had strategic superiority over the Soviet Union. The subliminal message of the President's Strategic Defence Initiative was that it was possible for the United States once again to enjoy the kind of security provided by the Atlantic Ocean during the nineteenth century. Short of that, SDI would at least enable it to regain the strategic superiority that had characterised the first twenty years of the nuclear age.

By identifying himself and his policies with traditions, values and circumstances that had great appeal, Reagan guaranteed the popularity of his administration. Yet there was a negative side to this. The extent to which the Reagan administration exhibited what Hofstadter in 1965 termed 'the paranoid style in American politics' cannot be ignored. From the outset the administration engaged in what one analyst has described as 'political demonology'.[9] The particular focus of attention, notably in the first administration was the Soviet Union which was deemed to be an evil empire. Indeed, in his television address justifying the US military intervention in Grenada and commenting on the attack on the marine base in Beirut, Reagan linked together these disparate events by suggesting that the problems in the Middle East and the Caribbean could be traced back to Moscow.

With Gorbachev's accession to power, the Reagan administration softened its stance on the Soviet Union. There were other targets for the hard-line rhetoric, however, including Colonel Gaddafi (who was almost certainly given an inflated importance by the administration) and President Ortega of Nicaragua. US–Nicaraguan relations during the Reagan era were characterised by mutual paranoia. In view of the disparity of power between the two nations, the paranoia in Managua was perhaps more understandable. Yet the Reagan administration continued to demand support for the Contras on the grounds that they were freedom fighters against the forces of tyranny. When congressional opposition made this difficult, less orthodox approaches were initiated, resulting, of course, in the Iran–Contra revelations. Whether or not Oliver North was acting with the knowledge of the President, he was clearly in accord with the overall philosophy of the Reagan administration.

The third important element of the Reagan style, his essentially non-confrontational stance, derives from both the limited agenda and an optimistic, can-do approach. What is important here is the influence which this avoidance of conflict had on government operation and outcomes. Reagan's relations with the political community, even when Congress became overwhelmingly dominated by the Democrats, avoided as far as possible entrenched clashes and vetos, though this was to change under the pressure of Iran–Contra affair. The Great Communicator maintained, both directly and through his chosen personnel, close contacts with leaders in Congress (see Chapter 5, Louis Fisher, 'Reagan's Relations with Congress'). This non-confrontational approach to governing stemmed primarily, of course, from the advantages of a limited agenda. The Reagan presidency was not pressing for extensive new action in the domestic sphere – budget cutting not problem solving, and legislative inertia rather than proposing new programmes, were the agenda hallmarks – so that policy battles were avoided or diffused down through the federal system.

The reduced agenda approach was reinforced by the controlled appointment of key agency personnel, chosen on grounds of personal and ideological loyalty, and the subsequent slowing down of regulatory action (for example in the sphere of environmental regulation through the much-publicised actions of the Environmental Protection Agency, or the relaxation of guidelines in the Department of Housing and Urban Development). The use of appointments to the federal bench was again a key vehicle of policy (see Chapter 4, Tinsley E. Yarbrough, 'Reagan and the Courts'). In these ways the President attempted to avoid excessive conflict with Congress and involvement with its 'iron triangles' of committees, bureaucrats and interest groups. Especially during the early years of the Reagan presidency this made the relationship between the White House and Capitol Hill somewhat less acrimonious than it had been under Reagan's predecessors. Yet the President's desire to avoid conflict had less happy results within the administration. Reagan never took charge, for example, of his national security establishment, allowing feuding between the State Department and the Department of Defence to have a debilitating effect on United States policy.

Closely related to this desire to avoid confrontation was a fourth aspect of the President's style – his pragmatism. Reagan was a pragmatic ideologue, a President who combined strong conviction with a profound realisation of the need for compromise and flexibility. Although Reagan could be doctrinaire, he also had a capacity for rationalising shifts in policy that enabled him to avoid both rigidity and the appearance of inconsistency. This was perhaps most evident in foreign policy: the change in approach towards the Soviet Union and the embracing of what was, in effect if not in name, a new *détente*, was justified as the result of the administration's emphasis on negotiating from strength. Indeed, the course of Soviet-American relations in the mid-1980s revealed very clearly that Reagan was a pragmatist: a rhetorician who preferred anecdote to analysis but who when pressed, consistently put results over ideological purity.[10] He also recognised that the rise of Gorbachev offered opportunities for new and more constructive dialogue in Soviet-American relations.

If Reagan often displayed a degree of pragmatism that surprised his critics and dismayed his hard-line supporters, he was also a visionary politician. In what he regarded as basic areas, notably supply-side economics and the development of the Strategic Defense Initiative, Reagan defended his position tenaciously and it was difficult to convince him otherwise. As Elizabeth Drew's famous *New Yorker* article put it, 'Reagan understands the importance of having a vision and stating it forcefully, and knows that this can be far more powerful than the facts. People who intrude with the facts are "doomsayers" and "handwringers" who must be ignored'.[11] This aspect of Reagan's personality was encapsulated in the comment by New York Professor of Journalism Jay Rosen that 'Reagan *believes in belief*, while even his strongest supporters feel the need to modify their views when reality closes in. The heart of the Reagan legacy resides here: in a conception of the president as a man who is in history but exempt from it'.[12]

Closely related to this was the emphasis in the Reagan administration on presentation and packaging. The president's style not only governed the scope and direction of the policy agenda but was a major element in the restoration of the presidency. Reagan used the ceremonial opportunities with skill and panache. These occasions, like all his appearances, were grounded in very careful preparation and a great deal of management by speechmakers and others – the use of the cue screen for example – to focus on the immediacy, warmth and sincerity of the president's appeal to his audience. There were, of course, well-known difficulties that arose in these presentations because of the president's deafness. There were also queries about President Reagan's age, health and at times wandering and confused performance as these were revealed in the Mondale debates in the 1984 election campaign.[13] But the overall impression of the president and the presidency which was created was of confidence, exemplified and reinforced by the relaxed skill with which he dealt with the trauma of the assassination attempt and with surgery for cancer.

The problem with this emphasis on presidential personality and packaging was that it sometimes obscured or distorted very difficult policy issues as Reagan became not only the great communicator but the great illusionist. The vision Reagan presented often hid the hard choices that had to be made as well as the cost of following the prescribed path. At its worst, it led to distortions of reality which somehow did not undermine the President's standing or prestige.

A footnote to these personal factors came with the revelation by Donald Regan in his autobiography *For The Record* that Nancy Reagan's interest in astrology influenced the president's movements and their timing, particularly the signing of the INF treaty in Washington in December 1987. It appears, however, that the obsession was a deep and continuing one of the president himself and stretched back over a forty-year period. It was also a matter of public record: the Federation of American Scientists had expressed their concern about it in the 1980 presidential campaign though Reagan at that stage denied the charge.[14]

If Reagan's personal philosophy and style as well as his idio-syncrasies had a major impact on both the direction of his policies and the overall performance of his administration, it is also important to remember that Reagan represented and embodied strands of conservative thinking which had become very important in American political life in the late 1970s.

THE POLICY AGENDA AND THE NEW RIGHT

The Reagan years are often viewed as being the era of the new right, with its emphasis on individual freedom and market forces. Accordingly a fuller analysis of the new right in the 1980s is offered by Gillian Peele in Chapter 2 ('The Agenda of the New Right'). The impact of the new right on the Reagan agenda, however, is a mixed one. The Reagan administrations have conventionally been seen as coalitions made up of Conservatives, neoconservatives and the religious new right all of whom strongly influenced the conduct of the 1980 campaign and established the general ideological tone of the presidency.[15]

This was not surprising. During the 1970s, there was an upsurge of conservative 'think tanks'. Prominent amongst these was the Heritage Foundation, established in 1973, which launched massive publication and publicity drives to influence the political agenda. The Heritage Foundation was a vigorous critic of liberalism at home and communism abroad, and provided help for like-minded supporters throughout the administration. The Heritage Foundation produced a master strategy (Mandate for Leadership I) at the beginning of the Reagan presidency which was considered to have been influential on both individuals and the Reagan programme. Its counterpart in 1984, Mandate for Leadership II, had less force.[16]

Another major conservative 'think-tank' was the Hoover Institution at the University of Stanford (whose three honorary fellows were Friedrich Von Hayek, Solzhenitsyn and Ronald Reagan). Although Hoover was originally believed to be central to new right influence and dominated Reagan's campaign advisory committees in 1980 and many of the subsequent transitional task-forces, it provided only two – admittedly influential – members of his first administration: Martin Anderson as the President's Assistant for Domestic Policy Developments, and Richard Allen as National Security Adviser. And though both were identified with the Hoover's right-wing conservative tradition, both had also been members of the Nixon Administration (admittedly part of an extreme group purged by Ehrlichman and Haldeman).

The incoming President, however, did not rely on new right advisers to the extent which had been expected and his senior appointments included prominent figures from previous administrations. What was clearly of importance, however, as Joseph J. Hogan shows (Chapter 7, 'Reaganomics and Economic Policy), was the president's commitment to supply-side economic policy as the main engine of his domestic agenda. The new right believes that economic growth depends on the interrelation of the free market and the enterprising individual. Supply-side economics takes the view that economic behaviour responds to financial incentives, generated by tax cuts and reduced government spending which returns income to the private sector. If resources are shifted to higher income groups and to industry, investment and productivity rise and the subsequent growth benefits all. This conviction underpinned the Reagan agenda. There was to be, in David Stockman's words, a clear break with past policy. The President's economic recovery plan would slow budget growth, reduce tax rates, curb monetary growth, and lighten the regulatory burden.[17] The irony was, of course, that by the end of the first term economic growth was the result of tax cuts, a consumer boom, and a rise in defence spending which observers labelled 'military Keynesianism'.

In national security the new right belief in strong defence was paramount. Although Reagan's anti-communism had deep roots, his views about the Soviet threat had been crystallised by the Committee on the Present Danger, a bipartisan group set up in 1976 to highlight the threat to American security posed by what was portrayed as the inexorable build-up of Soviet strategic forces and the failure of the Carter administration to react appropriately (see Chapter 10, Phil Williams, 'The Reagan Administration and Defence Policy'). Consequently, the administration's foreign policy and security agenda was dominated by antipathy towards *détente* and by condemnation of the policies of the administrations of the 1970s who had contributed to what was portrayed – in most respects wrongly – as a 'decade of neglect'.

The choice of this term, however, was not fortuitous. Underlying it was the belief that the American decline of the 1970s had resulted simply from a lack of will and the ineptitude of successive administrations. The corollary was that with a president in office who understood the challenge and was prepared to devote the resources to meeting it American decline could be reversed. Indeed, Reagan's foreign and defence policy was an attempt to regenerate American power and to transcend the limits of American will that had been evident since Vietnam. There were several ways in which this was to be done: through increases in defence expenditure and especially the strategic modernisation programme, through the use of force, albeit against targets of convenience, through tough rhetoric, and through the Strategic Defence Initiative. Indeed, the administration displayed a confidence and assertiveness that had not been evident in American diplomacy since the 1960s. This was even reflected in the way the Soviet challenge was defined: the concern with managing the rise of Soviet power that had been apparent in the 1970s gave way to managing the decline of Soviet power – a shift that was given credence initially by the Soviet leadership crisis and ultimately by Gorbachev's preoccupations with domestic reform.

In the event, the second Reagan administration displayed greater flexibility in its policy towards the Soviet Union than had appeared likely during the first term. This resulted from Reagan's pragmatism, from the belief that the hard-line policies had succeeded in making the Soviet Union more accommodating and restrained, and from domestic opposition (embodied both in the nuclear freeze movement and in increasing resistance to expanded defence budgets in Congress) to the hard line policies of the early 1980s. It also reflected the outcome of an internecine struggle within the administration between those who wanted to 'squeeze' the Soviet Union and those who thought it more prudent to 'deal' with Moscow through negotiations. Perhaps above all it reflected Reagan's willingness to grasp the opportunities that were opened up by Gorbachev's accession to power and the subsequent change in Soviet diplomacy.

The result was that the President who had arrived in the White House as a vitriolic critic of *détente* left office having had more summit meetings with his Soviet counterpart than any previous US president. Not only did Reagan's shift in policy bear out the prediction of Samuel Huntington that moderation in practice could prove to be the child of extremism in rhetoric, but it also earned Reagan the scorn of former supporters from the new right, who claimed that he had been duped by Gorbachev.[18]

If Reagan had his share of successes in foreign policy however – and in a direction that few would have expected at the outset – he also had failures. Two stand out. The first was the involvement in and subsequent withdrawal from Lebanon. Yet even here Reagan succeeded in limiting the divisions caused by what was always a controversial commitment of American forces. In October 1983 President Reagan avoided what might have been a traumatic division of the country caused by the death of 241 marines in a terrorist attack on their Beirut barracks and by the Grenada invasion only two days later by being, in David Broder's words, fully presidential in both the ceremonial and the substantive sense, providing national leadership of a very high order.[19] The subsequent decision to disengage US forces – presented as a redeployment to offshore positions – highlighted the administration's remarkable capacity to limit the damage to its credibility resulting from stark policy reversals.

The second and more important failure was Irangate. This cast a shadow over the last two years of the administration and highlighted the shortcomings of Reagan's detached style of leadership. There has been much speculation about the extent of the President's foreknowledge of the shipment of arms to Iran and the diversion of funds to the contras. Even if Reagan's denials were accepted, however, the disclosures undermined the image of strength and decisiveness the administration had tried to portray. The willingness to trade arms for hostages, for example, ran against a declaratory policy that had frequently been reaffirmed by Reagan and his chief advisers. Furthermore, as the Tower Commission pointed out, the NSC staff was insensitive, if not indifferent to the legal and constitutional issues involved in the dealings with both Iran and the contras.[20] And though the tone of the Commission's criticism of Reagan himself was muted, the President's managerial style was identified as a crucial source of the problems.

The Commission concluded that the basic National Security Council machinery was more than adequate but that the President

did not force his policy to undergo the most critical review of which the NSC participants and the process were capable. At no time did he insist upon accountability and performance review. Had the President chosen to drive the NSC system, the outcome could well have been different. As it was, the most powerful features of the NSC system providing comprehensive analysis, alternatives and follow-up – were not utilized.[21]

Even the circumspection of the language could not obscure the damning nature of the indictment. At the very least, Reagan was guilty of gross incompetence.

For his more severe critics, the same was true about the President's management of the economy where Reaganomics became the dominant theme. As Joseph Nye has noted, part of the problem was that Reagan spent like a Democrat on defence yet taxed like a Republican. He embarked upon the largest ever increase in American military spending while making tax reductions that gave away the revenue base to finance this increase.[22] Partly because Congress was unwilling to make the level of cuts in social programmes demanded by the President, and partly because of the need to service the debt, the Reagan administration ended up with massive increases in the budget deficit. Nor was this the only difficulty:

> the administration turned to financing its deficits through foreign borrowing, and to attract foreign funds it raised interest rates. Not only did the United States become the world's largest debtor country but also the influx of capital pushed up the value of the dollar, encouraging imports and discouraging exports. That, in turn, contributed to massive trade deficits, the erosion of the US manufacturing sector and rising domestic protectionist pressures.[23]

The influence of the new right can also be seen in the approach to welfare benefits and the debate on Workfare, though the new right's moral concerns had less success. The domestic agenda, as Dilys M. Hill shows in Chapter 8 ('Domestic Policy in an Era of "Negative" Government'), sought to withdraw the federal government from its involvement in services as these had developed from the New Deal onwards. The reduction in the growth of domestic expenditure was significant and the outcomes evident in reduced services and a widening gap between rich and poor. But major elements of the Reagan agenda were not realised. The 'New Federalism' proposals which sought to reverse federal government involvement in favour of state and local (and private) provision was effectively abandoned by the end of the first term. The pledge of the State of the Union Address of 1982 that major budget savings would be achieved by dismantling the Departments of Education and Energy was also unrealised as these Departments, and the Small Business Administration, remained in being.

Policy goals also suffered from the conflict between President Reagan and Paul Volcker, Chairman of the Federal Reserve Board, and between the administration's fiscal expansionism and Volcker's tight monetary policy, particularly in the first term. The conflict was eased in August 1987 when Volcker was not selected for a third term and Alan Greenspan, Chief Economic Advisor to President Ford, became Chairman.

President Reagan made tax reform the major domestic policy issue of his second term. The tax bill, which switched the burden of the taxation system from individuals to corporations, was carefully aimed to be 'revenue neutral', that is, to conform with the President's vehement commitment not to raise taxes. At the same time, Congress sought to attack the budget deficit by legislation forcing a balanced budget, through the Gramm–Rudman–Hollings Amendment. President Reagan, a long-term opponent of high personal tax rates, was powerfully committed to tax reform even though, it was alleged, he was ignorant of the specifics of his tax proposal and consistently misrepresented or misunderstood the effect of the reform on business.[24]

Reagan put forward his 'tax simplification' plan at the end of May 1985, but the proposal made very slow progress. In 1986 tax reform gained momentum, securing bipartisan backing, with Democrats supporting the removal of tax loopholes for the privileged and Republican supply-siders defending lower tax rates. Although Ronald Reagan did not play an active part in the two-year congressional struggle for tax reform, his support was of tremendous symbolic significance. Reagan was determined to be remembered as the President who cut the top tax rate at least in half and he was willing to remove business tax shelters and see corporate taxes rise if that would ensure the passage of tax reform.[25] The success of the tax bill in 1986 was regarded as a major refutation of charges of a lame-duck second-term presidency. The tax reform took a significant number of lower income families off the tax rolls while attacking individual and corporate tax havens.

POLICY AND PERSONNEL

In view of the revolutionary nature of at least parts of his agenda, President Reagan's strategy depended crucially on his choice of personnel. Here, three factors were crucial. First, the White House staff provided the core of direction for policy, particularly in the early years under the so-called Troika of Edwin Meese III, Counselor to the President, James Baker, Chief of Staff and Michael Deaver, Deputy Chief of Staff. Michael Deaver was closest to, and had the longest links with, both Ronald and Nancy Reagan. The Troika, often criticised for an air of mutual mistrust, in fact forced Reagan to be exposed to differing views and actions. There was also an admitted Californian network (though only Meese and Deaver had served in the Reagan Governor's office) but the main stress was on competence and ideological support. Their power over policy direction was enhanced by the President's focus on a few key items from which the details and the implementation were the responsibility of staff to pursue.

At the same time, Meese stood at the head of a Cabinet process which enabled the President to manage policy issues directly, and Meese's staff was given a key role in co-ordinating the work of the Cabinet. Baker, as Chief of Staff, conducted the 'external relations' of the White House machine, and controlled the press office. His role as a political strategist and his ties with Congress created a major success for President Reagan making him 'Mr Indispensable' according to Ken Duberstein (chief lobbyist for the White House on Capitol Hill). The other key personnel in instituting an effective White House apparatus at the start of the Reagan regime were Max Friedersdorf as head of legislative liaison and David Gergen as director of communications. The second crucial factor was that control over the policy agenda was reinforced by the use of Cabinet Councils (see below).

The third crucial factor was that the Reagan presidency was marked by the skill, from the administration's point of view, with which the Senior Executive Service (SES) of the bureaucracy was used to increase the number of appointees who did not fall within the career civil service rules. The 1978 Civil Service Reform Act allowed 10 per cent of SES to be held by non-career staff and, in any one department, the figure could rise to 25 per cent. Reagan made full use of this provision and many more Reagan appointees were made than in previous administrations, particularly in key agencies such as the Office of Management and Budget (OMB), Justice, Housing and

Urban Development (HUD) and Health and Human Services. The result was to reinforce the policy thrust of the Reagan agenda and to create what Richard Nathan has called the 'administrative Presidency', where achievements came from administrative action rather than costly and conflictful attempts to pass radical legislation through Congress.[26]

At this sub-cabinet level, both ideological loyalty and experience in government were key factors and far greater effort was exerted by the Reagan transition team to scrutinise personnel than had been evident in previous administrations. In office, the appointment of staff at lower levels was carefully controlled through the White House Office of Presidential Personnel under E. Pendleton James and later John Herrington. The stress was on personal loyalty and ideological commitment to the Reagan agenda which would prevent Departmental policy and bureaucratic inertia distorting the president's objectives. This emphasis on loyalty and ideological commitment proved an extremely successful appointment strategy.[27] It was reinforced by the use of judicial appointments to ensure the Administration's goals: by 1988 President Reagan, had appointed more than half the 744 federal judges.

Presidents come into office committed to Cabinet Government and a collegial style. In the case of Ronald Reagan this reflected his method of working in California and was also part of the strategy to ensure that Cabinet members were not deflected by bureaucratic politics and Departmental priorities. Counselor Meese was responsible for setting up a new system of Cabinet Councils which President Reagan chaired and which allowed him a hands-on surveillance of the policy process. Five Cabinet Councils, for Economic Affairs; Commerce and Trade; Human Resources; Natural Resources and Energy; Food and Agriculture, were set up in April 1981. A further two, for Legal Policy and Management and Administration, were added in January and September 1982. The Cabinet Councils worked under the general supervision of Office of Policy Development, which replaced the Domestic Policy Staff of Carter (which in turn had replaced the Domestic Council of Nixon and Ford). The Cabinet Councils, generally judged by the Administration to have fulfilled their policy purpose in the early years (though only that for Economic Affairs met with any degree of frequency), underwent substantial change in 1985 when Chief of Staff Donald Regan amalgamated them into two Councils: for Economic Affairs and Management and Administration (see Chapters 3 and 8 of this volume). The effect was judged to be a further centralisation of power within the White House.

The appointment of staff was not without its difficulties, especially in the field of foreign policy and national security. Reagan's first choice of Secretary of State, Alexander Haig, aware of the difficulties that had resulted from divided authority in foreign policy in the Carter administration wanted to be the 'vicar of foreign policy'. Yet Haig's inability to get on well with the White House staff and the lack of personal affinity between him and the President undermined this aspiration. The result was that in the foreign and defence fields the initial procedures left a great deal to be desired. Nor were the problems ever fully overcome. George Shultz, who replaced Haig, was much more of a team player and became an increasingly important influence on Reagan's own thinking, especially about East–West relations. With President Reagan having five National Security Advisers during his two terms in office, Shultz did not face a serious challenge to his authority from the White House staff. Yet, as the chapters by Ray Moore and Phil Williams point out, Shultz did have a series of clashes with Secretary of Defence Weinberger, both on East–West issues and questions relating to the use of force. Ironically, on the one issue where Shultz and Weinberger agreed – that the sale of arms to Iran was a misguided policy – their advice was ignored.

The second Reagan term saw notable problems of presidential staff management on domestic as well as foreign policy responsibilities. The first Reagan administration had displayed remarkable stability, with 13 of the 18 Cabinet rank officials serving the full term. Continuity was one of the main themes of the re-election campaign, and President Reagan subsequently asked top officials to stay on for the second term. In practice, however, there were major changes. In 1985, Meese became Attorney-General, Donald Regan and James Baker exchanged their posts of Treasury Secretary/Chief of White House Staff (a move initiated not by the president but by the two men themselves and widely attributed to the president's detached style of leadership and his reluctance to make personnel changes). There were major resignations in 1985: Michael Deaver, deputy chief-of-staff; Budget Director David Stockman; William French Smith, Attorney-General; William Clark, Interior; T. H. Bell, Education; Jeanne Kirkpatrick, United Nations Ambassador; and, over Thanksgiving weekend, Robert McFarlane, National Security Adviser. The star players were then seen to be Shultz taking the lead in foreign

policy and Regan concentrating his power over the White House staff
and acting as the key to the economic policy agenda. At Treasury,
James Baker's skills as a legislative tactician were crucial for the
proposed revision of the tax system in 1986.

But it was not long into the second term before there was a fear of
an early 'lame-duck' presidency: the Bitberg blunder, the inept
dealings with Gorbachev, the clash with Congress over funding for
the Nicaraguan Contras, the attempt to do a budget deal with the
Senate Republicans, all pointed to failing staff control. By contrast
with the first-term 'Troika' and Reagan's acknowledged dependency
on his aides – which shielded the president and restored the presidency – the new advisers lacked political instinct and sensitivity. This
was particularly noticeable in Regan's abrasive style and in his
deputy, Patrick Buchanan's (who had also taken over the Office of
Public Liaison) fervent ideological stance. These problems were
exacerbated by the more confrontational stance of the President
compared with earlier years: over Iran and the Gulf reflagging
mission, over the Iran–Contra revelations, and above all with Congress over the trade and budget deficits and the nomination of Judge
Robert H. Bork to the Supreme Court.

To some extent these difficulties were offset by the effectiveness of
James Baker at Treasury and the continued adroitness of George
Shultz's approach to the summit with the Soviet Union. Relationships
with Congress, however, remained strained, lacking the masterly
legislative liaison which had marked the early stages of the Reagan
presidency. Power appeared to move from the White House to
Capitol Hill and, within Congress, to a new set of leaders known to
be independent men. This was exacerbated when the Republicans
lost control of the Senate after the 1986 congressional elections.

The situation reached its nadir with the resignation of Donald
Regan on 28 February 1987, the day following the publication of the
Tower report, and his replacement by former Senate majority leader
Howard H. Baker Jr as Chief of Staff. The ousting of Regan followed
what was seen as a paralysing four-month crisis in the presidency
resulting from the Irangate affair and the doubts raised by the
President's increasingly rare public appearances following his prostate
operation in January 1987. The image the President had projected
had made him uniquely popular: decent, honest and reasonable. That
image now appeared to be fatally flawed as the Tower report was
published and the White House staff was in turmoil.[28] While it has
been normal for individuals to leave an administration in its final

months as officials seek lucrative private employment, the Reagan presidency took on a particularly beleaguered air with the resignations of communications director Patrick Buchanan, CIA Director William Casey and White House spokesman Larry Speakes. The problem was exacerbated by the departure of Donald Regan, given that Mrs Reagan's reported 'fury' with the Chief of Staff made his resignation inevitable.[29] The departures of Richard Perle and, some time later, of Caspar Weinberger, however, probably made it easier to develop greater coherence in foreign policy – especially towards the Soviet Union. This though was as belated as it was welcome.

An element within the working of the Reagan presidency was the role of the first Lady. Mrs Reagan was not the first president's wife to be seen to be a close part of the outward manifestation of the office. And, like all First Ladies in the modern period, she espoused a public cause, in Mrs Reagan's case drug abuse (supported by President Reagan through the Anti-Drug Abuse Act of 1986). Nancy Reagan acted as the zealous guardian of the president's strength, public schedule, and accessibility. Her closeness to certain staff members, notably Michael Deaver, was well known, as was her criticism during the second Reagan term of the disservice which staff allegedly perpetrated, culminating in the Iran–Contra affair and Donald Regan's departure from the White House.

There was also the problem of the 'sleaze factor', going back to the belated resignation in the spring of 1984 of Raymond Donovan, Secretary of Labor, charged with corruption in relation to the New York construction industry. The problem was not confined to Cabinet members. Other staff, including a deputy budget director (Joseph Wright) and the president's Assistant for Policy Development (Jack Svahn) appeared before congressional investigating committees in 1985. By late 1986 more than a hundred members of the Reagan administration had either resigned or left office under allegations of wrongdoing. President Reagan tended to dismiss allegations as unfair or unimportant, and had little regard for ethics-in-government laws governing conflict of interests of public officials.[30] Not surprisingly, therefore, the problem persisted. By the spring of 1988 White House former Deputy Chief of Staff Michael Deaver was awaiting conviction on perjury charges and Attorney-General Meese's financial affairs had been under criminal investigation for a year (Meese was subsequently cleared). There were a dozen vacancies in the top echelons of Meese's Department, many because staff believed the Attorney General's legal problems 'were undermining the work of the Justice Department'.[31] The President, through his press spokes-man Marlin Fitzwater, consistently maintained support for Attorney-General Meese. The Wedtech affair (involving defence contracts) and former press secretary Lyn Nofziger's investigation by a Special Prosecutor, added to the trauma.

The President fought to limit the damage caused by the Meese affair, aided by his own transparent honesty and sincerity which deflected much of the damage. By contrast, Larry Speakes's reve-lations in *Speaking Out* (including claims that he fabricated quota-tions for the president during his time as Press Secretary at the White House) had a hostile reception, eventually leading to Speakes's resignation from his position at stockbrokers Merrill Lynch. Never-theless, the overall impression in the last two years of the Reagan Presidency was of an administration which had lost much of its momentum and sense of direction.

THE VULNERABLE PRESIDENCY

Problems over staff, organisation and charges of corruption, although important, were overshadowed by the Iran–Contra affair. For the first time in his presidency, Reagan's own integrity was seriously questioned. But even here the damage appeared limited: his personal popularity continued, even while a *Newsweek* poll in May 1987 found that more than 60 per cent of those interviewed believed the President was lying over Irangate.[32] The Irangate crisis seemed to paralyse the President, making him despondent and withdrawn.

As discussed above, the Tower Report, while blaming the National Security Council staff for acting without adequate legal authority, did not absolve the President from responsibility. Yet perhaps the harshest criticisms in the report were reserved for Donald Regan. 'More than almost any Chief of Staff in recent memory, he asserted control over the White House staff and sought to extend this control to the National Security Adviser. He was personally active in national security affairs, and attended almost all the relevant meetings regard-ing the Iran initiative'.[33] While this indictment is both accurate and justified, there was a sense in which Regan became the sacrificial lamb to save the administration. Yet President Reagan, while conceding that mistakes had been made, continued to allege that the Iran–Contra affair had been misunderstood, that no hostage deals were intended, that private individuals, not the Iranian government, were involved. He referred to Lt. Col North as a 'hero' and did not condemn North's or Poindexter's actions. The result, however, was a serious decline in both the President's personal credibility and the effectiveness of the administration in dealing with domestic opposition.

If the administration in early 1987 appeared to be in unprecedented disarray, it was able to survive partly because of the success of Howard Baker as the new Chief of Staff. If foreign policy had brought the Reagan administration close to the point of collapse, however, foreign policy was also to be its saviour. The Irangate hearings, the endless stream of resignations, the indictments, were pushed off the air and on to the back pages by the prospect of an arms control agreement and the 'Thanksgiving Summit'. With Gorbachev's visit to Washington in late 1987 and the signing of the INF Treaty Reagan had a major arms control achievement that went at least some way to restoring the administration's rather tattered image (see Chapters 9 and 10).

Even so the period from mid-1986 was clearly not a happy one for the administration. The President's prestige was damaged not only by Irangate, but also by the Senate's rejection of Reagan's nomination of Robert H. Bork to the Supreme Court, by the Wall Street crash of October 1987, and by the continued and mounting budget and trade deficits. By mid-1988 the Reagan presidency appeared to be a caretaker one, focusing on Reagan's peacemaker role while keeping alive the image of an expanding economy. How it had reached this point, its achievements and its deficiencies, are dicussed more fully in the following chapters which consider in some detail both procedural and substantive aspects of the Reagan presidency.

Notes

1. P. Jenkins, 'Last line of the Ronald Reagan Story', *The Independent*, 17 August 1988.
2. J. D. Barber, *The Presidential Character*, 2nd edition, (Englewood Cliffs, New Jersey: Prentice-Hall, 1977) p. 7.
3. J. Mayer and D. McManus, *Landslide* (London: Collins, 1988).
4. J. Nye, 'Understating US Strength', *Foreign Policy* No. 62, Fall 1988, pp. 105–129 at p. 109.
5. L. Cannon, 'Underrating the Gipper is a Mistake', *International Herald Tribune*, 24 January 1985.

6. D. S. Broder, 'The Insulated Presidency: Why is Reagan Shielded?', *International Herald Tribune*, 15 October 1984.
7. G. Wills, *Reagan's America: Innocents at Home* (London: Heinemann, 1988).
8. See J. K. Tulis, *The Rhetorical Presidency* (Princeton, New Jersey: Princeton University Press, 1987) for a sophisticated and original treatment of the evolution of the presidency in relation to rhetoric.
9. M. Rogin, *Ronald Reagan, the Movie and other Episodes in Political Demonology* (London: University of California Press, 1987).
10. F. I. Greenstein (ed.), *The Reagan Presidency: An Early Assessment* (Baltimore, Maryland: Johns Hopkins University Press, 1983) pp. 11–14.
11. E. Drew, 'A Political Journal', *New Yorker*, 20 February 1984, p. 132.
12. J. Rosen, 'The sleep of reason', *New Statesman and Society*, 24 September 1988, p. 25.
13. J. Reston, 'In Fairness, Age Really is an Issue', *International Herald Tribune*, 15 October 1984.
14. D. Campbell, 'Reagan's secret computer', *New Statesman and Society*, 14 October 1988, p. 14.
15. A. J. Reichley, 'The Reagan Coalition', *The Brookings Review*, Winter 1982, pp. 6–9.
16. M. Shapiro, 'Heritage Panels' Ideas May have Less Impact in Reagan's New Term', *International Herald Tribune*, 22 November 1984.
17. Statement of David A. Stockman, Director, Office of Management and Budget, before the Senate Appropriations Committee, 23 January 1981, pp. 3–4.
18. S. P. Huntington, 'Renewed Hostility' in J. Nye (ed.), *The Making of America's Soviet Policy* (New Haven: Yale University Press, 1984), p. 289.
19. D. S. Broder, 'Reagan's Proud Image: It Isn't Quite Enough', *International Herald Tribune*, 3–4 November 1984.
20. *The Tower Commission Report* (New York: Bantam and Times Books, 1987), p. 78.
21. Ibid., pp. 79–80.
22. Nye, 'Understating US Strength', pp. 111–13.
23. Ibid., p. 113.
24. A. R. Hunt, 'Introduction', in J. H. Birnbaum and A. S. Murray, *Showdown at Gucci Gulch: Lawmakers, Lobbyists, and the Unlikely-Triumph of Tax Reform* (New York: Random House, 1987) p. xiv.
25. J. H. Birnbaum and A. S. Murray, ibid., p. 286.
26. R. P. Nathan, *The Administrative Presidency* (New York: Wiley, 1983).
27. L. Lynn, Jr., 'The Reagan Administration and the Renitent Bureaucracy', in L. M. Salamon and M. S. Lund (eds), *The Reagan Presidency and the Governing of America* (Washington DC: Urban Institute Press, 1984).
28. H. Johnson, 'Future of Reagan Presidency in Doubt', *Washington Post*, 1 March 1987.

29. B. Weinraub, 'Regan Days Were Numbered After Clash With First Lady', *New York Times*, 1 March 1987.
30. Mayer and McManus, *Landslide*, pp. 249–50.
31. P. Shenon, 'Meese Choice for No. 2 Post Withdraws', *New York Times*, 21 April 1988.
32. A. Brummer, 'A tide of greed that laps the White House doorstep', *Guardian*, 6 May 1987.
33. *The Tower Commission Report* (New York: Bantam and Times Books, 1987) p. 81.

0268444

Part II

Aspirations and Constraints

2 The Agenda of the New Right

Gillian Peele

THE NEW RIGHT AGENDA

One of the most distinctive features of the Reagan presidency was its ideological character. In contrast to the majority of American administrations, the Reagan years were associated with a self-conscious and organised political movement which remained active and vocal, even though its influence waned over the course of the 1980s. What made the phenomenon all the more remarkable was that the movement was a conservative one which rejected many of the assumptions of the liberalism which had dominated American political philosophy since the Second World War.[1]

It is important, however, not to exaggerate the role of the conservative movement in shaping the Reagan administration's policies. Although the ideological impulses behind the presidency were strong, the conservative movement itself was not monolithic. The movement was very much a broad church and each part of it had its own agenda and priorities. Furthermore, the American policy-making process is highly fragmented so that in addition to the disagreements about the details of foreign or economic policy the multiplication of actors in the policy process added a degree of complexity to the discussion of proposals.

As the administration wore on, the initial clarity of tone therefore became modified by pragmatism – especially in the field of arms control – and the executive experienced the customary need to bargain and accommodate its opponents to secure any policy agreements. The loss of the Senate by the Republicans in 1986 together with the effect of the Iran–Contra scandal stymied the executive even more than would have been the norm in the last two years of a presidency.

In addition to the familiar loss of direction which even the Reagan administration suffered towards the end of its period of office, there was early opposition to some aspects of its agenda from the Congress and more significantly from the courts. In the 'new federalism' proposals which formed part of the Reagan economic strategy there was substantial opposition from the states. Thus in a number of areas where the Reagan administration would have liked to see major changes the lead given within the administration was blocked by legislative or judicial action. This was especially true of those issues designated 'social' or 'family' issues by the right. Even the major initiatives of the administration in the field of budgetary control and taxation and the realm of federal relations encountered successful opposition from Congress and the states.

However, it is important to remember in trying to assess the Reagan years that there *was* a conservative agenda; and even if it was only partially implemented, it set the tone for much public policy debate. And a review of its fate underlines the difficulty within the political system of the United States of translating any clear and coherent set of ideas into policy.

THE CONSERVATIVE COALITION

The coalitional and loose nature of the conservative movement was an important factor in shaping the conservative agenda. Different elements of the coalition had different priorities and even within the various streams of the movement one could find divergences of emphasis. Thus the 'neoconservatives' who gave important intellectual leadership and legitimacy to the conservative movement frequently differed among themselves over domestic policy issues, although it is arguably in the field of foreign policy that their influence was most important.[2] Some interest groups which operated within the framework of the broader conservative movement – for example Paul Weyrich's Committee for the Survival of a Free Congress or Jerry Falwell's Moral Majority (which was renamed the Liberty Foundation in 1986) – themselves had a broad range of issues on their agenda. Other groups with conservative sympathies might be more concerned with single issues such as gun control or abortion. The think-tanks and institutes which were an important part of the conservative policy network themselves had different specialisms as well as varying levels of resources and expertise.

It is not necessary here to present an elaborate typology of the conservative movement. The interaction of the neoconservatives, business groups, economic conservatives, new right entrepreneurs and the religious right has been discussed in a number of places and the literature will doubtless expand further.[3] What should be under-lined however is the extent to which three themes dominated conservative concerns at the advent of the Reagan era. These themes were the role of America in the world, the character of the economy, and social policy – a theme which covered both a range of problems relating to welfare policy and the so-called 'social' or 'family' issues which were perhaps the distinctive feature of the new right's agenda.

THE INTERNATIONAL ARENA

The first issue of major importance to conservatives was the global position of the United States and the spread of communism. Here the neoconservatives – scholars and publicists such as Irving Kristol, Norman Podhoretz, Charles Krauthammer, Jeanne Kirkpatrick and Daniel Patrick Moynihan – had voiced major criticisms of the direc-tion of American foreign policy during the Carter years. Conserva-tive analysis of the American security situation saw the 1970s as a decade in which the United States had not merely lost its will to lead the West in the fight against communism but had also been overtaken by the Soviet Union in the battle for strategic superiority. In addition the 1970s had seen the growth of Soviet adventurism in Africa and the formation of regimes hostile to vital American interests in the Middle East and Latin America. The conservative remedy for this decline involved at the minimum a hard-nosed assessment of the character of international conflict, a willingness to spend additional money on defence and a readiness to intervene with force if necessary when communist expansion threatened American interests anywhere in the world.

Common to these critiques was a belief that the Soviet Union was an expansionist power and that communism was an aggressive ideology. It has been pointed out that the 'neoconservatives' were in many ways reflecting their own domestic roots in the Democratic party by urging on Reagan a new version of the Truman doctrine.[4] But whatever the truth of that assertion it is clear that for the 'neoconservatives' there was no question of drawing a distinction between vital and peripheral American interests or seeing foreign policy in wholly pragmatic terms. Foreign policy was about a world in which American values could prosper and inevitably had an ideolo-gical dimension.

It should be emphasised that in terms of foreign policy debates the conservative agenda was highly influential. Not merely were the arguments of the 'neoconservatives' adopted in large part by the Reagan administration but key figures associated with the movement either became important members of the new administration or were regularly consulted by it. Thus Jeanne Kirkpatrick, a political science professor who had done much to expose what she saw as the hypocrisies of the Carter administration on human rights and to sharpen Republican awareness of the extent to which international organisations had become hostile to the United States, was made Ambassador to the UN.[5] Richard Allen, who had been a prominent member of the Committee on the Present Danger – a high profile pressure group dedicated to exposing America's strategic weakness *vis-à-vis* the Soviet Union – became Reagan's National Security Adviser. Elliot Abrams became Assistant Secretary of State for Latin American Affairs and Richard Perle was made Assistant Secretary of Defence – a post in which he would have major influence over the progress of arms control.

This initial infusion of conservative ideas – and personnel – into the Reagan administration had two consequences for the conduct of foreign policy. First it had a decisive impact on the rhetoric of the new administration and of the President. Even if the language of 'evil empires' is discounted as specially tailored for domestic consumption, there was a stark contrast with the language of the Carter years with its elevation of concerns about human rights.

Secondly it had – as it was designed to have – a reinvigorating effect both upon the morale of the United States itself and upon the Nato alliance. Much had been made of the humiliations heaped upon the United States around the globe in the late 1970s culminating in the Iran hostages tragedy. There was clearly a demand for strong leadership in the international arena. Within the Western alliance also, President Reagan, in combination with an ideologically sympathetic British premier, was able to provide firm direction in the matter of upgrading nuclear weapons and defence budgets to meet the threat of Soviet developments.

The problem for the Reagan administration was that the strategies that counted as realistic in terms of the 'neoconservatives' ' perception of the world were not realistic either in terms of the complexities of the international situation or the constraints of the domestic political arena. In terms of the international arena, while it was true that America could not ignore the emergence of unfriendly regimes such as Nicaragua in Latin America, it was equally clear that many of the methods of influence which America had at its disposal would be counter-productive if the aim was to establish a set of stable, democratic regimes friendly to the United States.

As far as domestic constraints were concerned, the Reagan administration had to confront the paradox that Americans wanted a strong and reassertive United States only if it was cost-free in terms of military personnel and money.

The tangible symbol of change in the international environment was for the conservatives a massive increase in the defence budget. This had been the goal of the neoconservatives in the late 1970s and the primary aim of the major pressure group the Committee on the Present Danger. Norman Podhoretz, the editor of the New York based magazine *Commentary* published a number of attacks on American defence policy including one work *The Present Danger* which was endorsed by Reagan himself.[6] International events – especially the Soviet invasion of Afghanistan in 1979 – had seemed to prove at least some of the conservatives' arguments about the nature of Russian intentions to have merit. President Carter's last budget had already acknowledged the need for additional defence spending but the charge that the Democratic administration was endangering American national security was too useful politically to let pass. Reagan's campaign commitments in 1980 made it highly likely that there would be major defence increases if he took office and that these would be more dramatic than those envisaged in the military build-up which Carter had projected.

What in fact occurred was that there was a massive defence build-up over the next five years, which then slowed slightly in the face of Congressional opposition and deficit constraints. In current dollars, expenditure on defence climbed from $116.3 billion in 1979 to $209.9 in 1983 and to $273.4 in 1986.[7] Defence as a percentage of GNP rose from 4.8 in 1979 to 6.3 per cent in 1986. (Figures 2.1–2.3 present an overview of the rise in US defence spending in current terms and real terms.) Of course, as one authority on the budgetary process has pointed out, this trend has to be set against the background of the years from the late 1950s to the late 1970s when the proportion of GNP devoted to defence declined from roughly 10 to 5 per cent.[8] However if the measure of commitment to an assertive role in the world is America's defence budget this item on the conservative agenda was certainly not neglected.

Critics of this level of defence spending over the years of the

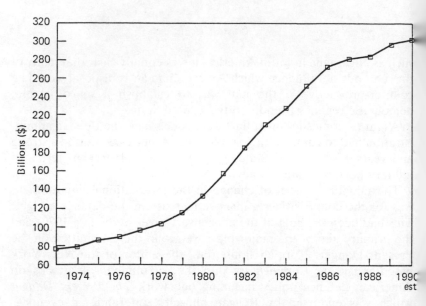

Source: H. W. Stanley and R. Riemi (eds) *Vital Statistics on American Politics* (Washington, DC: Congressional Quarterly Press, 1988).

Figure 2.1   US defence spending (in current dollars)

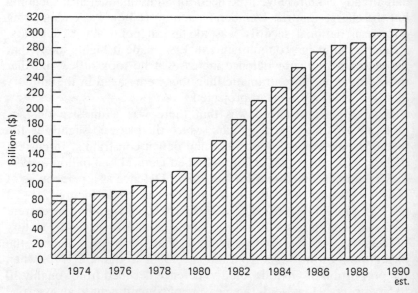

Source: H. W. Stanley and R. Riemi (eds) *Vital Statistics on American Politics* (Washington, DC: Congressional Quarterly Press, 1988).

Figure 2.2   US defence spending (in current dollars)

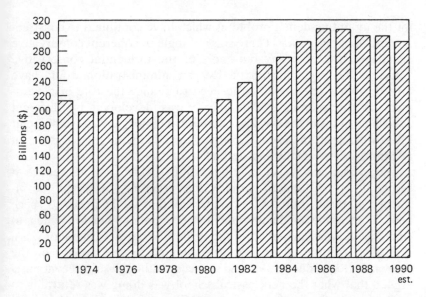

Sources: US Bureau of Labor Statistics, *Consumer Price Index* (see *Statistical Abstract of the United States*, GPO; and *Monthly Labor Review*, Bureau of Labor Statistics).

Figure 2.3   US defence spending (in 1989 dollars)

Reagan administration have pointed to the extent to which its spread caused 'chaos' in the Pentagon and neglected the need to ensure that military commitments were backed by economic strength.[9] This level of defence increase was difficult to sustain politically and it is hardly surprising that defence should now be the subject of close budgetary scrutiny both within the Congress and within the administration. However, it is perhaps arguable that the initial conservative push for major defence increases – which amounted in real terms to a 50 per cent increase allowing for inflation over the first five years of the Reagan administration – enabled a major modernisation of weapons systems and a renewed feeling of strength from which to bargain with the Soviets even if along the way the rapid increases caused political and practical difficulties.

THE CONSERVATIVE ECONOMIC AGENDA

Certainly the major rise in defence spending coupled with massive tax cuts and later failures to increase taxes were in large part responsible for the mounting deficit problems which have continued to constrain American public policy. There was no single or coherent conservative agenda on the economy but most of the influential conservative voices at the beginning of the Reagan administration would have united around one theme – the need to reduce the role of government in the economy. This theme was developed by different advocates in different ways but here it is helpful perhaps to pinpoint the key elements in the conservatives' agenda on the related issues of taxation, spending cuts and deregulation.

The conservative agenda on taxation – which was to reduce it across the board and to simplify the structure – reflected the influence of the so-called supply-side economists. There is no space here to examine in detail the 'new economics' which seemed to challenge Keynesian models in the 1970s.[10] What was called for was a shift away from levels of aggregate demand to an emphasis on the propensity to produce goods and services. Although some economists argued that what the neoclassical school was doing was returning to basics rather than setting out into hitherto uncharted intellectual territory, this theory seemed radical for two reasons. First, it rested on assumptions about the impact of changes in tax rates on personal behaviour which were difficult to test. Secondly, the theory ran counter to egalitarian assumptions about what a tax system should do at two different levels. By highlighting the deleterious effects of taxation on the efficiency of the economy, supply-side economics subtly shifted the bias against new expenditures generally and against the heavy costs of welfare programmes in particular. And by focusing on the relationship between the tax rate and economic activity, it shifted the argument away from concerns of taxation equity.

The major figures in developing supply-side ideas on the economy in the 1970s were Milton Friedman and Arthur Laffer, both of whom contributed not merely to an intellectual debate about the relationship between high levels of taxation and incentive but also to a popular revulsion against high taxation. Laffer in particular argued that tax cuts would be self-financing.[11]

More general political arguments – linking neoclassical economics to the survival of capitalism and liberty – were put forward by George Gilder and Jude Wanniski and had an extensive impact on public opinion.[12] Devotees (or apparent devotees) of supply-side economics were taken into the administration notably at Treasury and at the Office of Management and Budget where former Congressman David Stockman became the keeper of the administration's financial conscience.[13] In Congress Jack Kemp and Senator William Roth introduced what was in many ways the most symbolic piece of Reaganite legislation – the Economic Recovery Tax Act of 1981.

The Economic Recovery Tax Act was dramatic in design and dramatic in effect. It reduced the highest tax rate to 50 per cent and implemented an across-the-board reduction of tax rates by 25 per cent. The effect of inflation on changing the tax brackets into which individuals fell (bracket-creep) was tackled by the introduction of inflation-indexed tax brackets. In addition to these major changes in income tax, there were reductions in capital gains taxes (from 28 to 20 per cent), in estate and gift taxes and an increase in the opportunity to set capital costs against tax.

From the perspective of supporters of tax reduction much of the beneficial influence of these tax reductions was undermined by subsequent increases in such taxes as the payroll-tax as well as by the delayed phasing in of the new tax brackets. From the perspective of opponents of these tax reductions, the inequitable spread of benefits and the contribution towards the mounting deficit were serious flaws in the Reagan administration's approach.

The Kemp–Roth tax reduction was in a sense the high water mark of achievement in the conservative economic agenda. After 1981–82 the conservative coalition in Congress began to disintegrate and the President's control of the budgetary process weakened. Although the second term of the Reagan presidency saw a major simplification of the tax structure with the Tax Reform Act 1986 the conservative initiative on tax reduction had by then fallen far behind concern about the size of the deficit and the adequacy of such remedies as the Gramm–Rudman–Hollings bill to control it.

The conservative agenda on the economy included a number of important issues apart from tax reduction. Many of these issues (for example on international trade or on anti-trust policy) had been considered in detail by the free-market oriented think-tanks which had become so influential over the 1970s. Apart from the influential American Enterprise Institute, there was the Heritage Foundation (which published a set of highly detailed policy prescriptions for the administration under the title *Mandate for Leadership*), the Cato Institute and the Institute of Contemporary Studies.[14] But two general questions ran through all the discussions of economic policy in conservative circles. The first related to the level of public expenditure on domestic programmes especially welfare. The second concerned the extent to which the regulation of various areas of industrial activity – airlines, food and drugs, banking and communications for example – could be removed in order to reduce the bureaucratic restrictions on important sectors of the economy and encourage competition.

The two questions were clearly linked in that conservative thinking in America (as in Britain) had come to view the extension of government activity as economically inefficient and politically dangerous. Many of the adherents of the public choice school saw government bureaucracy as a flawed instrument of policy-making because its primary goal would be to protect its own interests rather than to promote any 'rational' policy objective.[15] Moreover many on the right argued that government agencies were unresponsive to consumer choice (unlike the market where the consumer was king) and the incremental accumulation of power by federal government had a distorting effect on the constitutional system.

In the process of dismantling the Leviathan which the United States had created in the twentieth century many observers focussed on welfare programmes as an area which should be cut.[16] Not merely were these programmes costly but they also in the eyes of a number of writers created undesirable effects upon those who received them. Welfare recipients effectively became dependent on the subsidies and programmes administered by government in a way which was itself disabling and demoralising.[17] It was far better in the eyes of these theorists that the poor (including the female heads of families who constituted a major sector of the poor) should work for their livelihood even if the remuneration was low.

The hostility of conservatives towards welfare programmes meshed nicely with the conservative concern to control public expenditure. David Stockman during the 1980 transition period co-authored (with Jack Kemp) a memorandum which emphasised the importance of cuts in domestic programmes as a complement to tax cuts. Without major spending reductions there would be an 'economic Dunkirk'. Indeed it seems that one reason for Stockman's support of the radical tax cutting measures demanded by the supply-siders was the pressure which such cuts would put on domestic expenditure.[18]

The problem with cutting domestic programmes was two-fold. First a very substantial portion of that expenditure fell into the 'uncontrollable' category. Secondly there was likely to be resistance to programme cuts within Congress as programmes dear to the hearts of special interests and constituencies came under review.

The major initial effort to prune domestic expenditure was contained in the first Reagan budget presented to Congress in March 1981. This budget was in effect the new administration's alternative to Carter's budget for the fiscal year 1982 and involved cuts in about 300 programmes. While useful from the perspective of those who wanted to reduce the level of spending, they were not so much real cuts as slow-downs in the rate of growth of many programmes. The fact that defence and social security were effectively 'off limits' for cuts meant that this operation was inevitably unequal to the task of balancing the major tax cuts proposed by the administration. Yet for all its inadequacies this first Reagan budget was a radical one and unusually it was able to withstand Congressional scrutiny. However, thereafter the administration's ability to control Congress weakened and its attempts to reduce domestic expenditure were severely limited.

Surveying the efforts of the economic conservatives to secure public expenditure reductions over the course of the Reagan presidency it is difficult to avoid the conclusion that the budget machinery – both inside the administration and in Congress – compounds the problem of controlling public expenditure in a system where such a large proportion of expenditure is taken by entitlement programmes which operate fairly rigid formulae to determine how much federal government is obligated to pay. In addition some inside observers of the economic policy-making process have suggested that not merely were there few consistent fiscal conservatives within the Reagan administration but that failure to reconcile different priorities in economic policies led to the fatal error of separating the tax cutting measure and the spending cuts.[19] Tax cuts should have been made dependent on spending cuts to avoid exacerbating the deficit.

If the conservative agenda on spending cuts was doomed to failure the same could not be said of the conservative strategy with regard to regulation. Deregulation was a central component of the Reagan economic strategy from the beginning following major pressure from groups such as the American Enterprise Institute and Heritage. Vice-President George Bush was put in charge of the task-force to cope with deregulation; when this Task Force on Regulatory Relief disbanded in 1983 its report concluded that its efforts had led to a one-off saving of between $15 and 17 billion and to annual savings of between $13 and $14 billion – findings which were highly controversial. In reality deregulation did not begin with the Reagan administration and although eagerly espoused by the conservatives they had no monopoly on the movement. Despite the push from both conservative ideological groups and from business interests anxious to be free from bureaucratic rules, by the beginning of the Bush administration there was a substantial demand for re-regulation especially in areas such as occupational safety and environmental protection. The issue of environmental protection resurfaced particularly strongly at the end of the Reagan presidency and it was noticeable that Bush's choice as Director of the Environmental Protection Agency (Reilly) was closely associated with conservationist groups. In the area of banking also it was noticeable that the movement to free the banks from regulatory controls (and especially the movement to repeal the Glass–Steagall Act) was weakened by the experience of the crash of October 1987.

THE SOCIAL ISSUES

A third major theme of the conservative movement was the concern to reverse tendencies which were seen as permissive and to recreate support for traditional, often religiously-based, morality. The prominence of this third concern gave the conservative movement of 1970s and 1980s a crusading quality and distinguished it from the conventional Republican Party. In part the priority accorded to social, moral or family issues may have reflected a shrewd awareness of the kinds of themes which would find an echo in American public opinion and might shift votes and money behind conservative causes and candidates. In part though these concerns represented two highly significant developments: the growth and political mobilisation of conservative Christians and the more general reaction against the cultural liberalism of the 1960s.[20]

The particular issues which dominated the conservative social agenda were abortion and school prayer but there was also concern about homosexual rights, women's liberation, pornography and the need for censorship in schools and public libraries, and sex education. Bussing and affirmative action were also deeply opposed by the conservative movement which sought to reverse the general stance on civil rights taken by the federal government from 1960 onwards.

One important aspect of the prominence of the conservative social agenda was the extent to which it brought conservatives into conflict with the courts. The Supreme Court had been the source of many of the policy initiatives which the right disliked – from school integration as mandated by *Brown* v. *Board of Education of Topeka* in 1954 to the legalisation of abortion in 1973 by the decision in *Roe* v. *Wade*. For many on the right the assumption of what was seen as an extensive policy-making agenda over the post-war period was a usurpation of power and a distortion of the proper role of the judiciary. Conservatives argued that the Reagan administration should seek to reverse the trends of the previous thirty years by paying special attention to judicial appointments and selecting for all federal judicial slots (but especially the Supreme Court) only judges who subscribed to the philosophy of judicial restraint. Sometimes conservative theorists went further and argued for a litmus test either on the basis of adherence to a particular theory of constitutional interpretation (the theory of original intent which argued that judges ought to base their interpretation of the constitution on what the clause meant when it was enacted) or on a single issue (usually abortion).[21]

The priority accorded to judicial issues on the conservatives' agenda was underlined by the existence of specialists in judicial politics in a number of the conservative think-tanks and by the growth of right of centre law foundations anxious to pursue issues of interest to the conservative movement in the courts.[22] The major law schools also (especially Chicago which was the centre of the influential movement which rooted its jurisprudence in economic analysis) had produced a range of conservative scholars with their own legal agendas. Together these developments ensured that there was a ready cadre of recruits both for the various levels of the judiciary and for the sensitive political positions within the Department of Justice.

The injection of a strong conservative political character into questions of judicial administration was not problem free, however. Within the Department of Justice there were clashes as career appointees attempted to resist partisan interpretations of the law and to continue policies which the officials thought reflected Congressional intent.[23] Civil rights activists became angry as the Reagan administration seemed to drag its feet on enforcing a wide range of laws designed to reduce the degree of discrimination in American life. And the courts – including the Supreme Court – rebuffed the administration when it tried to alter its policies in the middle of a suit as it did in the case of the attempt by Bob Jones University to challenge an Internal Revenue Service ruling that certain fundamentalist colleges could not have charitable status because their admissions policies and practices discriminated against negroes.[24]

Conservatives for their part thought the effort to alter the composition of the courts and to give effect to a different view of civil rights was perfectly proper. They believed the Reagan administration had been elected with a mandate in 1980 to reverse many of the civil rights policies inherited from previous administrations. Enforcement policy should reflect the popular will which was hostile to affirmative action and hostile to such remedies as bussing to achieve desegre gation.

The struggle over civil rights policy and the conduct of the judiciary took a number of twists and turns during the Reagan administration. An early indication of the seriousness with which Congress viewed the conservative agenda on civil rights was the refusal to confirm William Bradford Reynolds as Associate Attorney-General.[25] Reynolds had been the Assistant Attorney-General in charge of the Civil Rights Division of the Department of Justice and, although he had no previous experience in the field, he rapidly became a zealous advocate of a highly conservative approach to civil rights issues. The controversy over the nomination of Robert Bork to the Supreme Court further indicated the widespread concern in Congress at the extent to which the American judicial system had indeed become the object of a carefully planned conservative strategy. Bork, if confirmed, would have tipped the balance on the Court in a conservative direction and once this was realised the normal expectation that presidents' nominees to the Court will be confirmed was no longer operative. The Senate rejected Bork's nomination in 1987 in a move which many saw as further politicising the process of judicial appointments.[26]

On the particular issues which were of most concern to the conservative movement there were few victories but a good deal of rhetoric. Abortion was by far the most important of the social issues on the conservative agenda.[27] The Right to Life movement – though itself by no means monolithic – was an influential part of the various coalitions put together within the general framework of the conservative movement. But the Supreme Court, although it narrowed the margin of support for *Roe* v. *Wade*, refused to overturn it and the availability of abortion remained a constitutional right though not one to be funded by taxpayers.

Efforts to introduce constitutional amendments to restrict abortion died in the Senate as did numerous efforts to secure restrictions on the federal courts' jurisdiction in the matter. And, while many politicians became reluctant to support abortion, there was a sense in which the Republican loss of the Senate in 1986 ended their best chances of securing the political changes the pro-life movement desired. By the end of the Reagan administration indeed the Surgeon General (Everett Koop) had shifted his position on a number of issues related to sexual morality in the wake of the Aids epidemic and had accordingly lost much of his support among movement conservatives.

There was little progress for the conservative social agenda in other areas – like school prayer. Although there was initially some hope that the courts might reverse the trend of court decisions of the 1940s on the need to separate church and state, the Supreme Court remained adamantly supportive of the need to maintain that wall of separation. Thus in an important case – *Jaffree* v. *Board of School Commissioners* – in which an Alabama court had offered the Supreme Court an opportunity to rule on the revisionist theory of the First Amendment, the Court disappointed a range of religious groups and legal foundations (such as the Rutherford Institute anxious to overturn the strict separationist construction of the constitution outlined in the *Everson* and *McCollum* cases).[28]

Where the conservative agenda was more successful was in relation to issues which had increasingly worried all Americans – crime and drugs. Many of the legal think-tanks had promoted much harsher penal measures and the Reagan administration responded to demands for a more vigorous war against crime. Similarly the explosion of drugs and drug-related crime found the conservative agenda on these issues very much the agenda of the administration.

It should be noted here that the explicit failure of conservatives to implement their social agenda on many social issues at the federal level in the years 1981–88 does not completely convey the movement's strength or its achievements. For one thing the success of conservatives could be seen in shaping the terms of political debate and moving those who wanted to argue for traditional liberal causes into a marginal position. Certainly the various organisations associated with the women's movement for example felt during the Reagan years that they were in a position of having to defend hard-won gains against the odds and could not really contemplate much forward movement on their agenda.[29]

Secondly, many of the achievements of the conservatives' causes would not be visible. For example on the issue of textbook censorship – where groups like that led by the Graebners vetted textbooks for elements of moral relativism and anti-Americanism – the anticipation of highly vocal criticism in such states as Texas probably caused textbook publishers to avoid including controversial material in their publications.[30]

Finally it is too early to tell what the impact of the vast number of judicial appointments made by the Reagan administration will be on the future course of legal decision making. The expansion of the number of judges in order to cope with the workload of the courts had occurred under Carter. Its beneficiary was Ronald Reagan who had in his two terms as President the opportunity to appoint over 50 per cent of the federal bench.[31]

THE CONSERVATIVE AGENDA: SUCCESS OR FAILURE?

It is clear that the Reagan years occasioned mixed reactions in the American conservative movement. On the one hand conservatives had the excitement of access to power – of feeling that this really was an administration with which they could identify. On the other hand much of the conservative agenda was either not implemented at all, despite the verbal support from the President, or stalled as the administration aged. As a result there was a marked divergence of opinion within conservative opinion about the political achievement of the administration. The 'players' who had entered government or who considered themselves realists in relation to the political process tended to congratulate the Republican administration for what had been achieved while urging more radical action in certain fields. The ideologues by contrast criticised the Reagan administration for failing to implement the conservative agenda and threatened withdrawal of conservative support. Thus Paul Weyrich, Richard Viguerie and in a different way Senator Jesse Helms provided an opposition to the Reagan administration on the right.

In seeking to explain the disappointments of the conservative movement it is important to remember that it was perhaps the victim of three features of American government which it is difficult to see changing. First the fragmentation of power between Congress, the Executive and the Courts and between the federal and state levels meant that despite a clear administrative lead policies met institutional obstacles. This was true as far as Congress was concerned of some of the administration's foreign policy (e.g. over arms to the contras) and after the brief honeymoon of 1981–2 over the budget.

The courts offered opposition to the novel interpretations of affirmative action offered by the administration (for example in the Stotts case). And state resistance to the idea of 'swaps' of programmes between the federal and state level killed much of the new federalism. Secondly, the Reagan administration encountered the inevitable problems of any radical administration which threatens vested interests. Congressional support for many of the programmes threatened by budget cuts was extensive in both parties. New right analysis of the power of the welfare lobby was in one sense extremely accurate. Without a clear consensus there is no reason for Congress to vote against programmes which benefit its constituents or to take unpopular measures for an administration to which they owe little.

Thirdly the difficulty of retaining direction and a sense of priorities within an American administration is enormous and daunting. The conservative movement had prepared itself thoroughly for the opportunity provided by the Reagan administration but it could not counteract the inevitable fragmentation and decentralisation which occurs once an administration becomes subject to the daily pressures of politics.

The conservative movement has over the last eight years lost much of its momentum. Some of its leaders have lost their ideological bite as a result of absorption into the mainstream of Congress. Others – especially the leaders of the so-called religious right – lost their credibility in the wake of personal scandals. Yet whatever the changed status of the conservative movement the experience of the period 1981–88 will provide an important legacy both for conservative activists and their opponents in the next administration.

Notes

1. For a general overview of the American conservative movement and its agenda see G. Peele, *Revival and Reaction: the Right in Contemporary America* (Oxford: Oxford University Press, 1984).

2. Apart from Peele, ibid, further information on the neoconservatives can be found in P. Steinfels, *The Neoconservatives*: The Men Who Are Changing America (New York: Simon & Schuster, 1979) and in S. Blumenthal, *The Rise of the Counter-Establishment: From Conservative ideology to Political Power* (New York: Times Books, 1986).

3. Recent work includes, for example, R. Liebman and R. Wurthnow, *The New Christian Right: Mobilization and Legitimation* (New York: Aldine, 1983) and S. Bruce, *The Rise and Fall of the New*

Christian Right in America 1978–1988 (Oxford: Oxford University Press, 1988).

4. On this see C. Layne, 'Requiem for the Reagan Doctrine', in D. Boaz, *Assessing the Reagan Years* (Washington DC: Cato Institute, 1988).

5. The character of Jeanne Kirkpatrick's ideas on foreign policy can be gleaned from her own essays and lectures in J. J. Kirkpatrick, *Dictatorships and Double Standards: Rationalism and Reason in Politics* (Washington DC: American Enterprise Institute, 1982).

6. N. Podhoretz, *The Present Danger* (New York: Simon & Schuster, 1980).

7. H. W. Stanley and R. Niemi (eds), *Vital Statistics on American Politics* (Washington DC: Congressional Quarterly Press, 1988).

8. A. Wildavsky, *The New Politics of the Budgetary Process* (Glenview, Illinois: Scott, Foresman, 1988).

9. On the defence budget generally see L.J. Korb, 'The Reagan Defense Budget and Program: The Buildup that Collapsed', in D. Boaz, *Assessing the Reagan Years*.

10. On this see N. Ture, 'The Economic Effects of Tax Changes: A Neo-Classical Analysis', in R. H. Fink, *Supply-Side Economics: A Critical Appraisal* (Frederick, Maryland: University Publications of America, 1982)

11. For Laffer's ideas see A. B. Laffer and J. P. Seymour (eds), *The Economics of the Tax Revolt* (New York: Harcourt Brace Jovanovitch, 1979); also his own chapter 'The Laffer Curve', in R. H. Find, *Supply-side Economics*. For a hostile account of supply-side economics see R. Lekachman, *Greed is not Enough: Reaganomics* (New York: Pantheon, 1982).

12. For an understanding of Gilder and Wanniski's works see G. Gilder, *Wealth and Poverty* (New York: Basic Books, 1981) and J. Wanniski, *The Way the World Works* (New York: Simon & Schuster, 1978).

13. An inside account of the early Reagan budgets from this perspective can be found in D. Stockman, *The Triumph of Politics* (New York: Harper & Row, 1986); see also W. Greider, 'The Education of David Stockman', *Atlantic Monthly*, November 1981.

14. The heritage 'mandate' documents (of which there are now three) are excellent source material for the conservative agenda; see C. L. Heatherley *et al.*, *Mandate for Leadership: Policy Management in a Conservative Administration* (Washington DC: The Heritage Foundation, 1981).

15. On the new right's ideas about bureaucracy, see W. A. Niskanen, *Bureaucracy: Servant or Master: Lessons from America* (London: Institute of Economic Affairs, 1973), and W. A. Niskanen, *Bureaucracy and Representative Government* (New York: Aldine Atherton, 1971).

16. For a stimulating overview of the problems of twentieth-century American government see R. Higgs, *Crisis and Leviathan* (New York: Oxford University Press, 1987).

17. On welfare see C. Murray, *Losing Ground: American Social Policy 1950–1980* (New York: Basic Books, 1984).

18. See W. A. Niskanen, *Reaganomics: An Insider's Account of the Politics and the People* (New York: Oxford University Press, 1988).
19. Ibid.
20. For the background to this see G. Peele, *Revival and Reaction* and S. Bruce, *The Rise and Fall of the New Christian Right in America 1978–1988.*
21. Some of the conservative agenda on the judiciary can be seen from P. McGuigan and R. Rader (eds), *A Blueprint for Judicial Reform* (Washington DC: The Free Congress Research and Education Foundation, 1981). Two excellent scholarly considerations of the constitutional theory and judicial policies favoured by the Reagan administration are H. Schwartz, *Packing the Courts: The Conservative Campaign to Rewrite the Constitution* (New York: Scribner, 1988) and L. Levy, *Original Intent and the Founders Constitution* (New York: Macmillan, 1988).
22. On the extent to which the right has been able to press its causes in the legal system see L. Epstein, *Conservatives in Court* (Knoxville, Tennessee: University of Tennessee Press, 1985).
23. For a general discussion of the Reagan administration's handling of legal issues see L. Caplan, *The Tenth Justice: The Solicitor General and the Rule of Law* (New York: Knopf, 1987).
24. The Bob Jones case is discussed in L. Caplan, ibid.
25. For the arguments over the Reynolds nomination see US Senate: Judiciary Committee: *Hearings on the Nomination of William Bradford Reynolds to be Associate Justice of the United States* (99th Congress: 1st Session), June 1985.
26. For the debate about the Bork nomination see US Senate: Judiciary-Committee: *Hearings on the Nomination of Robert H. Bork to Associate Justice of the Supreme Court of the U.S.* (100th Congress: 1st Session), September 1987.
27. For an overview of the political significance of abortion in American see K. Luker, *Abortion and the Politics of Motherhood* (Berkeley, California: University of California Press, 1984).
28. For an overview of the religious right's approach to the constitution see D. Dreizbach, *Real Threat and Mere Shadow* (Westchester, Illinois: Crossway Books, 1987). Also J. McClellan, 'The Making and Unmaking of the Establishment Clause', and S. Ball, 'Religious Liberty: New Issues and Past Decisions', in P. McGuigan and R. Rader (eds), *A Blueprint for Judicial Reform.*
29. On the dilemma of the women's movement in the Reagan years see G. Peele, 'Women's Issues', in P. Davies (ed.), *Issues in American Politics* (Manchester: Manchester University press, 1987).
30. For a discussion of this campaign see S. Bruce, *The Rise and Fall of the New Christian Right in America 1978–1988.*
31. See D. O'Brien, 'Background Paper', in *Judicial Roulette (Report of the Twentieth Century Task Force on Judicial Selection)* (New York: Priority Press, 1988).

3 Managing and Organizing the Reagan White House

Marcia Lynn Whicker

REAGAN AS A DRAMATIC MANAGER

Innovatively, Kets de Vries and Miller, in their book, *The Neurotic Organization*, have applied psychological terms to managers of large, complex organizations to describe aberrant managerial styles.[1] These authors analyzed the impact on large corporations of chief executives with paranoid, compulsive, dramatic, depressive, and schizoid management styles.

Subsequently, Whicker and Moore classified modern twentieth-century presidents from Hoover through Reagan according to their tendency towards mismanagement, using the Kets de Vries and Miller typology.[2] Whicker and Moore acknowledged that their classifications as to primary and secondary mismanagement styles fit some presidents better than others, and that generally, the classifications represented tendency rather than degree of mismanagement.

Paranoid managers are characterized by suspiciousness and mistrust of others, and their style results in organizational emphasis on intelligence, threats, and controls, with centralization of power in the hands of top executives. Presidents who exhibited a paranoid approach as their primary mismanagement style included Richard Nixon and Lyndon Johnson.

Compulsive managers are perfectionist, preoccupied with trivial details, insistent on pursuing their own approach to problems, meticulous and dogmatic. Managers with this style see professional relationships in terms of dominance and submission, and create organizations wedded to formal ritual and policies, rules and procedures. Presidents Herbert Hoover, Harry Truman, and Jimmy Carter all exhibited a compulsive style at times.

Depressive managers exhibit feelings of guilt, worthlessness, self-reproach, inadequacy, and helplessness. The organizations they oversee tend to be inactive, lack confidence, and exhibit extreme conservatism, passivity, and bureaucratic insularity. Gerald Ford, the accidental president, was the only modern president to exhibit a depressive management style.

Schizoid managers are detached, withdrawn, not involved, and demonstrate a sense of estrangement, lack of excitement or enthusiasm, and indifference to praise or criticism. They appear cold and unemotional, and the organizations they manage experience a leadership vacuum. The top executive discourages interaction for fear of involvement, and second tier management engages in gamesmanship from lack of top leadership. Shifting coalitions try to influence the often indecisive leader. The main characteristics of organizations headed by schizoid managers are the dispersal of power and delegation of decision-making power to managers just below the top executive, the development of independent fiefdoms in alienated departments and divisions, and the absence of effective collaboration. While only Dwight Eisenhower exhibited schizoid leadership as a primary mismanagement style, Ronald Reagan exhibited enough schizoid management to be classified as having this as a secondary mismanagement style, along with Richard Nixon.

Finally, dramatic managers tend toward self-dramatization, excessive expression of emotions, incessant drawing attention to themselves, and narcissistic preoccupation. These managers crave attention and excitement, and alternate between idealization and devaluation of others. They exhibit an exploitative incapacity for concentration or for sharply focused attention. Organizations headed by dramatic managers tend to be hypersensitive, impulsive, dramatically venturesome, and dangerously uninhibited. Decision-making reflects hunches and impressions rather than facts. A wide array of projects is addressed in a desultory fashion. The dramatic flair of the top manager causes top echelons to centralise power to be able to initiate ventures independently. The themes of dramatic management are boldness, risk-taking, and diversification, yet with an unreflective and impulsive decision-making style. Modern presidents exhibiting this style include Franklin D. Roosevelt, John F. Kennedy, and Ronald Reagan.

Ronald Reagan is the only recent president to exhibit the primary-mismanagement style of dramatic leadership and the secondary style of schizoid leadership. This chapter examines the impact Reagan's primary and secondary mismanagement styles had on the organization and functioning of the Reagan White House. The chapter will first analyze the major Reagan successes, and then the major administration failures. It will conclude with a discussion of the relevance of the Reagan experiences in managing and organizing the presidency for reforming the presidency.

REAGAN ADMINISTRATION SUCCESSES

The White House Troika of the First Administration

Since the Brownlow Committee urged the appointment of additional staff within the White House to assist the president in his expanding duties, concern has evolved over the staff size question of 'how big is big enough?' Proponents of an expanded White House staff believed that doing so was necessary to provide the president with sufficient personnel loyal to his policies and programs to allow the president to manage effectively. Others expressed concern over the imposition of a large, independent White House staff between the departments and the president and advocated greater reliance on cabinet governance.

Increasingly, as the size of the White House staff has continued to grow in the post-war period, from a staff of 50 in 1943 serving FDR to a staff of 575 serving Reagan in 1986,[3] the question of whether or not a large staff is necessary has been replaced by the issue of how to best organize a large staff to serve the president effectively. Plainly, the managerial style of the president greatly affects the organization of the White House, an organization that changes from one administration to the next, as well as during the course of single administration.[4]

In keeping with his dramatic management style and in sharp contrast to his predecessor, President Carter, Reagan perceived his role in the White House as 'head of the board' – a manager of managers.[5] Classified by James Best as an outsider in terms of Washington experience and as passive in his orientation toward his management role, the 'head of the board' role freed Reagan to pursue speechmaking, communications, and activities where he was in the public eye. This role was a continuation of the management orientation he had assumed as governor of California, one that had worked well for him there.[6]

Indeed, in 1986, *Fortune* magazine lauded Reagan's managerial and policy successes in an attempt to extract lessons for managers in the private sector and elsewhere. Reagan told a *Fortune* reporter that his managerial principles were few, and included surrounding himself with the best people he could find, delegating authority, and refraining from interfering as long as his policies were being carried out. Reagan was painstaking in choosing subordinates, but otherwise eschewed details. Also in keeping with his dramatic style, Reagan reportedly encouraged staff members to speak their minds, and diffused tension with an endless repertoire of jokes.[7]

The Reagan strategy of extreme delegation of authority worked well when Reagan's choice of subordinates produced a capable and functioning team, each assigned duties that meshed with their talents and personalities. When the match of subordinate to job was a poor fit, the delegation strategy foundered badly. One of Reagan's managerial successes, however, was his appointment of the Troika of top advisors consisting of James Baker, Michael Deaver, and Edwin Meese during his first term.

Both Deaver and Meese had served Reagan throughout his career, and Baker, the quintessential polished political actor, had served Vice-President George Bush. The functional division of labor among the three matched their respective talents and abilities. While Baker initially handled 'administration' and implementation, Deaver, the closest to the President, handled scheduling, travel, support services and the First lady's office. Meese was left to develop policy and articulate the administration's New Right agenda, including handling the cabinet and national security.[8] The administration's successes in the early years in implementing its agenda and priorities may be, in part, attributed to the success of the Troika arrangement.

Although Deaver was not particularly interested in policy issues, and preferred the roles of presidential image maker and guardian of the president's time, a potential conflict could have developed between Baker and Meese over policy issues. Immediately after Reagan's 1980 electoral victory, however, these two came to an agreement that they committed in writing, allocating responsibilities between them. Meese was to assume cabinet rank and to coordinate the work of the Domestic Policy Staff and the National Security Council staff, while Baker assumed the traditional office of chief of staff with its control over the flow of paper to the president and its concomitant hiring and firing authority over White House staff.[9]

Despite this allocation of initial responsibilities, and daily breakfast meetings by the Troika during the first year of the Reagan adminis- tration, Baker's dominance of budget and legislative strategy and control of day-to-day operations allowed him eventually to assume control of policy.[10] Baker, viewed by the press and Reagan's New Right constituency as a pragmatist rather than an ideologue, became the first among equals in White House policymaking. Baker's orient- ation, coupled with Deaver's similar pragmatic views, left only Meese as the defender of right-wing politics. This situation did not please the New Right constituency, but enhanced the ability of the administra- tion to achieve its immediate agenda in Congress and other pragmatic political battlegrounds in the nation's capital.

Coupled with the smooth-functioning Troika of the first term was Reagan's willingness to bring Washington insiders and old hands into his administration from the start.[11] This willingness provided a refreshing, necessary, and stark contrast to the early days of the Carter administration, when President Carter, having run a national campaign boasting of his base as a Washington outsider, failed to expand his inner circle to include Washington insiders in order to run the White House effectively. While Carter remained surrounded by Georgia aides such as Hamilton Jordan, Bert Lance, Stuart Eisen- stat, and Jody Powell who had few contacts and connections in Washington before being catapulted into national prominence in their administration roles, Reagan not only included Baker, but also others with Washington experience, such as Richard Darman, Max Friedersdorf, Kenneth Duberstein, and David Stockman.

By the end of the first term, despite some impressive legislative victories, strain was appearing in the White House command struc- ture. White House insiders began to complain that the functionally specialised Troika left no one to give commands except the President. Yet Reagan's dramatic managerial style left him inattentive to the daily details of policy development and implementation. Insiders noted that Reagan handled conflict by allowing trusted aides to 'fight it out'. Coordination between the members of the Troika, in part, disintegrated into individual fiefdoms. For the White House Troika command system, 1983 was the beginning of the end.

Reawakening National Pride

Ronald Reagan's communication skills and immense popularity were potential assets in his command of the White House. Following the compulsive and detail-obsessed management style of Jimmy Carter, Reagan's dramatic style provided a welcome relief to a weary citizenry, tired of speeches about malaise, caution, cutbacks, restraints – particularly during the energy crisis of the mid and late 1970s. Reagan's dramatic expression of national pride, patriotism, and traditional American values appealed to the public.

Defeating incumbent president Jimmy Carter by winning 44 states and 90 per cent of the electoral vote in 1980, Reagan entered office with a considerable popular mandate for his policies. The mandate was extended in the 1984 election when Reagan trounced Democratic candidate Walter Mondale by securing 98 per cent of the electoral vote and carried 49 states.

However, Reagan's popular vote margins, while substantial, remained considerably less (50.7 per cent to Carter's 41 per cent in 1980, and 58.8 per cent to Mondale's 40.6 per cent in 1984).[12] Plainly, despite the Reagan landslide in the electoral college, the popular vote revealed that only a subset of the voting public formed the Reagan constituency. Nor was Reagan's appeal, while broad, universal. Despite some inroads in 1980 into four groups that traditionally vote Democratic – blue-collar whites, union members, Catholics, and southerners[13] – much of the Reagan constituency reflected traditional Republican interests of large business, professional, high and middle income, and non-minority groups, those groups most likely to benefit from his New Right agenda, supply-side policies and tax cuts.

The nature of the support for Reagan is demonstrated by Ornstein, Kohut, and McCarthy, who categorize the voting public into several groups.[14] Four groups voted more heavily for Reagan than any others. First, there were the Enterprise Republicans ('Enterprisers') who constituted 10 per cent of the adult population and 16 per cent of the likely electorate. This group is primarily affluent, educated and 99 per cent white. 'Enterprisers' voted for Reagan by margins of 93 per cent in 1980 and 96 per cent in 1984. The group's top concern was budget deficits. Its members overwhelmingly disapproved of tax increases to cut deficits; opposed spending increases for health care, aid to the homeless, and the elderly; and supported Star Wars and aid to the Contras.[15] A second group that supported Reagan by margins of 92 per cent in 1980 and 97 per cent in 1984 were Moral Republicans ('Moralists'). This group is middle-aged, middle income, heavily southern, 94 per cent white, regular church-goers, and very conservative on social and foreign policy. The group is pro-defense, pro-social spending except when targeted to minority groups, and concerned about deficits and unemployment. Moralists constitute 14 per cent of the likely electorate.[16]

The two remaining groups are the 'Upbeats' and the 'Disaffecteds'. Upbeats formed 9 per cent of the likely electorate, and voted for Reagan by margins of 78 per cent in 1980 and 86 per cent in 1984. Middle-income, 94 per cent white, young and optimistic, this group identified the deficit and economic concerns as the major national problems, and supported Star Wars. Disaffecteds, a fourth group that supported Reagan by margins of 69 per cent in 1980 and 81 per cent in 1984 were alienated from big business as well as big government, felt financial pressure despite being middle income, and were dissatisfied with the role of government in society.[17]

These voting groups, combined with special interest groups and PACs, formed the political support for the 'Reagan Revolution' and provided the context within which the management of the White House rested on the relaxed populist style of the Great Communicator. And in the event Reagan, through his reliance on hunches, instincts, gut feelings and emotion, was able, even in spite of cold facts, to maintain his ebullient, optimistic attitude throughout his administration, even in the face of considerable failures in his second administration, and to appeal broadly enough to these and other groups to keep the myth if not the reality of the Reagan Revolution alive.

The Appointment of David Stockman to OMB

A major element in Reagan's management of the White House was the initial pivotal role played by the Director of OMB. Once regarded as a major source of non-partisan technical advice to the president, the Office of Management and Budget (OMB) has become increasingly politicized since the Reagan administration. Shifting its name from the Bureau of the Budget (BOB) to OMB, to reflect the change, Nixon began the process of imposing several levels of political appointees between top agency officials and budget examiners. Increasingly, the OMB became involved in policy advice and priorities as well as technical budget detail.

Yet politicisation of OMB undermined its earlier prestige. Despite the elevated importance of budgetary issues in the last two decades, its director does not hold cabinet status, a policy recommended by close observers of economic policy-making in Washington.[18] Further, since the establishment of the Congressional Budget Office by the

1974 Congressional Budget and Impoundment Control Act, OMB must compete with CBO to articulate national spending priorities. Because of the politicization of OMB, CBO estimates and economic forecasts have been more accurate and have been regarded as more reliable in recent years.

With the appointment of David Stockman, former congressman from Michigan and 'enfant terrible' of the administration, Reagan temporarily restored the OMB to greater national prominence. More akin in management style to Jimmy Carter than to his boss, Ronald Reagan, Stockman became compulsively obsessed with budgetary detail. His obsession did not prevent him from making a major error in White House negotiations with Congress over Social Security spending – a mistake that subsequently contributed to the deficit in the first Reagan term. None the less, Stockman, an early proponent of Reaganomics and supply-side policies, gained wide respect for his mastery of technical budget detail. In the first Reagan term, OMB was a force to be reckoned with, both within the administration and on Capitol Hill.

Besides Stockman, Jack Kemp, a Republican Congressman from New York and Arthur Laffer, an economics professor at the University of Southern California were early names associated with supply-side economics, as well as sociologist George Gilder, author of the supply-side Bible *Wealth and Poverty*,[19] Jude Wanniski, author of *The Way the World Works*, the second supply-side Bible,[20] and Paul Craig Roberts, Assistant Secretary of the Treasury for economic policy in the Reagan administration.

During the first year, it became apparent that supply-side theory meant different things to different proponents, a potentially damaging threat to the White House dominance of the making of economic policy. While Kemp's group believed that supply-side tax cuts would pay for themselves, Stockman, as early as February 1981, after spending two months at OMB poring over the budget figures, defected from this view, and began to believe that tax cuts without large spending cuts were insufficient. Stockman quickly elevated his concern over federal deficits to greater importance on the economic agenda.

Reagan, the loyalist, retained Stockman as OMB director, despite his defection from basic components of supply-side economics, not because he believed Stockman was correct in his pessimism about the impact of supply-side prescriptions on federal deficits. Rather, Reagan's dramatic style was fueled with impressions, hunches, and anecdotes, and his administrative course remained essentially unaltered by the troublesome facts and figures Stockman kept bringing to his attention.

Clashing with Kemp, who believed economic recovery would eventually obviate the need for substantial spending cuts, Stockman appeared on the cover of *Atlantic Monthly* of 11 November 1981 in a William Greider story, 'The Education of David Stockman'. In the article, Stockman discredited the supply-side economic policies of the Reagan administration. After being reprimanded, Stockman publicly repented and stayed in his position as OMB director, an action he later justified as an effort to clear his name and help correct the fiscal shambles he had helped to bring about that resulted in growing deficits. In the first administration, Stockman remained a voice of reason in a surrealistic world of supply-side rhetoric. By 1985, he admits to 'out-and-out subversion – scheming with the congressional leaders during the first half of 1985 to force a tax hike'.[21] When those efforts failed, Stockman resigned in August 1985. Here we see Reagan acting in a very detached 'head of the Board' role, rather than as a hands-on manager.

The Early Cabinet Council System

An innovative element of the Reagan White House was the institution by Ed Meese of the Cabinet Council system. Reaganomics was highly successful in shifting national priorities from social spending to defence. Defence spending as a percentage of GNP increased from 5.1 during the five years preceding the Reagan administration to 6.5 per cent during the first five years of Reagan budgets, while defence spending as a percentage of total federal spending increased 23.8 to 27.9 per cent, and by the end of the Reagan term in office, exceeded 30 per cent. Total non-defence spending as a percentage of GNP rose slightly from 16.4 to 16.9 per cent during the same two time periods, but declined relative to defence spending when considered as a share of total federal expenditures (from 76.2 to 72.1 per cent).

This mammoth shift in national priorities was achieved, in part, through the use of a cabinet council system during the first term.[22] In keeping with the tendency of dramatic managers to centralise power to the top echelons, as well as his desire to implement his conservative agenda, Reagan kept strong control of subcabinet appointments, feeling that Carter and Nixon had both lost control over this bureaucratic level. In exchange, participants in the 18-member

Reagan cabinet (including the heads of major departments, Meese, the directors of OMB and Central Intelligence Agency, the US Trade Representative and the US representative to the United Nations) were assured of access to the President and of participating in administration decisions.

On economic issues, several 'Councils' were established to offer advice, with the primary and most active one being the Cabinet Council on Economic Affairs (CCEA). Other councils established in 1981 included those on Commerce and Trade (CCCT), Human Resources (CCHR), Natural Resources and Environment (CCN-RE), and Food and Agriculture (CCFA). In 1982, cabinet councils on Legal Policy (CCLP) and Management and Administration (CCMA) were created. Cabinet councils consisted of six to eleven cabinet members. Meetings were chaired by the President and other interested cabinet members were invited to attend.

The cabinet council system allowed Reagan to delegate issues to these bodies, but in exchange issues of concern were to be discussed there first and not brought bilaterally to the President. Despite complaints by Alexander Haig and others that this system allowed White House domination, it worked well in conjunction with the Troika during the first term to implement Reagan's agenda. It required an atmosphere of trust, however, between the White House and cabinet officials. Trust was undermined in the second term when Donald Regan replaced Baker as Chief of Staff, and virtually all the cabinet secretaries were replaced. During the second term, the cabinet council collapsed under its own weight.[23]

REAGAN ADMINISTRATION FAILURES

The Baker–Regan Job Swap

In previous administrations, cabinet members had been shuffled from post to post as the needs of the president dictated. Rarely, however, has such a dramatic and ultimately disastrous reshuffling occurred as the Baker–Regan job swap at the beginning of Reagan's second term when Jim Baker, White House Chief of Staff and Donald Regan, former marine, chief executive officer for Merrill Lynch, and then Secretary of the Treasury, exchanged jobs. The initiative for the shift came not from the President, but from the two men themselves. Essentially, Baker was weary of the strain of White House duties, and Regan was envious of powerful White House staff serving in closer proximity to the President.[24]

The move was salutary for Baker, taking him from one important and highly visible job, Chief of Staff, that he handled well to a second important, but somewhat less visible job, Secretary of the Treasury, that he also handled well. In his capacity at Treasury, Baker negotiated the 1986 tax bill, began the process of devaluing the dollar, and helped to restore some international confidence in US economic management. The countermove was disastrous, for both Regan's ego and the smooth functioning of the White House. In contrast to Baker, Regan moved from a job he handled adequately if, at times abrasively, to the Chief of Staff job where he performed poorly.

In direct opposition to Franklin D. Roosevelt's observation that presidential aides should have a passion for anonymity, Regan had a passion for personal power and self-glorification, but did not have a personal agenda beyond that.[25] Reagan and Regan were both from Irish ancestry, and had a similar generational outlook and taste in jokes. Yet Regan drove away other senior aides and contributed to a chaotic White House, as documented by the Tower Commission report. His rough style and lack of political skills alienated much of Washington. He refused to reach out to Capitol Hill, hired a weak staff, and isolated the President.

Despite Nancy Reagan's advice, the President resisted dismissing Regan until the Iran–Contra scandal broke. During his last three months as Chief of Staff, Regan was plainly a liability to Reagan. The day after the release of the Tower Commission report, Nancy won her point against Regan with the President. Regan stormed from the White House, leaving behind a one sentence resignation and ill will.

Regan wrote his memoirs of his Reagan experience with a tone of bitterness.[26] In contrast to the decorum of early administrations, Regan and other top administration officials, including David Stockman,[27] Michael Deaver,[28] and Larry Speakes[29] released their insider reports while Reagan was still in the Oval Office.[30] Several of the reports revealed shocking disarray and mismanagement inside the White House resulting from Reagan's hands-off style of extreme delegation. Former Press Secretary Speakes, for example, revealed that he had routinely made up and attributed quotes to the President without first clearing the quotes with Reagan.

Even more dismaying was Regan's report that the President's schedule was almost totally dominated by Nancy Reagan's communications with an astrologer in California. While Reagan insisted that astrology had not determined policy, Regan and others made an effective argument that adherence to it and superstition had significantly hindered Reagan's effectiveness as President by sharply curtailing his schedule. Further, it indicated the unusual extent to which Nancy Reagan became involved in scheduling and interfered with the normal conduct of the presidency.[31]

In February 1987, Howard Baker, former G.O.P. Senate Leader, followed Regan as Chief of Staff, amidst expectations that he would rescue a then foundering president.[32] Within nine months, Baker's effectiveness as Chief of Staff was being questioned by conservatives who accused him of abandoning the Reagan agenda, and by friends on Capitol Hill, who criticized him for not saving Reagan from the Bork and Ginsburg rejections.[33] Others noted that Baker, having been a decision maker himself during most of his professional career, had never held a significant staff job, and that Chief of Staff of the White House was an unusually tough staff training post. By June 1988, Baker resigned as Chief of Staff, citing family reasons. He was superseded by his deputy, Kenneth M. Duberstein, for the brief remaining months.[34]

The Iran–Contra Scandal

The greatest blunder and case of mismanagement in the Reagan White House was Iran–Contra scandal. In this scandal, which became public knowledge in 1986 and 1987, officials in the Reagan administration secretly agreed to exchange arms for Iranian hostages, in direct opposition to formal US policy to never negotiate with terrorists. Further, other arms were sold secretly to Iran to secure funds to support Nicaraguan contras – guerilla soldiers fighting the pro-Marxist Nicaraguan Sandinista government – despite Congressional refusal to continue such funding. The scheme was risky, bold, impulsive, dramatically venturesome, incredibly arrogant, and illegal. It represented a foreign policy out of control and running amok.

Perpetrating the scheme, and eventually indicted by Independent Counsel Lawrence Walsh were Reagan's former National Security Advisor John Poindexter, former National Security Council Aide Lt. Col. Oliver North, and two arms dealers, former Air Force Major General Richard Secord and Iranian-born businessman Albert Hakim.[35] In addition to the investigation of the independent counsel, national televised congressional hearings were held that represented high political drama at its worst. Dashing, young, attractive, and pleading patriotism as the motive for illegal actions, Oliver North, in particular, captured both media and public attention.

The four defendants in the Iran–Contra scandal were also charged with theft of government property, for siphoning off more than $17 million in profit from US sales to Iran. These monies were run through Swiss bank accounts, and an unknown amount of the funds were transferred to the Nicaraguan contras. North was also accused of embezzling $4300 worth of traveler's checks, receiving an illegal gratuity of a $13,800 home-security system from Secord, and defrauding the IRS by using the tax-exempt National Endowment for the Preservation of Liberty to solicit $3.2 million in contributions that he used to buy lethal contra aid.

In analyzing how the Iran–Contra affair emerged, with US foreign policy essentially being made by a Lt. Colonel in the White House, Edward Muskie, a member of the Tower Commission that conducted a separate investigation into the affair, noted that the Iran initiative was handled with an informality that degenerated into chaos.[36] The Tower Commission report provided a stunning indictment of a White House decision system that failed because of the people who ran it. The report noted that formal discussions between the President and his foreign policy advisors were rarely conducted and that skimpy records were kept. Further, during the investigation, Reagan reported that he could not remember many key meetings. While Reagan was not personally implicated in the criminal activities surrounding the scandal, the inadequacy of the loosely controlled, poorly coordinated, and improperly documented foreign policy decision-making apparatus in the White House was laid bare.

Reykjavik

Poor foreign policy management was further illustrated in the administration's approach to the Reykjavik summit in October, 1986. Reagan, almost off the cuff, proposed perhaps the most sweeping and important arms reduction in history – the abolition of all offensive ballistic missiles within 10 years – with little forethought or analysis.[37]

Generated by two aides during the Reykjavik summit, Assistant Secretary of Defense Richard N. Perle and National Security Council arms expert Robert B. Linhard, the sweeping proposal was promptly presented to Reagan by Secretary of State George Shultz, who, in turn, presented it to the Soviet leader Mikhail Gorbachev within 30 minutes of the time he first heard it. This action represented impulsive foreign policy decision making in the extreme.

Nor was the administration well prepared at the summit on other issues. Preparatory meetings in Washington had not resulted in the development of any new strategy or fallback positions on the Strategic Defense Initiative (SDI), even though this was clearly an issue of major concern to the Soviets. Under a strict interpretation of the Anti-Ballistic Missile (ABM) treaty, the Soviets could demand a ten-year adherence, yet the administration had no position on this issue either. The improvization of US negotiators and the poor preparation of Reagan at the summit reflected the poorly coordinated style of foreign policy decision making used throughout Reagan's two terms.

The Bork/Ginsburg Rejections

Rarely has a president had the opportunity to shape the US Supreme Court that Reagan enjoyed. President Carter waited for his Supreme Court appointment that never materialized. By contrast, Reagan has made three appointments of associate justices, plus a new chief justice. Each of these has reflected Reagan's dramatic management style.

During his first term, Reagan appointed the first woman, Sandra Day O'Connor, to the courts – a dramatic gesture to a group long excluded from that august body, in keeping with his dramatic, impulsive, uninhibited management style. After her appointment, O'Connor's tendency to vote with the conservative block on the court upheld Reagan's impression that his new appointment was in keeping with his New Right agenda to reorient national priorities and reduce the role of government. His first term appointment of Antonin Scalia, the first American of Italian ancestry on the court, was more subdued but still somewhat dramatic. Like the O'Connor appointment, Reagan correctly perceived Scalia to reflect conservative views.

An associate justice since 1972 and the court's most conservative member for 15 years, William H. Rehnquist was selected by Reagan to become Chief Justice, to replace the retiring Chief Justice Warren Burger. A controversial selection, Rehnquist once complained that most of his fellow clerks had 'liberal' views, including 'extreme solitude for the claims of Communists and other criminal defendants'.[38] Rehnquist's appointment was bitterly opposed by liberals during his Senate confirmation hearings, but he was nonetheless confirmed.

None of these appointments, however, approached the high drama that surrounded Reagan's nomination of Robert H. Bork to fill Rehnquist's then vacant associate justice position. Bork was a strict constructionist in his interpretation of the US constitution and an extreme conservative in his view of social and economic issues. He was a Yale law professor who had served briefly in the executive branch during the Nixon administration in the Justice Department, achieving notoriety by executing Nixon's decision to fire special prosecutor Archibald Cox.

In elaborate, nationally televised hearings before the Senate Judiciary Committee, chaired by Senator Joe Biden (D–Del.), both Bork's facility for complicated and contorted legal reasoning, as well as his willingness to reexamine major decisions advancing the civil rights of previously disadvantaged groups became obvious. Day after day on national television, liberal and civil rights groups testified against the Bork appointment. A major lobbying effort left Senate Judiciary Committee members inundated with mail. When Senator Howell Hefflin from Alabama, a Democratic member of the Judiciary Committee, announced his willingness to vote against the appointment, administration officials recognized that the Bork battle was lost.

Conservative proponents of Bork accused the White House of failing to lay sufficient groundwork to secure his appointment. The Bork débâcle, however, did not imbue Reagan with greater caution, who continued to shoot from the hip with his next court nomination. Rejecting Chief of Staff Howard Baker's advice to nominate Anthony M. Kennedy, who was perceived to be less ideological and more moderate, Reagan adhered to the advice of Edwin Meese, then Attorney-General and representative of the hard right ideologues, to nominate little known Douglas H. Ginsburg. Within two days, the fact that Ginsburg had continued to use marijuana while a young law professor became known nationally. This information was a major source of embarrassment for an administration that had launched a campaign advocating getting tough with and saying no to drugs. Within another day, the controversial Ginsburg nomination was withdrawn.

Even more than previous appointments, the Ginsburg appointment demonstrated Reagan's impulsive, unreflective decision-making style. Angry over the Bork rejection, Reagan's intention was to cram an even more conservative and ideological court nominee down collective Congressional throats. His intention was undermined by the Ginsburg revelations, and in the end, Anthony Kennedy was appointed to the court after all.

The Defense Department Scandal

After the largest peacetime increases in defense spending ever, a major scandal was revealed in 1988 at the close of Reagan's second term in the US Defense department. A nationwide investigation uncovered 'rampant bribery' in military contracts.[39] Under the Reagan buildups, the Defense Department annually spent $160 billion on purchases of both sophisticated weapons systems and more mundane supplies, making it the largest 'business' in the world. Previously, the administration's $2.2 trillion defence buildup had been characterized by cost overruns, and non-working weapons systems. Yet never before had such high-ranking Pentagon officials been suspected of graft on such a large scale.

Much of the investigation focused on the Navy and was conducted by the Naval Investigative Service. Navy Secretary John Lehman (who resigned before the scandal was revealed), Defense Secretaries Caspar Weinberger and Frank Carlucci, and the White House were all unaware of the probe until shortly before it was made public. FBI Director William Webster, and his successor, William Sessions approved the investigation. In the Justice Department, William Weld, chief of the criminal division, and Deputy Attorney-General Arnold Burns also approved it, although both resigned before the investigation became public, charging that Attorney General Edwin Meese had violated conflict of interest laws.

Over 275 subpoenas were issued in the case, with indictments for violating antibribery, mail fraud, antitrust, and antiracketeerring laws expected as Reagan's second term drew to a close.[40] While Defense Department scandals are as old as the Defense Department iself, the size and magnitude of this scandal was both shocking and demoralizing. Its coincidence with an administration that tended to throw money at defence, headed by a dramatic president inattentive to managerial details, is hardly accidental.

Ethics Scandals and Sleaze

By the end of the Reagan administration, the ethics of the administration were under siege. The *Washington Post* reported that more than 110 senior officials had been accused of unethical or illegal conduct since Reagan took office in 1981, excluding officials charged in the Iran–Contra scandal, and in the Wedtech scandal surrounding Attorney-General Edwin Meese. In the Wedtech scandal, two colleagues of Meese were indicted in New York on federal charges of racketeering, fraud, and conspiracy, and Meese was investigated for personal involvement. Previously, White House aides Michael Deaver and Lyn Nofziger had both been convicted on charges of influence peddling.[41] Rep. Pat Schroeder (D–Col.) compiled an even larger list of 225 Reagan administration personnel or nominees who had been the subject of allegations of ethical infractions.[42]

Administration proponents contended that before passage of the 1978 Ethics in Government Act, many of the charges against administration officials would not have been prosecuted. However, critics charge that Reagan failed to set a moral tone and that his failure to condemn influence peddling and appearances of impropriety, as well as his inattentive management style contributed to an 'anything goes' atmosphere. By the end of the second term, charges of corruption in the administration were occurring almost daily, and had clearly become a significant public concern. Reagan received relatively low grades on moral and ethical standards in public opinion polls. In July of 1988, only 16 per cent polled nationally said such standards were higher in government because of his presidency, and 28 per cent said they were lower.

LESSONS FOR REFORMING THE PRESIDENCY

As the second term of his administration drew to a close, Reagan received mixed reviews on his eight years in office.[43] Most citizens in a national poll believed the country was better off because of his presidency, but were disappointed in the Iran–Contra affair and believed Reagan was a poor manager who did not control his aides.

Reagan's dramatic management style, with his flamboyant reliance on hunch and impression rather than meticulous attention to administrative detail, worked better in the first term, when he had a well-functioning administrative team in the White House, than in the second term, when his personnel choices were much less sanguine. While Carter veered too far toward micro-management, by the end of his second term, Reagan had veered too far toward macro-generalities, with the ensuing consequences of scandal, faulty decision making, and even illegal activities in the White House itself. Reagan restored America's belief in itself, only to see his own mismanagement erode that belief.

To reformers of the presidency who wish constantly to reshape the organizational structure of the White House, the Reagan lesson seems to be that actual organizational arrangements are less important than the quality of people close to the president, making key decisions and providing crucial advice. Yet rarely do White House reformers emphasize the selection of presidential aides and advisors as much as their institutional arrangements once in place.[44] Clearly, such institutional arrangements are important. The first term of the Reagan presidency, however, shows that even cumbersome institutional arrangements, such as the Troika, which violated administrative principles of clear hierarchy and chain of command, can work if the personalities and management styles of the president and his advisors mesh as an effective team.

Reagan's dramatic management style worked best in tandem with complementary styles – such as the political operative style of Jim Baker and the compulsive style of Deaver. It worked worst when Reagan was paired with other dramatic management styles – such as that of Donald Regan and Oliver North. Perhaps as the ultimate failing of Reagan's dramatic, inattentive management style, he grasped this idea only intuitively, and did not analyze his own strengths and weaknesses well enough to appoint advisors with complementary styles throughout his two terms.

Notes

1. M. F. R. Kets de Vries and D. Miller, *The Neurotic Organization: Diagnosis and Changing Counterproductive Styles of Management* (San Francisco: Jossey-Bass, 1984).
2. M. L. Whicker and R. A. Moore, *When Presidents Are Great* (Englewood Cliffs, NJ: Prentice-Hall, 1988).
3. J. M. Burns, J. W. Peltason, and T. E. Cronin, *Government by the People* (Englewood Cliffs, NJ: Prentice-Hall, 1987) p. 329.
4. S. Hess, *Organizing the Presidency* (Washington DC: Brookings Institution, 1976) p. 158.

5.   J. J. Best. 'Presidential Learning: A Comparative Study of the Inter-actions of Carter and Reagan', *Congress and the Presidency*, Vol. 15, Spring 1988, pp. 25–48.
6.   L. Cannon, *Reagan* (New York: G. P. Putnam's Sons, 1982).
7.   A. R. Dowd, 'What Managers Can Learn From Manager Reagan', *Fortune*, September 1986, pp. 33–41.
8.   J. P. Pfiffner, *The Strategic Presidency: Hitting the Ground Running* (Chicago, Illinois: Dorsey Press, 1988) pp. 30–40.
9.   L. Barrett, *Gambling With History* (Garden City, New York: Double-day Publishers, 1983) pp. 760–77.
10.   M. Kondracke, 'Baker Takes the Cake', *The New Republic*, 20 February 1984, p. 10.
11.   Pfiffner, *The Strategic Presidency*, pp. 30–40.
12.   S. J. Wayne, *The Road to the White House: The Politics of Presidential Elections* (New York: St. Martin's Press, 3rd edn, 1988) p. 302.
13.   G. R. Orren and E. J. Dionne, 'The Next New Deal', in J. I. Lengle and B. E. Shafer (eds), *Presidential Politics: Readings on Nominations and Elections* (New York: St. Martin's Press, 2nd edn, 1983) pp. 391–405.
14.   N. Ornstein, A. Kohut, and L. McCarthy, *The People, the Press, and Politics* (Reading, Mass.: Addison-Wesley Publishing Co., Inc., 1988), pp. 16–19.
15.   Ibid., p. 13.
16.   Ibid.
17.   Ibid., p. 14.
18.   C. Schultz, Comments on 'Executive Office Agencies and Advisory Policy Units' (Washington DC: Georgetown University Conference on Executive Leadership, September 6, 1988).
19.   G. Gilder, *Wealth and Poverty* (New York: Basic Books, 1981).
20.   J. Wanniski, *The Way the World Works* (New York: Simon & Schuster, rev. edn, 1983).
21.   D. A. Stockman, *The Triumph of Politics: The Inside Story of the Reagan Revolution* (New York: Avon Books, 1987), p. 408.
22.   M. Genovese, 'The Presidency and Styles of Economic Management', *Congress and the Presidency*, Vol. 14, Autumn 1987, pp. 151–67; see also Pfiffner, *The Strategic Presidency*, pp. 58–67.
23.   Pfiffner, *The Strategic Presidency*, pp. 58–67.
24.   D. Regan, *For the Record: From Wall Street to Washington* (New York: Harcourt Brace Jovanovich, Publishers, 1988) pp. 218–30.
25.   J. Alter, with T. M. DeFrank and M. G. Warner, 'The Final Days of Donald Regan', *Newsweek*, 9 March 1987, p. 23.
26.   Regan, *For the Record*.
27.   Stockman, *The Triumph of Politics*.
28.   M. K. Deaver, with M. Herskowitz, *Behind the Scenes* (New York: Morrow Publishers, 1987).
29.   L. Speakes, with R. Pack, *Speaking Out: The Reagan Presidency from Inside the White House* (New York: Scribner, 1988).
30.   J. Alter, with H. Fineman and E. Clift, 'White House Tattletales', *Newsweek* 16 May, 1988, pp. 18–19.

31. B. Seaman, 'Good Heavens!', *Time*, 16 May 1988, pp. 24–5.
32. J. V. Lamar Jr, with L. I. Barrett and H. Gorey, 'The Right Man at the Right Time', *Time*, 9 March 1987, p. 27.
33. L. Cannon, 'Howard Baker May Have Become Part of the Problem', *Washington Post National Weekly Edition*, 23 November 1987, p. 12.
34. J. Johnson, 'Can the White House Do More Than Wait for January?', *New York Times*, 19 June 1988, p. E4.
35. J. Lamar, with A. Constable, 'Conspiracy, Fraud, Theft and Cover-up', *Time*, 28 March 1988, pp. 16–18.
36. R. Watson, with J. Barry, 'A Stunning Indictment: The Tower Report Exposes a System Betrayed by the People Who Ran It', *Newsweek*, 9 March 1987, pp. 25–31.
37. D. Oberdorfer, 'Reykjavik: The Rest of the Story', *Washington Post National Weekly Edition*, 2 March 1987, pp. 10–11.
38. S. Taylor, Jr, 'Rehnquist's Court: Tuning Out the White House', *New York Times Magazine*, 11 September 1988, pp. 38–41.
39. E. Magnuson, with E. Shannon and B. van Voorst, 'The Pentagon for Sale', *Time*, 27 June 1988, pp. 16–18.
40. P. Dwyer, D. Griffiths, and S. Payne, with L. Helm, 'We've Got Some of These Guys Dead to Rights', *Business Week*, 4 July 1988, pp. 31–4.
41. G. Lardner, Jr., 'Conduct Unbecoming an Administration', *Washington Post National Weekly Edition*, 3 January 1988, p. 31.
42. 'Administration "Sleaze Factor" is a Clear Question of Ethics', *Richmond Times-Dispatch*, 20 December 1987, p. A-14.
43. D. Broder, 'Mixed Grades on Eight Years in Office', *Washington Post National Weekly Edition*, 11–17 July 1988, p. 13.
44. B. A. Rockman, 'Reforming the Presidency: Nonproblems and Problems', *Political Science*, Vol. 20, Summer 1987, pp. 643–9.

4 Reagan and the Courts

Tinsley E. Yarbrough

More than any other recent president, Ronald Reagan and his administration challenged the federal human rights orthodoxy of the post-World War II era – an orthodoxy forged to some degree by the Congress and the White House but mainly by the federal courts. The administration's stance had a variety of roots. First, it can be viewed as a continuation of the 'Southern Strategy' which GOP presidents and would-be presidents have pursued with varying degrees of enthusiasm since Harry Truman's years in the presidency. Playing to white southern resentment of school desegregation and related modern civil rights developments, Republican leaders have attempted to woo dissident southern Democrats into the GOP fold with attacks on such policies and promises of change. Especially in his attacks on court-ordered school bussing to achieve integration, President Richard M. Nixon vigorously courted white southern votes. But no other Republican candidate or president matched Reagan's effectiveness in winning white southern hearts.

Second, the administration's opposition to numerous human rights trends also undoubtedly reflected its appreciation for the growing organizational and voting clout of the religious right – those people vehemently opposed to Supreme Court decisions banning devotional programs from the public schools, recognizing rights of sexual privacy, extending broad constitutional protection to erotica, and guaranteeing women a right of abortion. While the influence of Jerry Falwell's Moral Majority and other such groups can easily be exaggerated, the movement is clearly better organised, more vocal, and better financed than it was ten to fifteen years ago. This is especially so as a result of the easy access to voters that the explosion in satellite cable technology and computer-generated mailings has afforded television evangelists and other leaders of the religious right. Neither that trend, nor the antagonisms against modern human rights doctrines which have helped to fuel it, was lost on the Reagan administration.

Combined with Reagan's attempt, as candidate and president, to capitalise on the irritations of white southerners and the religious right was a campaign for the hearts of a more amorphous, yet potentially even larger, group – voters incensed at Supreme Court rulings expanding the rights of suspects and defendants in criminal cases. Candidate Nixon had begun that campaign with his vow to appoint to the Supreme Court 'strict constructionists' who would 'interpret', not make, law, who would be dedicated to 'law and order', and who could be counted on to 'strengthen the peace forces as against the criminal forces of the land'. Reagan's civil liberties agenda, like Nixon's, was an appeal to this segment of the electorate as well.

Finally, the Reagan administration's challenge to modern civil liberties orthodoxy reflected the philosophical leanings of the president and, perhaps to an even greater degree, key members of his administration, especially his second Attorney-General Edwin Meese, III, and William Bradford Reynolds, his Assistant Attorney General for civil rights. Whatever the political motivations underlying the administration's stance, it was also consistent with the thinking of administration leaders. Many of these leaders repeatedly affirmed for the record their opposition to race- and gender-conscious hiring and university admissions, the application of Bill of Rights safeguards in state criminal cases, judicial interpretations of the Constitution going beyond the (in their eyes, inevitably narrow) 'original intent' of its framers, bans on devotional programs in the public schools, the exclusion of illegally seized evidence and confessions from criminal trials, expansive concepts of constitutionally protected privacy, especially in the abortion field, and legalized pornography.

Just as the administration's assaults on civil liberties policies stemmed from numerous sources, they also took a variety of forms. Certain of its efforts were directed at congressional civil rights policies. Most notable was the administration's campaign, early in Reagan's first term, to secure repeal of the 'pre-clearance' provisions of the 1965 Voting Rights Act, which the Supreme Court had upheld in a 1966 case.[1] Under the law, states and counties with a history of racially discriminatory election and voter registration practices were required to obtain the approval of the Attorney General or the federal district court in Washington DC, before enforcing new election regulations. Application of the 'pre-clearance' provision was limited almost entirely to the states of the deep South, and southern officials resented the requirement and especially the presumption that discriminatory practices common in the 1960s would resurface in the 1980s, were the requirement dropped. They could also cite statistics indicating that 34,798 proposed election law changes had been submitted to the Department of Justice, 1965–1980, yet the Department had objected to only 815, or about 2.3 per cent.

In April 1981, Charles McC. Mathias (R–Md.), Edward M. Kennedy (D–Mass.), and six other Senators introduced legislation to continue the pre-clearance and other key provisions of the 1965 law until 1992. A similar proposal was introduced in the House of Representatives. Despite pressure from civil rights groups, President Reagan took no position on the legislation prior to its passage by the House. Instead, on 15 June he released a letter he had written to Attorney-General William French Smith, asking that the Justice Department conduct a thorough study of the law and submit a recommendation to him by 1 October. At that point, he endorsed the 'principle' underlying the law but declined to endorse the pending legislation.

In early November, however, the President announced that he favored a ten-year extension of the Act, providing that the revised version included amendments incorporating 'reasonable "bail-out" provisions' for states and political subdivisions no longer likely to engage in discriminatory election practices. Under the existing law, states and counties could be relieved of further compliance with the pre-clearance and related regulations only if they could convince a three-judge panel of the US District Court for the District of Columbia that they had not engaged in discrimination for at least five years prior to the statute's 1965 enactment – a condition no deep South state could meet. President Reagan wanted a more liberal 'bail-out' arrangement. Southern congressmen, among others, contended, moreover, that bail-out hearings should be conducted by three-judge panels in the jurisdictions seeking a bail-out rather than in the District of Columbia district court, so long as judges from the specific area involved were excluded from such suits. After considerable debate, Congress enacted a bill which extended the law for 25 years rather than the ten years the administration had favoured, but did include provision for the bail-out of states, counties, and local governments which established, to the satisfaction of the District of Columbia district court, a clean voting rights record for the previous ten years. The old law required the states to show clean records. On 29 June 1982, President Reagan signed the bill into law.[2]

When Congress enacted legislation overturning Supreme Court decisions which narrowed the reach of statutory rights, the administration also moved to intervene. Following the Supreme Court's 1980 conclusions that the 1965 Voting Rights Act extended only to *purposeful* discrimination,[3] Congress provided that voting rights violations could be demonstrated by a showing that an election law or procedure operated in a manner that *resulted* in voting discrimination. In making such determinations, the revised law stipulated, courts were to look at the 'totality of the circumstances'. The administration vigorously opposed this legislation, complaining that the new law amounted to a *de facto* requirement of proportional representation in the election process. It opposed, moreover, Congress's reversal of a Supreme Court plurality judgement, in 1984, in the *Grove City College* case that Title IX of the 1972 Education Act Amendments – and presumably three other federal laws containing virtually identical language – banned discrimination only in a particular education 'program or activity' receiving federal aid, not the entire institution housing the program or activity at issue.[4] When a bill to overturn the Court's construction was introduced in Congress, President Reagan's Education Secretary said that he could support it with certain modifications. At a press conference, however, the President expressed concern about the proposal's undue breadth, indicating that he might be obliged to veto it, while William Bradford Reynolds testified before a joint hearing of the House Judiciary and Education and Labor Committees that the Justice Department would oppose the legislation. The proposal's vague language, Reynolds asserted, would substantially broaden the government's power to penalize private institutions and state and local governments which discriminated on the basis of race, sex, age, or handicap, despite the nation's long tradition of one-sex educational and athletic programs as well as other practices potentially vulnerable to the proposed law's reach. The legislation was finally enacted, in early 1988, but over the President's veto.

Disturbed by its criticisms of his administration's civil rights policies, President Reagan also sought to strengthen presidential influence over the US Commission on Civil Rights. Members of the Commission, which was created under the 1957 Civil Rights Act to monitor the status of civil rights in the nation, served open-ended terms of office. In 1974, Theodore M. Hesburgh resigned at President Nixon's request so that the President could select his own commission chairman. Otherwise, the six Commissioners had been replaced only as they left voluntarily or died in office, and the governing law was silent on the matter of tenure.

The Commission had no enforcement power; instead, it compiled

reports and recommendations for new legislation and other governmental responses to civil rights problems. Over the years, moreover,
individual members and the body itself had frequently criticized the
administration in power. Attacks on what was claimed to be the
Reagan administration's failures to enforce existing laws, as well as
its challenges to such policies, had been particularly intense. On 26
May 1983, the President announced that he was replacing three
members of the Commission, including Howard University law
professor Mary Frances Berry, perhaps his most vocal Commission
critic, with prominent civil rights lawyer Morris Abram, John Bunzel
of the Hoover Institution, and Robert Destro, a Catholic University
law professor and vigorous abortion critic. The incumbents would,
however, continue to serve until their successors had been confirmed
by the Senate.

A lengthy battle ensured, with liberal congressmen and lobbyists
led by Ralph G. Neas, executive director of the Leadership Conference on Civil Rights, an umbrella organization for 165 groups,
seeking to insulate the Commission from political removal. The
President's congressional supporters called such efforts an 'infringe-
ment' on executive authority, while, on the other hand, Berry and
another ousted Commissioner initiated a law suit to block their
removal. The President's critics insisted their concern was purely
over the administration's threat to the commission's independence,
not the qualifications of the Reagan nominees or their commitment
to civil rights. During a Senate Judiciary Committee hearing on the
President's choices, for example, Joseph R. Biden (D–Del.) told the
nominees, 'You are not the issue. . . . The question hanging over
your head is, if and when you disagree with the president, will you be
summarily fired?'[5]

Extended negotiations between the White House and congressional leaders led finally to adoption of a compromise under which
the Commission's size was increased from six to eight, the President
and Congress were each given four appointments, the Commissioners
were to serve staggered, six-year terms, and Berry was retained as a
congressional appointee. At one point during the bargaining,
however, the President fired the Commissioners he was seeking to
replace. Even after the compromise was adopted, moreover, he
backed away from what some considered an agreement to appoint to
the reconstituted Commission a Republican incumbent who had
often criticized the administration's policies.[6]

In the main, however, the Reagan administration's challenge to the human rights orthodoxy of the past three decades centered on the federal courts. It proposed constitutional amendments designed to overturn objectionable judicial constructions of the nation's basic law. It supported legislation to restrict the courts' jurisdiction over abortion and other civil liberties issues. As a party litigant and *amicus curiae* (friend of the Court), it urged the Supreme Court to reverse or modify its own precedents. It undertook a largely successful effort to convert the office of the Solicitor General into an advocate for its human rights agenda. Most significantly perhaps, Reagan and his advisers systematically attempted to use his control over judicial appointments to perpetuate and expand his human rights legacy. This chapter focuses on such efforts.

ATTACKING JUDICIAL DOCTRINE

Ironically, one of the first Reagan administration confrontations with prevailing civil rights doctrine was mounted against policy imposed by the Nixon administration in the face of pressure from the courts. By 1970, more than 600,000 southern youths were attending white-only private schools, the vast majority of which had been established to avoid integrated education. The Internal Revenue Service (IRS) initially granted tax-exempt status to such schools – and tax deductions for their financial supporters – so long as they were not receiving state aid. After a federal court enjoined tax exemptions for segregated private academies in Mississippi, however, President Nixon issued an order to the IRS in 1970 denying exemptions to any school with discriminatory admissions policies. During the Nixon years, private schools found it relatively easy to satisfy the IRS they were no longer discriminating; essentially all that was required was a statement to that effect, whatever an individual school's actual racial composition. When Jimmy Carter was president, though, the service attempted to impose relatively strict compliance standards. In his 1980 campaign, Ronald Reagan sought to capitalize on resentment the policy had aroused among white southerners. The GOP platform promised, for example, to halt President Carter's 'vendetta' against private schools, and a campaign position paper emphasized Reagan–Bush opposition to 'the IRS's attempt to remove the tax-exempt status of private schools by administrative fiat.'[7]

An attempt to keep that campaign promise, however, was to embroil the administration in a politically embarrassing battle with lower court rulings upholding the denial of exemptions to discriminatory private schools and the government's own position in those suits. In 1980, a three-judge panel of the Court of Appeals for the Fourth Circuit had upheld the IRS's policy against the claims of lawyers for Bob Jones University, a South Carolina school, that it interfered with the religious liberty of sectarian institutions.[8] Within little more than a month of President Reagan's inauguration, moreover, the claims of Goldsboro Christian Schools, a segregated North Carolina academy, met the same fate in another Fourth Circuit proceeding.[9]

But the President's vow to stop IRS 'harassment' of such schools was not to be forgotten. While officials in the Treasury Department initially recommended that Secretary Donald Regan defend the policy, congressional critics, including Senator Jesse Helms (R–N. Car.), Senator J. Strom Thurmond (R–S. Car.), and especially Republican House whip Trent Lott of Mississippi urged the White House to keep the President's promise. William Bradford Reynolds and other Reagan Justice Department appointees also opposed the IRS's position. In a memorandum to Deputy Attorney-General Edward C. Schmults, for example, Schmults's assistant Bruce Fein, along with Reynolds perhaps the Department's most articulate conservative ideologue, complained that the policy had a tenuous statutory basis, at best, and 'daunting' implications. Federal law regarding tax-exempt organizations was largely patterned after the common law of charitable trusts, which, by definition, were to be dedicated to the general welfare and conform to the law and government policy. In defending its tax-exemption policy, the IRS was arguing that discriminatory private schools were engaged in practices inconsistent with a prevailing national policy of non-discrimination and thus were not entitled to an exemption. Such a theory, Fein warned, could be used by courts to deny exemptions 'to the institutions that did not accommodate the handicapped, the aged, women, and other groups currently favored in federal statutes on the ground that a tax exemption would be inconsistent with national policy'. In his judgement, moreover, such thinking seemed 'to conflict with the attorney-general's view that the Department should discourage rather than encourage judicial activism and policymaking, except when clearly mandated by statute of the Constitution'.[10]

Ultimately, congressional and administration opponents of the policy prevailed with the President. On 8 January 1982, Treasury

Department officials announced that the 1970 regulation was being abandoned. No longer would the IRS revoke or deny exemptions to nonprofit organizations 'on the grounds that they don't conform with certain fundamental public policies'.

While hailed by Jesse Helms, Senator Thurmond, and others who considered the president's decision a triumph, as conservative columnist James Jackson put it, for the First Amendment, the announcement generally provoked a firestorm of harshly negative reaction. Journalists and civil rights leaders charged that the action bordered on racism, especially given the administration's mounting record of opposition to bussing, affirmative action, and other human rights policies. In the Justice Department, 204 employees of the civil rights division, including more than a hundred lawyers, signed a petition protesting at division head William Bradford Reynolds's role in the decision, and several division personnel resigned in protest. When IRS staffers were informed that they were no longer to deny exemptions to discriminatory schools, the judge who had enjoined the granting of exemptions to Mississippi's segregated academies warned that they should grant those institutions tax-exempt status only if they 'like jail'.[11] On 22 February, moreover, a three-judge Court of Appeals panel hearing a nationwide class action suit seeking more vigorous IRS enforcement of nondiscrimination policies enjoined the service from granting exemptions to any racially discriminatory schools.[12]

When asked by the press whether the administration planned to seek congressional legislation granting the IRS power to deny exemptions to discriminatory private schools, Treasury officials who issued the 8 January announcement ending the 1970 policy had replied that it would be inappropriate for the administration to attempt to influence Congress on the issue. In the wake of hostile reaction to the announcement, however, the administration hastily submitted such a proposal to Congress. Insisting that he was 'unalterably opposed to racial discrimination in any form', President Reagan asserted that he was simply trying to eliminate government by 'administrative fiat' and expressed regret there had been 'a misunderstanding of the purpose' underlying his decision. But congressional conservatives were hardly interested in clothing the IRS with the authority the President was now seeking, and liberals contended that the service already possessed ample authority to deal with segregated private schools. So, apart from hearings at which congressional critics of the President's action bombarded administration officials with embarrassing questions, Congress merely sat on the issue.

The administration's experience with the tax-exemption issue in the *Bob Jones University* and *Goldsboro Christian Schools* cases was equally embarrassing. In the lower courts, of course, the government had defended the IRS's policy. When the Reagan administration decided to rescind the policy, Assistant Attorney-General Reynolds recommended that the Solicitor General's office file a confession of error in the cases with the Supreme Court. Under that rarely used procedure, the Solicitor General 'confesses' that a decision favorable to the government in the lower courts was in error and petitions the Supreme Court to reverse the erroneous ruling. Since he had been involved in the tax-exemption issue before his appointment, Solicitor General Rex E. Lee had excused himself from participation in the cases. Acting Solicitor General Lawrence G. Wallace, a veteran Justice Department staffer who had clerked for Justice Hugo L. Black, had defended the 1970 policy in responding to the Bob Jones University and Goldsboro Christian Schools petitions for Supreme Court review. Wallace refused to confess error in the cases. Instead, the government moved unsuccessfully for a dismissal of the cases on the grounds that, given the Reagan administration's position, the dispute between the government and the schools was now moot. Wallace later did sign the government's brief in the cases but attached a notation disassociating himself from the argument that the 1970 policy had no statutory basis.

Ultimately, the Supreme Court was to assume the same position. Since the government was no longer challenging the schools' claims to tax exemptions, it was doubtful, as the administration had argued, that the cases continued to present a true controversy. Nor, of course, were any of the current litigants now willing to argue the IRS's position. But the Court seemed determined to reach the issues the cases had raised. On 19 April, 1982, it denied an NAACP motion to intervene as a party to the litigation but permitted the organization to file an *amicus curiae* brief. More significantly, it also allowed William T. Coleman, a prominent black attorney, member of the Ford cabinet, and head of the NAACP's Legal Defense Fund, to both file a brief and argue orally in the cases as a friend of the court. Coleman's unstated responsibility was to defend the IRS policy before the Court.

Late in its 1982 term, the Court held eight-to-one that the IRS possessed adequate statutory authority for the 1970 policy. It voted unanimously, moreover, to reject claims that the policy interfered with the First Amendment rights of racially discriminatory sectarian schools. Only Justice William H. Rehnquist, the Court's most conservative member, for whom a Justice Department staffer who played a substantial role in preparing the government's challenge to the 1970 policy once clerked, registered a dissent.[13]

As I have attempted to demonstrate elsewhere,[14] the administration's claims probably deserved greater weight than the Court accorded them in its ruling. Politically, however, the battle over the exemption issue had been a disaster for the President, a success only in 'Southern Strategy' terms, if that. Many saw the administration's position as purely an attempt to appease racist voters and conservative congressmen. 'What an enormous disservice is done the President', New York Democrat Daniel Patrick Moynihan admonished administration officials during a Senate hearing, 'all to placate two Senators and one Congressman. My Lord. My Lord, the Presidency isn't worth it nor are your jobs'.[15] Moynihan's statement well captured the prevailing public and congressional reaction to the administration's exemption gambit.

In other areas, however, the administration's challenge to judicial human rights policies was more sustained. In cases involving state aid to parochial schools and related religious establishment issues, the administration urged the Court to abandon what it termed 'wooden' constructions of the Court's 1971 conclusion in *Lemon* v. *Kurtzman*[16] that, to withstand establishment challenges, laws affecting religion must promote a secular purpose, have a primary effect which neither advances nor inhibits religion, and avoid an 'excessive entanglement' between religion and the state. On occasion, it was partially successful in its efforts. In *Lynch* v. *Donnelly* (1984),[17] for example, the Supreme Court declined the recommendation of the government's *amicus curiae* brief that the *Lemon* test be abandoned, but did uphold on narrow grounds the display on public property of a nativity scene along with other, secular symbols of the Christmas season. Reversing lower court findings that the nativity scene had a religious purpose and effect, Chief Justice Warren Burger concluded for a majority of Justices that, in the context of the entire display, the nativity scene was simply part of a 'legitimate secular' celebration of the holiday season.

On the more sensitive issue of devotional exercises in the public schools, the administration's efforts bore considerably less fruit. Despite the government's support as *amicus curiae*, for example, a six-to-three majority struck down an Alabama law setting aside a minute of silence 'for meditation or voluntary prayer' in the public schools.[18] Nor were other efforts to reverse or modify the Court's 1960s decisions banning devotional exercises in the public schools successful. Early in his first term, the President proposed that the Constitution be amended to provide: 'Nothing in this Constitution shall be construed to prohibit individual or group prayer in public schools or other public institutions. No person shall be required by the United States or any state to participate in prayer'. But that and related proposals failed, and moves by Senator Helms and others to deny the federal courts jurisdiction over school prayer issues met the same fate.

Following the Supreme Court's ruling in *Widmar* v. *Vincent* (1981)[19] that state colleges which provided forum facilities for student groups could not deny religious groups access, an administration-supported move to extend this equal access requirement to secondary schools surfaced in the Congress. As the 1984 election season was beginning, Congress adopted a law requiring public high schools which set aside time and space for meetings of extracurricular student groups to grant religious groups equal access. The Act also provided, however, that federal funds were not to be withdrawn from schools which failed to comply with its provisions. Moreover, the *Widmar* Court had drawn a sharp distinction between public colleges and secondary schools, and several courts had struck down state versions of the congressional enactment; the statute's constitutionality was thus doubtful at best.

The administration's efforts in an area of equal importance to the religious right, as well as to a broader segment of the electorate, proved almost as unproductive. In a line of decisions which had begun to develop before President Reagan's inauguration, the Supreme Court had upheld the power of government to deny public funding for abortion, even where childbirth and maternal care were provided for indigent women and their offspring.[20] The Court also reaffirmed, however, the broad right of abortion it had first recognized in *Roe* v. *Wade* (1973).[21] In an *amicus curiae* brief filed for a number of 1983 cases, the administration urged the Court to defer to the political process on the abortion issue, leaving 'further refinements' of the law to state legislatures and Congress. Declining that invitation, the Court struck down requirements that abortions after the first trimester be performed in acute-care, full-service hospitals; that parental consent be obtained for all abortions performed on minors under fifteen; that physicians inform women about the status of fetal development, possible abortion complications, and alternatives to abortion; that the physician alone inform the patient about particular risks associated with her own pregnancy and abortion; that a twenty-four-hour waiting period be observed between a woman's signing of an 'informed consent' form permitting an abortion and the procedure itself; and that fetal remains be given a 'humane' disposal.[22] The Court did uphold, however, a number of more narrowly drawn regulations. It validated, for example, a law requiring 'unemancipated' minors to secure parental or judicial consent and another stipulating that second-trimester abortions be performed in a licensed hospital, where that stipulation was broad enough to include outpatient surgical clinics.[23] In later cases, though, the Court continued to reaffirm *Roe*, despite further government briefs urging rejection of that controversial precedent. Congressional efforts to overturn the decision or leave the issue in state hands via a constitutional amendment or restrictions on federal court jurisdiction also failed.

The administration was perhaps least successful, however, in the affirmative action field. Near the end of President Reagan's first term, William Bradford Reynolds was asked to list the administration's major areas of progress in the field of civil rights. His response reflected the administration's attitude toward preferential employment and university admissions for minorities and women. 'I think', he said,

We have made a lot of progress in terms of reawakening the public debate on a number of issues. I have in mind, specifically, the whole question of affirmative action. It is, I think a monumental step forward that the majority of the people in this country are now willing to question responsibly whether preferential treatment on account of race or sex is a legitimate course for government to follow. As that public debate continues, I am confident it will ultimately influence a change in that policy.[24]

When the Supreme Court rejected a particular affirmative action program, Reynolds and other administration officials attempted to give the ruling at issue the broadest possible reading. When the Court concluded in 1984, for example, that the anti-employment discrimination provisions of the 1964 Civil Rights Act did not authorize the setting aside of a bona fide seniority system as a means of remedying

past patterns of discrimination, Justice Byron R. White couched the
Court's decision in very narrow terms closely tied to the facts of the
specific dispute.[25] Reynolds cited the ruling as evidence, however,
that lower courts should not support affirmative action programs.
Three federal appeals courts disagreed with him, but in 1985 he sent
letters to fifty jurisdictions, asking them to modify consent decrees
which included quotas as remedies for past discrimination. He and
Edwin Meese also urged the President to rewrite an executive order
issued in 1965 by President Lyndon B. Johnson, under which
government contractors were required to take 'affirmative action' to
ensure that workers were employed without regard to race, color, or
creed. Both actions infuriated liberal congressmen and civil rights
lobbyists. By the end of 1985, for example, 69 Senators and 175
House members had written to Reagan, urging him to leave the 1965
order alone.[26] Moreover, although in its 1978 *Bakke* decision the
Supreme Court overturned a racial quota for admissions to a state
medical school, it upheld the use of race and gender, among other
'non-merit' considerations, in public employment and university
admissions policies and later rejected contentions that the 1964 Civil
Rights Act prohibited racial hiring quotas entered into by a company's management and union representatives. Administration briefs
and oral argument urging rejection of such programs had little
impact.

In addition to attempting to persuade the Supreme Court to
reverse or modify controversial precedents, and supporting congressional action toward that same end, the administration also sought to
undermine public support for those precedents in a variety of fields.
In the abortion area, for example, President Reagan repeatedly
encouraged members of the right-to-life movement in their attacks on
Roe v. *Wade*. Each year when members of the group sent roses to
congressmen and Supreme Court Justices on *Roe*'s anniversary, then
gathered on the Ellipse across from the White House, the President
sent words of support. When pro-lifers conducted a funeral for
thousands of aborted fetuses, Reagan sent his condolences. He did
little, moreover, to discourage the growing number of bombings at
abortion clinics, and his rhetoric left no doubt where his sympathies
lay. 'I don't think', he observed on one occasion, 'that womanhood
should be considering murder a privilege'.[27]

As Attorney-General, Edwin Meese was even more outspoken. In
a series of addresses written by one of his more articulate staffers,
Meese attacked the Court's well-established position that most

guarantees of the Bill of Rights are implicit commands of the Fourteenth Amendment's due process clause and thereby binding on the states. He also charged the Court with making law rather than interpreting it, urged a construction of the Constitution based on the framers' intent rather than changing judicial notions of justice, and came close to suggesting that government officials have no obligation to obey judicial interpretations of the Constitution unless they themselves are subject to a court order. Several members of the Court registered vigorous rejoinders. Justice William J. Brennan asserted, for example, that appeals to 'original intent' were 'little more than arrogance cloaked as humility', adding that the Constitution's genius lay in the 'adaptability of its great principles to cope with current problems and current needs'.[28] In a controversial address to a lawyers' meeting in Hawaii, Thurgood Marshall assumed the same stance. In the long term, however, the administration's attacks on prevailing doctrine, like those of the religious right and other conservative groups, may have done as much damage to those policies as any courtroom-based challenge.

POLITICIZING THE SOLICITOR GENERAL

The administration also sought to convert the office of Solicitor General into a tool for advancing its human rights agenda.[29] The Solicitor General is the government's chief representative before the Supreme Court and largely determines what cases the administration will appeal to that highest tribunal. A high-ranking member of the Justice Department, he is appointed by the President and serves at the president's pleasure. Traditionally, however, the Solicitor General and his staff have been considered ultimately servants of the law, not the government – a position perhaps best reflected in the confession of error, by which the Solicitor General is expected to petition the Supreme Court to reverse what he believes to be the government's legally erroneous lower court victories.

President Reagan's first Solicitor General was Rex E. Lee, former clerk to Supreme Court Justice Byron R. White, head of the Justice Department's civil rights division, and Dean of the law school at Brigham Young University. Statistically, Lee compiled an excellent record as Solicitor General. During his last year in office, the Court agreed to hear about 80 per cent of the government's petitions for review and only 3 per cent of all other petitions; his office also won over 80 per cent of the cases it filed or participated in. Among Lee's victories were a number of rulings important to the administration's human rights agenda. At his urging, or at least consistently with it, the Court expanded the exceptions to the controversial exclusionary rule under which legally seized evidence is inadmissible in criminal trials. In one case, for example, the Justices permitted use of evidence collected through police misconduct if that evidence would 'inevitably' have been discovered anyway.[30] In others, the Court held that the fruits of a 'good faith' search were admissible even if the accompanying warrant was defective.[31] Lee's office may also have been instrumental in persuading the Court to uphold a state law allowing parents of parochial school students, as well as those attending public schools, to take tax deductions for educational expenses.[32]

Rex Lee is a conservative who shared his president's concerns about modern trends in civil liberties law. But he was also mindful of the restrictions tradition had placed on the political roles of his office as well as the likely limits of Supreme Court patience with repeated administration challenges to its precedents. Especially after the Court's 1983 rebuff of the administration's broadside attack on the *Roe* decision, Lee was convinced that his office must follow a prudent, selective course or run a serious risk of growing Court resistance to its contentions.

Lee's stance hardly pleased administrative officials favouring a more aggressive posture. He and William Bradford Reynolds differed repeatedly over the position Lee should assume in specific cases. Conservative leaders also became increasingly critical. Lee's success rate, they complained, was evidence that he was asking the Court, as one journalist put it, 'merely for what it would easily give'.[33]

Among New Right ideologues, James McClellan was founder of the Center for Judicial Studies and editor of *Benchmark*, the Center's bimonthly journal. Staff members of the Center and journal had close ties to the Reagan administration. During a brief stint as Attorney-General Meese's chief speechwriter, for example, *Benchmark*'s 1984 book review editor Gary McDowell drafted Meese's controversial addresses on the proper, limited role of the judiciary in a representative democracy. After leaving the administration, moreover, former Deputy Associate Attorney-General Bruce Fein became *Benchmark*'s Supreme Court editor.

McClellan was most disturbed apparently by Lee's strategy in a number of religion cases, especially *Wallace* v. *Jaffree*, the suit over Alabama's law requiring a daily minute of silence for prayer or meditation in the public schools. In his decision upholding the law, US District Judge Brevard Hand, who later was to ban more than forty textbooks containing 'secular humanist' values from Alabama's schools, challenged the incorporation thesis under which the First Amendment's safeguard against laws respecting an establishment of religion, among many other Bill of Rights guarantees, has been held to be binding on state and local governments through the Fourteenth Amendment's due process clause. Since Judge Hand's position flew in the face of nearly half a century of Supreme Court precedent, Lee and others in his office elected to defend the Alabama law on the narrow ground that it was a reasonable state accommodation of religion not forbidden by the Constitution. In a *Benchmark* editorial article, McClellan called for Lee's 'prompt removal'. Without mentioning Judge Hand's acknowledged 'indebtedness' for McClellan's 'vision', or informed speculation that he had actually drafted the judge's opinion, McClellan praised Hand's position and complained that the incorporation thesis was an historically baseless doctrine by which judges had acquired 'jurisdiction over civil rights disputes that were originally intended to remain under the exclusive control of the States'. By resting the government's position on narrow grounds and bowing to precedent, McClellan asserted, Lee had missed an excellent opportunity 'to lay the foundation for a conservative constitutional revolution'.

Nor was McClellan's assault confined to the prayer issue. Since Lee had once been asked for advice by the American Civil Liberties Union, McClellan wrote of his 'ACLU Connection'. He also charged that the Solicitor General had failed to take sufficiently strong positions on abortion and other issues of importance to 'the Administration he was appointed to serve'.[34]

Assistant Attorney-General Reynolds shared McClellan's concerns. Lee had persuaded Reynolds that the government should not file an *amicus* brief when Judge Hand's ruling was appealed to the Court of Appeals for the Eleventh Circuit. When the appeals panel reversed Hand, however, Reynolds argued that the government should mount in the Supreme Court a broad challenge to the Court's ban on voluntary devotional programs in the public schools. Lee and others in the Solicitor General's office were able to convince

Attorney-General William French Smith to agree to a more narrow strategy drawing a distinction between the state-directed spoken prayers forbidden by the Court's precedents and the moment of silent prayer authorized by the Alabama law. But the friction between Lee, Reynolds, and New Right leaders seemed irreconcilable. In June of 1985, the same month the Court decided the *Jaffree* case, Lee submitted his resignation. He cited financial pressures on a family with three college-age children. But he also reiterated his view that where precedents 'are well established and it's obvious that Court isn't going to depart from them, it isn't smart to lecture the Justices about where they went wrong'. He rejected, too, the notion that it was his 'job to press the Administration's policies at every turn and announce true conservative principles through the pages of my briefs. It is not. I'm the Solicitor General, not the Pamphleteer General'.[35]

During his first year as Solicitor General, Lee's successor Charles Fried enjoyed a much smoother relationship with other top Justice Department staffers than his predecessor had. A Harvard law professor who had clerked for Justice John Marshall Harlan, Fried, like Lee, had been a strong Reaganite from the beginning. In 1980, he was a member of Scholars and Educators for Reagan; in 1984, co-chairman of Law Professors for Reagan–Bush. Before his appointment as Lee's political deputy in the winter of 1985, he had served as consultant to Edwin Meese. In op-ed and magazine pieces with such titles as 'Curbing the Judiciary' and 'Questioning Quotas', he had essentially tracked the administration's position on a variety of issues.[36] Unlike Lee, moreover, Fried seemed entirely willing to use his office in ways the administration preferred. Nor, when the Court did not go his way, was he reluctant to voice his frustrations. He reportedly complained to a journalist after one ruling, 'Who knows what these clowns mean?'[37] Fried's success rate was lower than Lee's had been, but he vigorously pursued the administration's agenda.

Fried's stance may well have reflected his own conception of the Solicitor General's proper role, or the depth of his personal commitment to the goals he was advocating, rather than merely a desire to please his president. Whatever his motivations, however, his posture soon began to damage the image of his office. Three former Solicitors General complained that President Reagan had turned the office into a 'political mouthpiece' of the administration. Reports circulated that several Supreme Court Justices were finding it increasingly difficult to trust his interpretations of lower court rulings or other assertions.[38] Perhaps in an attempt to neutralize such concerns, or perhaps because Reagan as a lame-duck wanted to avoid further controversy, Fried began to moderate his positions and distance himself from Assistant Attorney-General Reynolds and other key Justice Department figures as the president's tenure neared an end. When the Supreme Court announced in the late spring of 1988, for example, that it would consider *Runyon* v. *McCrary*,[39] a 1976 precedent subjecting private discrimination to the provisions of a broadly worded Reconstruction-era civil rights statute, Fried decided not to take a position in the case. At least for a time, however, the administration had been successful in its efforts to convert the Solicitor General's office to its uses, if not in the results so achieved.

PACKING THE JUDICIARY

In its challenge to modern civil liberties policies, the Reagan administration devoted much of its time and resources to litigation, court-curbing moves in the Congress, and public attacks on controversial precedents. President Reagan's appointments to the federal bench may have the most enduring impact, however, on the future directions of civil liberties law. During his first six years in office, Reagan appointed 290 district and appeal court judges, nearly 40 per cent of the 741 total. By the end of his second term, he had a reasonable chance of filling a majority of the seats on the federal judiciary – a record matched only by Presidents Roosevelt and Eisenhower in this century. With the possible exception of Roosevelt during his first term, moreover, no president gave greater attention to the ideological leanings of his prospective nominees.[40]

To assure close scrutiny of judicial candidates and their likely decisional patterns, the administration developed a number of significant modifications in the traditional selection process. In previous administrations, the procedure for choosing nominees had been centered in the office of the Deputy Attorney-General. During the Reagan years, this role largely shifted to the Justice Department's Office of Legal Policy. In 1984, moreover, the position of Special Counsel for Judicial Selection was established in the Office of Legal Policy to advise the Assistant Attorney-General in charge of that division regarding details of the selection process. In an effort to maximize White House influence over the process, the President's Committee on Federal Judicial Selection was also created. Headed by the President's Counsel and including in its membership Reagan's

Chief of Staff, the Attorney-General, and other key White House and Justice Department figures, the Committee reviewed prospective nominees screened through the Office of Legal Policy and also served as an independent source of candidates. Finally, the President's Personnel Office began to conduct investigations of prospective nominees independent of the Justice Department's own review.

When Edwin Meese succeeded William French Smith as Attorney-General in early 1985, the selection process continued much as it had during Reagan's first term, but with the new Attorney General's significant influence increasingly evident. Before, the Assistant Attorney-General in charge of the Office of Legal Policy had reported to the Deputy Attorney-General on matters relating to judicial selection; now, that official reported directly to Meese. The position of Special Counsel for Judicial Selection in the Office of Legal Policy was also abolished and that official's responsibilities largely transferred to a Meese assistant. The President's Counsel continued to chair the Committee on Federal Judicial Selection in the White House, but Meese became the most influential figure on that Committee as well.

In contrast to every other Republican White House beginning with Eisenhower's, the Reagan administration also declined to seek pre-nomination evaluations of prospective judgeship candidates from the American Bar Association's Committee on the Federal Judiciary. Since the Committee's creation in 1946, Republican presidents had generally refused to nominate candidates not receiving at least a 'qualified' preliminary Committee rating. To further enhance its own control over the selection process, the Reagan administration stopped that practice, though continuing to maintain a close working relationship with the Committee during post-nomination evaluations of its candidates. There was probably another motivation for the administration's approach to the ABA as well. President Reagan frequently nominated younger judges (with better prospects for a long tenure) and conservative law professors who could be expected to be articulate and forceful appeals court advocates of views important to the administration. Traditionally, neither category had enjoyed the ABA ratings assigned older, practicing attorneys.

In an effort to assure nominees philosophically compatible with the President's agenda, the administration supplemented written files on prospective candidates with personal interviews. Such face-to-face encounters gave Justice Department staffers the opportunity to probe possible nominees for ideological trouble-signs, but they also gave rise to the charge that potential candidates were being subjected to a 'litmus test' of their thinking and removed from further consideration if their response to questions about abortion and other social issues important to the administration did not meet Justice Department expectations. Administration officials countered that they were concerned only with a candidate's general judicial philosophy and conception of the judge's role in constitutional cases. It would be improper, they agreed, to question candidates regarding issues likely to be raised in specific cases. But such concerns persisted throughout the President's tenure.

Attempts to secure ideologically correct nominees occasionally came into conflict, moreover, with political considerations which traditionally had played an important role in the selection process. Shortly after taking office, President Reagan abolished the circuit nominating commissions of lawyers and laypersons which President Carter had created to develop binding lists of candidates for court of appeals vacancies. But he was still subject to the dictates of 'senatorial courtesy', the custom by which Senators of a president's party exert a virtual veto (and thus *de facto* appointive power) over nomination to district judgeships and other federal offices in their state. Nor was he immune from the more flexible custom dictating that a state is entitled to one or more seats on the courts of appeals of the circuit in which it lies. While the administration seemed to respect such traditions, friction developed at times between such requirements and the ideological qualifications the administration wanted its judicial nominees to meet.

The administration's detractors not only complained about elements in the Reagan selection process; a number of nominees also proved extremely controversial. The 1986 nomination of Indiana attorney Daniel A. Manion to the Court of Appeals for the Seventh Circuit provoked bitter opposition. A former state senator whose law practice was limited largely to minor personal injury and commercial claims, Manion had never appeared before the court to which he was being appointed and his legal briefs were poorly written, riddled with spelling and grammatical errors. The ABA assigned him its lowest positive rating, and by a split vote. The Chicago Council of Lawyers, an organization of a thousand attorneys whose members practised regularly before the Seventh Circuit, found him unqualified for the position. His ideological leanings were a source of equal or greater concern to liberal congressmen and civil rights organizations, including People for the American Way, which mounted an extensive media campaign against his confirmation by the Senate. The son of Clarence Manion, a founder of the ultra-conservative John Birch Society, Manion had appeared regularly with his father on the 'Manion Forum', a radio and television program promoting conservative causes. On the program, the nominee was often critical of Supreme Court rulings, including those requiring states to obey Bill of Rights safeguards.

Although the Senate judiciary committee split nine – nine on Manion's nomination, the full Senate narrowly approved his appointment. Jefferson B. Session, III, was not so fortunate. As a federal attorney in Alabama, Session prosecuted several blacks on vote fraud charges which the defendants, who were acquitted, claimed were racially motivated. He had also called the NAACP and ACLU 'un-American' and 'Communist-inspired', thought the Ku Klux Klan was 'O.K.' until learning that some of its members were 'pot smokers', and termed a white civil rights lawyer 'a disgrace to his race'. The Judiciary Committee voted eight – ten against Session's confirmation for a district judgeship and nine – nine killing Senator Thurmond's motion to send the nomination to the Senate floor without a recommendation. Attorney-General Meese called the Committee's action 'an appalling surrender to the politics of ideology'.

But Sessions's nomination, of course, was not to be the administration's most significant Senate defeat. The President's elevation of William H. Rehnquist to the Supreme Court's center chair following Chief Justice Warren Burger's retirement aroused considerable controversy over the nominee's judicial record, charges that he had attempted to intimidate black voters in the 1960s, and his signing of illegal restrictive housing covenants. Rehnquist was ultimately confirmed by the Senate, but the 33 votes cast against him were the largest number ever cast by the Senate against a Supreme Court nominee who won confirmation. Although his judicial and constitutional philosophy appears largely to track Rehnquist's, the new Chief Justice's replacement, appeals court judge Antonin Scalia, easily won confirmation 98–0. But when Reagan sought to replace retiring Nixon appointee Lewis Powell with Robert Bork, another of his appeals court appointees and, like Scalia, a former law professor, Bork fell victim to perhaps the best orchestrated lobbying effort ever mounted against a judicial nominee. Bork's own well-documented opposition to constitutional protection for sexual privacy, even within the marriage relationship, and to First Amendment coverage for artistic expression, among other controversial positions, was no help to him either. Nor probably, given the long memories of those in political life, was his willingness, as President Nixon's Solicitor General, to fire Watergate special prosecutor Archibald Cox when Bork's Justice Department superiors resigned rather than follow the President's orders.[41]

The overwhelming majority of President Reagan's nominees made it through the Senate, however, with little or no opposition. Most apparently shared, moreover, the President's views regarding the proper role of judges in a majoritarian democracy. Few were black, and while the President named the first woman Supreme Court justice, Sandra Day O'Connor, and appointed significantly more women to the bench during his second term than in his first, at least one study has suggested that the ideological leanings of prospective women candidates may have been even more closely scrutinized than those of their male counterparts.[42] Most significantly perhaps, the oldest president in the nation's history tended, as noted earlier, to appoint younger judges than his twentieth-century predecessors, especially during his second term. The average age of his second-term appointees up to June 1987 was 48.1, compared with an average age of over fifty for Carter appointees. Thirty-nine per cent of his appointees for that period, in fact, were under 45. President Reagan thus not only made many appointments during his years in office; many of them can be expected to serve a lengthy tenure.

THE REAGAN JUDICIAL LEGACY

At this point, of course, it is difficult to assess the impact of Reagan's judicial appointments or related activities on the courts or the direction of modern civil liberties law. A study conducted by the Center for Judicial Studies of all published decisions of judges appointed by President Reagan during the first two years of his first term concluded that nearly all his appointees adhered to principles of judicial restraint favored by his administration.[43] An analysis of 1247 appeals court decisions found, however, that while Republican judges overall were much more conservative in their voting patterns than their Democratic counterparts, President Reagan's appointees were not significantly more conservative than other Republican judges. 'Public focus upon a few controversial nominations', the

study's authors concluded, 'may have led to an incorrect generaliza-
tion that all of President Reagan's appointees are rigid ideologues. In
fact, the decision-making of federal judges in the Reagan era reflects
the divergent attitudes represented by the mainstreams of the two
major parties and not, at least so far, the extremism of the far right'.[44]
Jon Gottschall arrived at somewhat the same conclusion in a separate
study. Gottschall found, for example, that the Reagan appeals court
appointees' average score of support for civil liberties claims was 31.5
per cent, while the score was 34 per cent for Nixon and Ford
appointees, 46 per cent for Kennedy–Johnson judges, and 53 per cent
for President Carter's judicial choices.[45]

Such findings suggest that the appointees of a Republican president
not so openly committed to the sort of ideological court-packing
President Reagan attempted might well have developed essentially
the same voting records the Reagan judges have. In fact, a more
circumspect president might have been even more effective in placing
such jurists on the federal bench, since the vigorous manner in which
the Reagan administration pursued its judicial agenda put opponents
on guard and undoubtedly stimulated their mobilization against the
President's more controversial nominees. Had President Reagan's
attempt to appoint judicial conservatives not been so well-defined
and obvious, for example, it is unlikely that Robert Bork's nomination could have been defeated by the Senate, at least in the absence
of the sorts of ethical improprieties which brought down the nominations of Abe Fortas and Clement Haynsworth, or the marginal
credentials that plagued G. Harrold Carswell.

It is questionable, moreover, whether many of the Reagan appointees, or others for that matter, will be willing to remain on the federal
bench without significant salary increases. According to one study,
federal district judges suffered a 34 per cent loss in real income,
1969–86, while senior corporate lawyers had a 16 per cent increase
during the same period. Primarily as a result of low salaries, the
resignation rate among federal judges has nearly doubled since the
early 1970s. Yet President Reagan recommended much lower
increases in judicial salaries than those proposed by the Commission
on Executive, Legislative, and Judicial Salaries in its 1986 report to
the president. For that reason, Sheldon Goldman has suggested that
by his indifference to the problem of relatively low judicial salaries,
President Reagan may have unwittingly undermined his efforts to
reshape the federal judiciary.[46]

In a more general way, however, President Reagan may already have had a significant impact on the courts and civil liberties policy. To a much greater degree than any president since Roosevelt, he lent attacks on the courts the enormous prestige of his office. No longer could such assaults be dismissed as the mere demagoguery of segregationist politicians, the ravings of the ultra-right 'lunatic fringe', or the eccentric notions of a minority of academics. Instead, they were now clothed with the prestige of the presidency – or at least of one president's administration. The climate of doubt and outrage the Reagan administration helped to create about the wisdom and propriety of modern human rights policies and the courts' role in their development may prove to be President Reagan's most enduring judicial legacy.

Notes

1. *South Carolina* v. *Katzenback*, 383 U.S. 301 (1966).
2. For an analysis of the administration's enforcement of voting rights legislation during President Reagan's first term, see C. S. Bullock, III, and K. I. Butler, 'Voting Rights', in T. E. Yarbrough (ed.),*The Reagan Administration and Human Rights* (New York: Praeger, 1985), pp. 29–54. Despite the administration's concerns about the preclearance requirement, Bullock and Butler concluded that the Reagan Justice Department at times demanded more than the law required of states and localities subject to federal voting rights regulations.
3. *Mobile* v. *Bolden*, 446 U.S. 55 (1980).
4. *Grove City College* v. *Bell*, 465 U.S. 555 (1984).
5. Quoted in *1983 Congressional Quarterly Almanac*, p. 294.
6. For an analysis of the controversy, see R. J. Thompson, 'The Commission of Civil Rights', in T. E. Yarbrough (ed.), *The Reagan Administration and Human Rights*, pp. 180–203.
7. For an analysis of the Reagan administration's involvement in the exemption issue, see T. E. Yarbrough, 'Tax Exemptions and Discriminatory Private Schools', in ibid., pp. 106–36.
8. *United States* v. *Bob Jones University*, 639 F. 2d 147 (4th Cir., 1980).
9. *Goldsboro Christian Schools* v. *United States*, 644 F. 2d 870 (1981).
10. Quoted in US Congress, Senate Committee on Finance. Hearing, *Legislation to Deny Tax Exemption to Racially Discriminatory Private Schools*, 97th Cong., 2d sess., 1 February 1982, pp. 60–61 (hereinafter cited as Finance Committee hearing).
11. *Washington Post*, 5 February 1982.
12. *Allen* v. *Wright*, 656 F. 2d 820 (d.C. Cir., 1982). Ultimately, the Supreme Court dismissed the suit on standing grounds, 468 U.S. 737 (1984).

13. *Bob Jones University* v. *United States*, 461 U.S. 574 (1983).
14. T. E. Yarbrough, 'Tax Exemptions and Discriminatory Private Schools', *The Reagan Administration and Human Rights*, pp. 125–9.
15. Finance Committee Hearing, p. 248.
16. 403 U.S. 601 (1971).
17. 465 U.S. 668 (1984).
18. *Wallace* v. *Jaffree*, 472 U.S. 38 (1985).
19. 454 U.S. 263 (1981).
20. See, for example, *Harris* v. *McRae*, 448 U.S. 297 (1980).
21. 410 U.S. 113 (1973).
22. *Akron* v. *Akron Center for Reproductive Health*, 462 U.S. 416 (1983).
23. *Planned Parenthood Ass'n* v. *Ashcroft*, 462 U.S. 476 (1983); *Simopoulos* v. *Virginia*, 462 U.S. 506 (1983).
24. 'A Defense of the Reagan Administration's Civil Rights Policies: An Interview with Assistant Attorney General for Civil Rights, William Bradford Reynolds', *New Perspectives*, Summer, 1984, p. 34.
25. *Firefighters Local Union No. 1784* v. *Stotts*, 467 U.S. 561 (1984).
26. For a summary of the Reynolds and Meese efforts, see *1985 Congressional Quarterly Almanac*, pp. 221–2.
27. For an analysis of the administration's first-term anti-abortion campaigns, see K. O'Connor and L. Epstein, 'Abortion Policy', in T. E. Yarbrough (ed.), *The Reagan Administration and Human Rights*, pp. 204–29.
28. 'Supreme Court Justices on Original Intent'. *Social Policy*, Vol. 18, Summer, 1987, pp. 24–8.
29. For an excellent critical study of the administration's efforts, see L. Caplan, *The Tenth Justice: The Solicitor General and the Rule of Law* (New York: Knopf, 1987).
30. *Nix* v. *Williams*, 467 U.S. 431 (1984).
31. See for example, *United States* v. *Leon*, 468 U.S. 897 (1984).
32. *Mueller* v. *Allen*, 463 U.S. 388 (1983).
33. A. Kamen, 'Not Right Enough?', *Washington Post National Weekly Edition*, 13 May 1985.
34. 'A Lawyer Looks at Rex Lee', *Benchmark*, 1, March–April, 1984, p. 1 f.
35. Quoted in Caplan, *The Tenth Justice*, p. 107.
36. See, for example, 'Curbing the Judiciary', *New York Times*, 10 November 1981.
37. Quoted in Caplan, *The Tenth Justice*, p. 275.
38. See ibid., ch. 15.
39. 427 U.S. 160 (1976).
40. For excellent analyses of Reagan judicial appointments, see the extensive research of Sheldon Goldman, including 'Reaganizing the Judiciary: The First Term Appointments', *Judicature*, Vol. 68, April–May, 1985, pp. 313–29; 'Reagan's Second Term Judicial Appointments: The Battle at Midway', *Judicature*, Vol. 70, April–May, 1987, pp. 324–39. This section draws heavily on Professor Goldman's findings and insights.

41. For an interesting analysis of Senatorial role-playing in confirmation proceedings, see G. Watson and J. Stookey, 'Supreme Court Confirmation Hearings: A View from the Senate', *Judicature*, Vol. 71, December–January, 1988, pp. 186–93; and, by the same authors, 'The Bork Hearing: Rocks and Roles', *Judicature*, Vol. 71, December–January 1988, pp. 194–6.

42. E. Martin, 'Gender and Judicial Selection: A Comparison of the Reagan and Carter Administrations', *Judicature*, Vol. 71, October–November, 1987, pp. 136–42.

43. Discussed in *National Journal*, 8 December 1984, p. 2341.

44. 'All the President's Men? A Study of Ronald Reagan's Appointments to the U.S. Courts of Appeals', *Columbia Law Review*, Vol. 87, 1987, pp. 792–3.

45. J. Gottschall, 'Reagan's Appointments to the U.S. Courts of Appeals: The Continuation of a Judicial Revolution', *Judicature*, Vol. 70, 1986, p. 54.

46. S. Goldman, 'The Age of Judges: Reagan's Second-Term Appointees', *American Bar Association Journal*, 1 October 1987, pp. 94–8.

5 Reagan's Relations with Congress

Louis Fisher

When President Reagan entered office in January 1981, Congress had just weathered four frustrating years with the Carter administration. Part of Jimmy Carter's campaign in 1976 had been directed against Congress and the bureaucracy. He seemed to pride himself on being an 'outsider', untainted by the compromises and deals practiced in the nation's capital. His congressional liaison team had little experience in dealing with Congress, often viewing it as not much more than a national version of the Georgia legislature. Relations with congressional leaders began poorly and never recovered.

Reagan, like Carter an ex-governor, had also campaigned against Congress and the bureaucracy. However, the complexity and size of California's political system was a better training ground for understanding Congress than Georgia. For eight years as governor, Reagan's ideological beliefs were compromised by consensus politics. His style seemed less sanctimonious than Carter's. Reagan assembled a professional team in the White House that worked effectively with Congress during the first year. Max Friedersdorf, part of the congressional relations staff in the Nixon and Ford administrations, was selected to head the Reagan liaison unit. Key support came from Powell A. Moore, responsible for the Senate, and Kenneth M. Duberstein, assigned to House members. Both Moore and Duberstein had substantial experience on Capitol Hill as congressional aides.

This team worked effectively and smoothly the first year in pushing Reagan's economic agenda through Congress. However, as the economy lurched into a recession and the Republican party lost 26 seats in the House in the 1982 elections, Reagan's control over Congress began to slip away. This chapter concentrates on three major issues during Reagan's administration: his economic recovery program, leading to a stunning increase in budget deficits; his Supreme Court appointments, culminating in the Senate's rejection of Robert Bork; and the Iran–Contra affair that surfaced in

November 1986 and colored the remaining years of the administration.

BUDGET POLICIES

Reagan was extraordinarily skilful in 1981 in forcing Congress to adopt his budget program. This achievement is especially remarkable when we recall the perpetual difficulties faced by the Carter administration. So bleak was the prospect of having Congress enact a presidential proposal that Lloyd Cutler, Carter's legal adviser, suggested in a famous 1980 article that the deadlock was constitutionally based:

> A particular shortcoming in need of a remedy is the structural inability of our government to propose, legislate and administer a balanced program for governing. In parliamentary terms, one might say that under the U.S. Constitution it is not now feasible to 'form a Government'. The separation of powers between the legislative and executive branches, whatever its merits in 1793, has become a structure that almost guarantees stalemate today'.[1]

A year after the appearance of this article, operating within the same constitutional system, Reagan and his assistants rammed through a revolutionary budget scheme that cut taxes, increased defense spending, and made significant reductions in domestic programs. These legislative actions were driven by the theory of supply-side economics. The cuts in taxes were supposed to stimulate new investments in the private sector and provide sufficient economic growth to generate increased tax revenues for the government. In an address before a joint session of Congress on 28 April 1981, Reagan promised that these measures would produce a balanced budget by 1984:

> Reducing the growth of spending, cutting marginal tax rates, providing relief from overregulation, and following a noninflationary and predictable monetary policy are interwoven measures which will ensure that we have addressed each of the severe dislocations which threaten our economic future. These policies will make our economy stronger, and the stronger economy will balance the budget which we're committed to do by 1984.[2]

This speech came less than a month after Reagan's dramatic recovery from the assassination attempt on 30 March. The strength of his victory in the 1980 elections had produced Republican control of the Senate for the first time in 28 years. Republicans also picked up 33 seats in the House of Representatives. Reagan could count on strict party loyalty in the Senate for the first year, and in the House he managed to stitch together a majority composed of Republicans and conservative Democrats. Through his communication skills and effective White House lobbying, Reagan was able to gain control of the budget resolution and use it for his own objectives. Unlike Carter, who announced a laundry list of legislative goals with little sense of priority, Reagan succeeded because he focused all of his skills on a single theme: economic recovery. Conservatives clamoring for action on school prayer, bussing, abortion, and the rest of their social agenda were told to wait.

Reagan was also assisted by his budget director, David Stockman, who quickly gained the reputation as a wizard with numbers and theory. We now know that Stockman was in over his head, using statistics and false information as a shield to cover his ignorance. He later admitted that he 'out-and-out cooked the books' to fabricate phony budget figures.[3] After leaving office he observed that 'a plan for radical and abrupt changes required deep comprehension – and we had none of it'.[4]

Stockman held a position of vast responsibility. He had an impressive ability to marshal facts and enunciate esoteric theory, but he lacked even an elementary understanding of the political and constitutional system. Although he had served as a staff aide to a Congressman and later as a member of Congress from Michigan, he acknowledges that it was not until years had passed in the Reagan administration that he discovered that the national government is one of checks and balances. In his own words:

> Governance was not a realm of pure reason, analysis, and the clash of ideologies. It really did involve the brute force of personality, the effrontery of bloated egos, the raw will-to-power. . . . Now the scales had fallen from my eyes. I was finally beginning to see that raw hunger for power was as important a part of the equation as pure ideas.[5]

His naivete is expressed in the following passage:

> The true Reagan Revolution never had a chance. It defied all of the overwhelming forces, interests, and impulses of American democracy. Our Madisonian government of checks and balances, three branches, two legislative houses, and infinitely splintered power is conservative, not radical. It hugs powerfully to the history behind it. It shuffles into the future one step at a time. It cannot leap into revolutions without falling flat on its face.[6]

Imagine that: a high-ranking official discovering that there are three branches of government, two Houses of Congress, and a substantial amount of fragmentation. That understanding should have come before, not after, Stockman's acceptance of the job as budget director. Reagan's budget policy in 1981 set the stage for an astonishing string of budget deficits. Although the Republican Party had long considered budget deficits as anathema, the budget package enacted in 1981 invited record deficits from one year to the next. Reagan's budget for fiscal 1982 projected a deficit of $45 billion; the deficit eventually reached $127.9 billion. The deficit for fiscal 1984, which was supposed to be a balanced budget, was $185.3 billion. The next two years produced deficits of $212.3 billion and $221.2 billion, before the deficit declined to $150.4 billion for fiscal 1987. The deficit for fiscal 1988 ended up at $155 billion.

When Reagan became President the total national debt (accumulated since 1789) was about one trillion dollars. After about five years of his administration the total debt exceeded two trillion dollars. By the time he leaves office it was approaching three trillion dollars. The general response by Reagan supporters was: 'So what? What's the harm? Deficits have not caused the predicted inflation or high interest rates, and the early deficits probably lessened the harsh effects of the 1981–82 recession and speeded economic recovery'.

Part of the cost of budget deficits is further rigidity of the budget. In 1974, President Nixon submitted a budget with 7 percent of outlays set aside to pay interest on the public debt. That is a fixed, uncontrollable cost. When Reagan submitted his budget in 1988, expenditures for interest on the public debt had doubled to 14 per cent. Because of restraints on domestic and defense spending and the persistence of budget deficits, an even higher portion of the federal budget will be set aside in the future simply to pay interest on the public debt. The more is paid for interest the less is available for other budget priorities. Increasingly, choices are being limited.

The Reagan administration was able to accumulate massive deficits without triggering a new round of inflation, but the successful record on inflation should be attributed to the policies of the Federal Reserve and Paul Volcker, not Ronald Reagan. The weapon against inflation was monetary, not fiscal. Moreover, Reagan was extremely lucky during his two terms. Both Gerald Ford and Jimmy Carter were hard hit by OPEC policies on oil. During Reagan's years, the oil cartel fell apart and oil prices tumbled. Agricultural and food prices decreased worldwide. Labor unions had less leverage to bargain for wage increases. These are secular trends and cannot be attributed to deliberate policies adopted by the Reagan administration.

The Federal Reserve's anti-inflation policy relied on high interest rates, high enough to attract foreign investors whose contributions helped the United States finance its budget deficits. As a result, the United States is more vulnerable to the decisions of foreign investors; more of its capital stock belongs to foreigners; and the returns on those investments will go to foreigners, not to the United States. There is serious concern that heavy borrowing will limit moderniza- tion, economic expansion, and improvements in U.S. living stan- dards. High interest rates are also a burden on Third World coun- tries.

The eight years of the Reagan administration divide into two periods for budget policy. In the first year Reagan put the country in an enormous quandary. For the next seven years he offered no solution for the deficits. He continued to submit budgets with huge deficits and vowed to veto any attempt by Congress to redress the situation through tax increases. Any lessening of the deficits came from congressional efforts, either through changes in tax rates or through cutbacks in defense spending. Reagan was content to sit on the sidelines and tell Congress: 'You figure it out.' In matters of budgeting, it is difficult to find a more irresponsible President in the twentieth century.

For its part, Congress helped undermine presidential responsibility by passing the Budget Act of 1974 and the Gramm–Rudman– Hollings Act of 1985. Without going into excessive detail on either statute,[7] the net effect has been less accountability for the President and the acceptance by Congress of duties it cannot discharge. Ironically, the new budget process adopted by Congress in 1974 to strengthen its prerogatives helped Reagan enact his budget package in 1981. The total result is an increase in presidential power and a decline in presidential responsibility.

The Budget Act of 1974 marked a turn from decentralized to centralized legislative action. Instead of acting in piecemeal fashion on individual appropriation, authorization, and revenue bills, Congress established Budget Committees in each House to prepare budget resolutions. The purpose of a budget resolution was to enable Congress to act on the budget as a whole, permitting comprehensive and systematic action. The Budget Act assumed that members of Congress will behave more responsibly if they have to vote on budget totals rather than on separate budget items.

The authors of the Budget Act believed that the new congressional process would restrain spending, reduce deficits, and lead to the timely enactment of appropriations bills. These goals have not been fulfilled. The level of spending before and after the Act has not been materially different, deficits have exploded, and Congress is much less able to pass appropriations bills on time.[8]

An unintended consequence has been to erode the significance and influence of the President's Budget. From 1921 to 1974, as a statutory duty, the president took personal responsibility for the budget he submitted. Congress could change the president's priorities, as it did, but over a period of decades the aggregates proposed by the president were generally the aggregates enacted by Congress. With regard to total spending, total revenues, and the level of surpluses and deficits, the president was the determining actor. He was the one person in the country who could be held accountable. There was only one budget: the president's. Congressional action could be easily analyzed by comparing committee actions with presidential requests. Each branch of government did what it was institutionally designed to do.

The 1974 Act changed this pattern. Now the Congress had to sort through multiple budgets: the president's, the first budget resolution, the second budget resolution, the second budget resolution revised (passed the following spring), and a mind-numbing assortment of other budgets produced to reflect changing baselines, reestimates, and updates. The phrases 'below budget' and 'above budget' no longer had meaning. The president's budget, as a visible benchmark to keep both branches accountable, had disappeared.

In fact, members of Congress claimed that there was only one budget: the one produced by Congress. During the debate in 1983, House Majority Leader Jim Wright made this statement:

This bill is not over the budget: the amounts proposed in this amendment are well within the budgeted figures. The amounts that we have agreed to and discussed are not in excess of the congressional budget resolution. That, of course, is the budget. Now they may be in excess of certain amounts requested by the President in his budget request of last January. But that, of course, is not the budget. Congress makes the budget; the President does not.[9]

Such statements invited Reagan to tell Congress: 'Since you make the budget, you figure it out.' The problem is that Congress is not institutionally capable of making and being held responsible for a budget. That takes unity, and Congress is inherently a decentralized body, permanently divided between two houses, two parties, and a plethora of committees and subcommittees.

Ironically, the decision in 1974 to centralize the congressional budget process by passing a budget resolution opened the door to greater executive influence. In 1981, Reagan was able to gain control over the budget resolution to impose his budget priorities: retrenchment of domestic spending, increases for defense, and a major tax cut. It is highly unlikely that his radical program would have survived the previous decentralized, fragmented process within Congress. By the time he had negotiated separately with the appropriation, authorization, and revenue committees, there would have been little left of supply-side economics. The incrementalism of the decentralized process made radical action practically impossible.

The 1974 Act simplified Reagan's task. Because Congress had to vote on an overall budget policy in the budget resolution, Reagan could accomplish his goals by gaining control of the resolution and using it to embody his principles. Stockman explained how the congressional budget process became a convenient handle to promote Reagan's goals. The constitutional prerogatives of Congress 'would have to be, in effect, suspended. Enacting the Reagan Administration's economic program meant rubber stamp approval, nothing less. The world's so-called greatest deliberative body would have to be reduced to the status of a ministerial arm of the White House'.[10] Congress 'had to forfeit its independence and accept the role of a rubber-stamping parliament if the whole plan was to work'.[11]

Legislative action in 1981 revealed serious weaknesses within Congress. Instead of relying on the estimates of its own institutional body, the Congressional Budget Office, or substituting a forecast of its own, Congress accepted the administration's facile economic assumptions. Although part of the purpose of the 1974 Act was to give Congress an independent technical capability, in 1981 Congress chose to embrace the administration's flawed and false premises. Anyone familiar with the budget in 1981 knew that Reagan's proposals risked enormous deficits.

The Reagan administration was very effective its first year in exploiting the congressional budget process. Unfortunately, the President's influence in producing record deficits was not used in subsequent years to reduce them. The budgets he submitted after 1981 were almost totally ignored by both houses. He did not submit budgets with the conviction that he wanted them passed. There was no indication that he personally believed that deficits of $150 billion or $200 billion a year are appropriate for the country, or that he would intervene whenever possible to defend his proposals. The budgets came to Capitol Hill with only tenuous connections with the President's office.

Why did Congress pass the Gramm–Rudman–Hollings Act of 1985? I think it was an admission that the process created by the 1974 Act, despite all the brave pronouncements defending it, was unreliable in controlling spending and deficits. Because of the political stalemate between President Reagan and Congress, it was necessary to enact a statute that gave both branches marching orders to eliminate deficits by fiscal 1991. Beginning with a deficit of $171.9 billion for fiscal 1986, the statute called for a decrease in the deficit by about $36 billion each year over a five-year period. Both the budget submitted by the President and the budget resolution passed by Congress had to adhere to these deficit targets. In short, a statute dictated a key aggregate in the president's budget, further undercutting the notion of executive responsibility.

One of the curious spinoffs from budget deficits was Reagan's request for item-veto authority. Repeatedly, in his State of the Union messages, he asked Congress to pass a constitutional amendment to give him the power to invoke not merely a general veto but also the deletion of specific items. As he said in the State of the Union message in 1988: 'Give the President the same authority that forty-three governors use in their states, the right to reach into massive appropriations bills, pare away the waste, and enforce budget discipline. Let's approve the line-item veto'.

The request was curious coming from a president who ushered in massive deficits and persisted in sending unbalanced budgets to

Congress. If balanced budgets were an important goal for Reagan, why didn't he do what was clearly within his power and send one up? Based on his performance in office, why should he be rewarded with new authority?

The appeal in 1988 was particularly bizarre because whoever drafted the speech for Reagan showed no understanding of the budget process. Standing in front of members of Congress and the millions of citizens watching on television, Reagan gave as examples of the waste that could be trimmed with an item veto 'millions for items such as cranberry research, blueberry research, the study of crawfish, and the commercialization of wild flowers'. In an important address given on national television, why single out such trivia? It does not take a budget expert to realize that the cumulative total of the four items were miniscule. The amounts come to $92,000 for research on the blueberry shoestring virus to be conducted in Michigan, $260,000 for cranberry/blueberry disease and breeding in New Jersey, $50,000 for native wildflowers in New Mexico, and $200,000 for crawfish research in Louisiana. When facing deficits of $150 billion to $170 billion, what purpose is served by zeroing in on $602,000? Reagan's preoccupation with these four items is even more fantastic because the four items were not in the bill presented to him. They were in the conference report. Even if Reagan had item-veto authority in December 1987 when the continuing resolution reached him, he would have been powerless to delete the cranberries, blueberries, wild flowers, and crawfish. You cannot veto what is not in a bill. OMB professionals knew that the passage in the State of the Union message was nonsense, but amateurism was in the driver's seat.

Reagan's successor has inherited a budget crisis ready to explode. A solution will take close cooperation and good faith between the legislative and executive branches. An essential step is to restore in the presidency a sense of personal accountability for submitting a responsible budget. If the president shows leadership in preparing budgets to reduce the deficit, Congress can be counted on to live within the presidential aggregates while rearranging his priorities. If this occurs, each branch will be fulfilling its institutional strengths.

SUPREME COURT APPOINTMENTS

Reagan had his first opportunity to appoint a Justice to the Supreme
Court when Potter Stewart sent his letter requesting retirement, with
effect from 3 July 1981. As Stewart's replacement, Reagan nominated Sandra Day O'Connor who had served in the Arizona state
senate and in the Arizona courts. During his campaign he promised
to name a woman to the Court. O'Connor, proposed as the first
woman on the Court, performed well at the hearings before the
Senate Judiciary Committee and was confirmed by a unanimous
Senate, 99–0. Senator Max Baucus, who had supported her nomination, was absent for the final vote. Although Reagan would name few
women to the federal courts, his nomination of O'Connor was a
personal triumph.

No other openings on the Supreme Court appeared until 1986,
when Chief Justice Warren Burger announced his intention to retire.
Reagan named Associate Justice William Rehnquist to replace
Burger, setting off a vigorous fight against Rehnquist's elevation. The
Senate finally confirmed Rehnquist's nomination 65–33, after lengthy
hearings and spirited floor debate. The votes in opposition were the
largest number ever cast against a Supreme Court nominee who won
confirmation.

To replace Rehnquist as Associate Justice, Reagan nominated
Antonin Scalia, who had served as a federal appellate judge on the
D.C. Circuit. Scalia had a relatively easy time with the Senate
Judiciary Committee, answering few questions during his single day
of hearings. So reticent was Scalia that he declined to comment even
on *Marbury* v. *Madison* (1803): 'I do not think I should answer
questions regarding any specific Supreme Court opinion, even one as
fundamental as *Marbury* v. *Madison*'.[12] Senators, remembering
Scalia's performance, would insist that the next nominee for the
Supreme Court be more forthcoming.

With these three appointments, Reagan made a substantial difference in the composition of the Court. O'Connor was thought to be
more conservative than Stewart, and Scalia more conservative than
Burger. Many of the decisions on defendants' rights, abortion,
church and state, and other cases that offended conservatives now
seemed in doubt. If Reagan could make one more appointment, it
seemed likely that some of these rulings could be overturned or at
least recast along lines favored by Reagan supporters.

The opportunity came in June 1987, when Associate Justice Lewis Powell, Jr., announced his intention to retire. To replace Powell, who had been a moderate voice on the Court and a swing vote, Reagan picked Robert H. Bork. Perhaps best known for his firing of Archibald Cox during the Watergate 'Saturday Night massacre', Bork was a conservative favorite. For several years he had served as a federal appellate judge from the D.C. Circuit. Alarm bells rang. It now looked as though major shifts in Court doctrine were likely.

Reagan tried to argue that (1) a judge's personal preferences should not influence constitutional interpretation, (2) Bork was chosen because of his personal beliefs, and (3) it was proper for the President, but improper for the Senate, to take into account a nominee's philosophy. The Senate should confine its attention solely to qualifications, not philosophy. Consider these conflicting announcements by Reagan:

> Judge Bork, widely regarded as the most prominent and intellectual advocate of judicial restraint, shares my view that judges' personal preferences and values should not be part of their constitutional interpretations.[13]

> . . . . he's not going to promote my political views; he's going to apply a superb legal mind to the task of interpreting the Constitution and the laws of the United States.[14]

> . . . a President, whether Republican or Democrat, liberal or conservative, seeks out the best qualified person who generally shares the president's judicial philosophy. The Senate then decides whether the nominee meets the qualifications to serve.[15]

The Senate rejected these restrictions on the advice and consent of Supreme Court nominees. The President took personal philosophy into account; so would the Senate. One mistake by the White House was the effort to paper over Bork's conservative views. Reagan said in a radio address to the nation: 'In truth, Judge Bork's philosophy of judging is neither conservative nor liberal'. Reagan agreed with the assessment of Lloyd Cutler that Bork was part of the 'moderate center'.[16] By painting Bork as a moderate, the message to conservatives was to stay in the shadows and not show their faces. Meanwhile liberal groups were mobilizing in full force.

The White House strategy backfired for another reason. At the hearings, Bork time and time again dissociated himself from views he had earlier propounded. Although administration officials begged Bork to keep his answers short, Bork preferred to talk at length. He was encouraged to do so by the chairman of the Senate Judiciary Committee, Senator Joseph R. Biden, Jr. The more Bork talked, the more ammunition he gave his opponents. Because Bork had earlier flirted with socialism and libertarianism, and now appeared to be in transition from a conservative to a moderate, Senators wondered what they were being asked to confirm. What would he be in six months hence? Did he have a consistent judicial philosophy? Were his statements at the hearings nothing more than a 'confirmation conversion', a clever effort to recant positions for no other reason than to attract committee votes? These shifts raised serious questions of integrity and honesty.

After Reagan had nominated Bork, he gave several speeches that emphasized Bork's strong record on law and order. Reagan said that the Supreme Court 'has always had a critical role in the administration of criminal justice at both the State and Federal levels. Criminal cases make up one of the largest categories of the highest Court's decisions'. As Solicitor General, Bork had argued in favor of capital punishment. His nomination, said Reagan, 'is a crucial opportunity to continue our progress in the war against crime'.[17] Beyond questions of Bork's scholarship and judicial qualifications, Reagan said 'there's nothing more significant for his confirmation than the war on crime'. Both as Solicitor General and as judge, 'Robert Bork has been a principled champion in the fight against crime. . . '.[18]

This tactic came to nothing when Bork was asked at the hearings to give his views on criminal law. He responded by saying that he was not an expert on criminal law and that the issue did not come up frequently when he was on the DC circuit. Lawyers in the Justice Department who had drafted the question, thinking it would be a softball laid across the middle of the plate, shook their heads in despair. One of them told me: 'He was supposed to hit it out of the park. Instead, he dribbled back to the pitcher'.

Bork encountered major resistance because of the strong positions he had taken on controversial issues, making him appear antagonistic to women's rights, civil rights, abortion rights, privacy, and freedom of speech. No issue gave Bork such difficulty as the question of privacy. He testified that the Constitution does not recognize a general right to privacy, and in his previous writings and public statements he had criticized Justice Douglas's decision in *Griswold* v. *Connecticut* (1965), which struck down a state law that prohibited the use of contraceptives. It is easy to ridicule Douglas's effort to discover a right to privacy in various 'penumbras' and 'emanations' in the Bill of Rights. But the right to privacy is a core concept that protects individuals from government. Citizens of every rank and station, of every level of education, whether liberal or conservative, hold strong views on the retention of what the Declaration of Independence calls 'certain unalienable rights'. They believe in a zone of privacy that prevents governmental intrusion.

The Bork nomination divided every sector of society. The American Bar Association Committee, after reviewing his record, supplied a split vote. Ten members of the committee supported him as 'well qualified'. Four found him 'not qualified'. One voted 'not opposed', which means minimally qualified and not among the best available. Bork was opposed by the National Association for the Advancement of Colored People, the American Civil Liberties Union, People for the American Way, women's groups, and other organizations. The Senate Judiciary Committee rejected him 9 to 5. The vote in the full Senate was 58 opposed and 42 in favor of the nomination.

After this exhausting and bruising battle, Senators were prepared to confirm the next nominee for the Court. Instead of sending up a name of a moderate conservative who could be quickly confirmed, Reagan decided to have another confrontation. On 29 October 1987, Reagan announced the nomination of Douglas H. Ginsburg, a conservative who had served less than one year as a federal appellate judge. Reagan's announcement was brusque and combative, but only by watching his performance on television can one appreciate the full measure of spite and vindictiveness. He even set a deadline for hearings by the Senate Judiciary Committee, suggesting that if the delay exceeded three weeks 'the American people will know what's up'.[19]

Ginsburg's credentials were not impressive. Other than his year on the bench, he had little experience with constitutional law beyond antitrust and government regulation. When he was nominated to be a federal appellate judge, he told the Senate that he had appeared in court 34 times to try a case to judgment. In fact, his total courtroom experience amounted to an hour-long appellate court argument. It was also revealed that when he handled cable television matters while working in the Justice Department he owned $140,000 in cable television stock. Serious questions of judgment and conflict of interest were raised by this disclosure.

The final blow to his nomination came when he admitted smoking marijuana while a professor at the Harvard Law School. Ginsburg's admission was particularly damaging because of Reagan's strong campaign against drugs. His wife, Nancy, had urged youngsters to 'just say no'. Moreover, the Reagan administration had placed a heavy emphasis on law and order. With the latest disclosure the supporters of Ginsburg took flight. It was only a question of when Ginsburg would save the administration from further embarrassment. Within nine days of the nomination, long before Reagan's three-week deadline could be breached, Ginsburg requested that his name be withdrawn.

Reagan's performance is strongly reminiscent of Richard Nixon's behavior in 1969. After having his nomination of Clement F. Haynsworth to the Supreme Court rejected, Nixon acted in a vengeful manner by sending up the name of G. Harrold Carswell. Nixon suggested that presidents could take personal philosophy into account, but not the Senate:

> What is centrally at issue in this nomination is the constitutional responsibility of the President to appoint members of the Court – and whether this responsibility can be frustrated by those who wish to substitute their own philosophy or their own subjective judgment for that of the one person entrusted by the Constitution with the power of appointment . . . if the Senate attempts to substitute its judgment as to who should be appointed, the traditional constitutional balance is in jeopardy and the duty of the President under the Constitution impaired.[20]

The Senate lost little time in rejecting Carswell. Nixon's third nomination, Harry A. Blackmun, was confirmed by a unanimous Senate.

After Reagan failed with Bork and Ginsburg, he turned to Anthony M. Kennedy, a federal appellate judge from the Ninth Circuit. Kennedy sailed through the hearings without difficulty. Instead of floundering the way Bork did on the question of privacy, Kennedy testified that privacy was a fundamental right. Here are excerpts from the hearings:

> *Senator DeConcini*: [I]t appears from reading your speech, that you have concluded, without question, that there is a fundamental

right to privacy. And I think the chairman had you state that, and that is your position, correct?
Judge Kennedy: Well, I have indicated that is essentially correct. I prefer to think of the value of privacy as being protected by the clause, liberty, and maybe that is a semantic quibble, maybe it is not.
Senator DeConcini: But it is there, is that . . .
Judge Kennedy: Yes, sir.
Senator DeConcini: No question about it being in existence?
Judge Kennedy: Yes, sir.[21]

Judge Kennedy elaborated on his response, indicating that he understood the important value of privacy as a constitutional concept: 'It is central to our American tradition. It is central to the ideal of the rule of law. That there is a zone of liberty, a zone of protection, a line that is drawn where the individual can tell the Government: beyond this line you may not go'.[22] He was confirmed by the Senate, 97–0.

THE IRAN – CONTRA AFFAIR

The issues discussed thus far were high-profile matters for Ronald Reagan: the defense buildup, cuts in domestic programs, tax reductions, and Supreme Court nominations. Two other matters occupied Reagan's thoughts: assistance to the Contra rebels in Nicaragua and efforts to free American hostages in Iran (with Carter's political embarrassment always in mind). The two issues became entwined, eventually causing the most serious crisis for the Reagan administration and producing a direct confrontation with Congress. To provide military aid to the Contras, the administration had to violate language that Congress had added to appropriation bills.

Congress agreed in the first year of Reagan's administration to provide covert assistance to the Contras. With the war in Central America on page one of the leading newspapers, assistance by 1982 had become overt, and bad-faith actions by administration officials prompted Congress to tighten the language giving aid to the Contras. After other transgressions by the administration, especially the mining of harbours in Nicaragua, Congress in October 1984 adopted the strict language of the Boland Amendment:

During the fiscal 1985, no funds available to the Central Intelligence Agency, the Department of Defense, or any other agency or entity of the United States involved in intelligence activities may be obligated or expended for the purpose or which would have the effect of supporting, directly or indirectly, military or paramilitary operations in Nicaragua by any nation, group, organization, movement, or individual.[23]

The tortuous language was adopted because Congress felt that it had been tricked and deceived by the administration and this time wanted to close all doors. Although Congress provided some humanitarian aid to the Contras in 1985, the prohibition on lethal aid continued until October 1986.

Members of Congress heard reports that the administration might be playing games again, trying to circumvent the Boland Amendment. However, in hearings in March and April 1985, an administration official assured Congress that there would be strict compliance with the Amendment.[24] In fact, at the very moment this official was testifying, the administration was supplying lethal aid to the Contras. When congressional committees asked National Security Advisors Robert McFarlane and John Poindexter if anyone in the administration, especially Colonel Oliver North, was violating the Boland Amendment, Congress was lied to. North later admitted, during congressional testimony, that he helped prepare documents for Congress that were 'erroneous, misleading, evasive and wrong'.[25] North also testified that, in an effort to conceal his activities, he destroyed the falsified official documents kept in the National Security Council. Despite these admissions, he received public praise from Reagan.

The Iran–Contra affair began to unravel on 5 October 1986, when a C-123 aircraft carrying military supplies to the Contras crashed in Nicaragua. The only survivor was Eugene Hasenfus, later found to be working for the CIA. The State Department issued press statements that the Reagan administration was not involved in the flight. This was the first of many lies.

On 3 November 1986, a Lebanese newspaper reported that the United States had secretly sold arms to Iran. Later reports indicated that the purpose of the sales was to free American hostages. On 13 November, President Reagan made a national address denying the reports:

The charge has been made that the United States has shipped weapons to Iran as ransom payment for the release of American hostages in Lebanon, that the United States undercut its allies and secretly violated American policy against trafficking with terrorists. Those charges are utterly false. The United States has not made concessions to those who hold our people captive in Lebanon. And we will not. The United States has not swapped boatloads or planeloads of American weapons for the return of American hostages. And we will not.

. . . Our government has a firm policy not to capitulate to terrorist demands. That no concessions policy remains in force, in spite of the wildly speculative and false stories about arms for hostages and alleged ransom payments. We did not – repeat – did not trade weapons or anything else for hostages nor will we.[26]

Every one of these statements by Reagan was a lie. During a news conference on 19 November, he said that 'everything that we sold them could be put in one cargo plane, and there would be plenty of room left over'.[27] That too was false. Another shoe fell on 25 November when Attorney-General Edwin Meese III announced that profits from the sales of arms to Iran had been 'diverted' to the Contras at a time when the Boland Amendment was in force.

Reagan could have taken control of the situation by asking the principal players – John Poindexter, Oliver North, Robert McFarlane, William Casey – for a full account. Instead, he moved in three directions: setting up the Tower Board, urging Meese to go to the courts to have an Independent Counsel appointed, and inviting Congress to conduct a fullscale investigation. As the months rolled by, it became clear that the operations of Iran–Contra had been in direct conflict with administration policies. Publicly, the United States was neutral on the Iran–Iraq war, it opposed the shipment of weapons to either side (Operation Staunch), and refused to trade arms for hostages or make concessions to terrorists. Privately, the administration violated everyone of these policies.

The Tower Board completed its investigation and released its report in February 1987, informing President Reagan that he had indeed traded arms for hostages. In another address to the nation, on 4 March 1987, Reagan gave this feeble explanation: 'A few months ago I told the American people I did not trade arms for hostages. My heart and my best intentions still tell me that's true, but the facts and the evidence tell me it is not'.[28] It took an outside study group to tell Reagan what he had done.

One of the extraordinary revelations of Iran–Contra was the theory pushed by some members of the Reagan administration that the President can conduct foreign and military affairs without appropriations from Congress. Under this theory, if Congress passed a Boland Amendment to prohibit the use of funds to assist the contras, the President could accomplish the same result by seeking funds from foreign governments and private parties. This was the testimony of Poindexter and North.[29]

Permitting the President to use funds obtained from foreign and private parties, thereby circumventing Congress and the appropriation process, would create a system of government the framers feared the most: union of the sword and the purse. Alexander Hamilton and James Madison explained that liberties in America would be safeguarded by placing the sword in one branch and the purse in the other.[30] Iran–Contra, as envisioned by William Casey, Oliver North, and others, represented a shadow government with its own system of transportation, communication, personnel, and military supplies, all operating out of sight of Congress and the public.

Beyond the question of uniting the purse with the sword is the prospect of debasing foreign policy. By soliciting funds to help the contras, as was done with Saudi Arabia and others, the United States was beholden to other countries. Obligations were incurred. In return for one favor, the United States would be expected to make a reciprocal gesture or concession. A quid for a quo. Congressman Ed Jenkins expressed concern that the foreign nation asked to contribute to the contras would be 'placed in a compromising situation'. McFarlane responded: 'What is worse, we would be'.[31] Nations who donate money to help the President conduct his foreign policy will expect the administration to compensate through arms sales, economic aid, trade concessions, or some other form of assistance. There is also the spectacle of the President going around the world with a tin cup, begging for funds that Congress had refused to appropriate.

Because of the death of William Casey and the destruction of so many official documents, we may never know the full story behind Iran–Contra. The reports by the Tower Board and the Iran–Contra Committees supply some of the details, yet there are still many loose ends and implausible statements from those who testified. Criminal prosecutions in the federal courts may uncover additional information.

Whatever the final outcome, the cost to President Reagan was enormous. Despite his repeated explanations about his role in Iran-Contra, public polls revealed that a majority of Americans, liberals and conservatives, did not believe him. It was not a question of being out of touch with events within his own administration. He had lost the precious commodity of credibility. The picture was of a president who went before the cameras and one occasion after another lied to the electorate.

The other cost of Iran–Contra was accountability. However much one might disagree with Reagan on the military buildup, budget deficits, resistance to tax increases, or the Bork and Ginsburg nominations, there was never any doubt of where he stood. He was visible and in charge. With Iran–Contra, many key events and decisions could never be traced back either to Reagan or to Vice-President George Bush. Lines of accountability seemed to disappear into thin air, never connecting to the two elected leaders of the executive branch. Iran–Contra shattered Reagan's reputation as a political leader.

CONCLUSION

This chapter describes only a fraction of Reagan's relationships with Congress. He came to office with important experience from a major state. His ability to communicate to the people was vastly superior to any president in the television age. One need only recall the discomfort of Lyndon Johnson, Richard Nixon, Gerald Ford, and Jimmy Carter before the television camera. Reagan was a master. His tone, expression, and delivery were unparalleled. Either by memorizing his lines or using a professional's technique to read the monitor, Reagan spoke with a directness, naturalness, and sincerity that touched millions.

The tragedy of Ronald Reagan is that these ample gifts came to so little. His program for economic recovery resulted in more than a doubling of the national debt. The trade deficit soared. Both of these deficits – budget and trade – became chronic problems over the eight-year period. Promises by the administration to cut the trade deficit came to nought. By the end of Reagan's second term the United States had become the world's leading debtor nation. Other countries had reason to doubt the health of the US economy. The praise that greeted Reagan's first year was now replaced by a decline in confidence. As Reagan's successor, President Bush inherited an economy beset by fundamental deficiencies, requiring decades to correct.

On his judicial nominations, Reagan made substantial changes in the makeup of district courts, appellate courts, and the Supreme Court. Although conservatives complained about the behaviour of some nominees once on the bench, it was never realistic to expect a wholesale change from the Warren and Burger years. Even if the 'liberal' decisions have not been overturned, they have been moderated to some extent and the votes are becoming so close on some issues that reversals may not be too far in the future. Even given the defeat of Bork and the withdrawal of Ginsburg, Reagan was able to put on the Court three conservatives: O'Connor, Scalia, and Kennedy. They have already made their presence felt. However, given the ages of other members on the Court, pivotal choices may well fall to President Bush, who is likely to be able to select three or more Justices.

With regard to Iran–Contra, the American public could have forgiven Reagan for trying and failing. Other presidents have made grievous errors in foreign policy and survived because they accepted personal responsibility. What could not be forgiven about Iran–Contra was Reagan's recourse to memory loss, confusion, and falsehood. Mistakes in the White House are costly but not fatal. Permanent damage comes from actions that break faith with the public, creating a rupture that prevents citizens from again believing in the words of a leader. This was the special dimension and magnitude of Iran–Contra.

Unlike Carter and Reagan, Bush did not run against Congress and the bureaucracy. Thus, for the first time in more than a decade, conditions are favorable for cooperative relations between the President and Congress. No doubt collisions and confrontations will occur, but if each side accepts the other as legitimate and is willing to reach accommodations in the public's interest, the United States can begin the process of restoring fundamentals in its economic and political systems.

Notes

1. L. N. Cutler, 'To Form a Government', *Foreign Affairs*, Vol. 59, Fall 1980, p. 127.

2.   *Public Papers of the Presidents*, 1981, p. 393.
3.   D. A. Stockman, *The Triumph of Politics* (New York: Harper & Row, 1986) p. 353.
4.   Ibid., p. 91.
5.   Ibid., p. 243.
6.   Ibid., p. 9.
7.   For further elaboration see L. Fisher, *The Politics of Shared Power* (Washington DC: Congressional Quarterly Press, 1987) pp. 198–209.
8.   Louis Fisher, 'Ten Years of the Budget Act: Still Searching For Controls', *Public Budgeting & Finance*, Vol. 5, August 1985, pp. 3–26.
9.   129 Cong. Rec. H7237 (daily ed., 22 September 1983).
10.   Stockman, *The Triumph of Politics*, p. 159.
11.   Ibid., p. 200.
12.   Senate Committee on the Judiciary, 'Nomination of Judge Antonin Scalia', 99th Cong., 2nd Sess. (1986), p. 33.
13.   *Weekly Compilation of Presidential Documents*, Vol. 23, No. 26, p. 761 (1 July 1987).
14.   Ibid., Vol. 23, No. 39, p. 1096 (30 September 1987).
15.   Ibid., p. 1097.
16.   Ibid., Vol. 23, No. 38, p. 1049, 19 September 1987.
17.   Ibid., Vol. 23, No. 36, p. 983, 28 August 1987.
18.   Ibid., Vol. 23, No. 39, p. 1097, 30 September 1987.
19.   Ibid., Vol. 23, No. 43, p. 1248, 28 October 1987.
20.   *Public Papers of the Presidents*, 1970, p. 332.
21.   133 Cong. Rec. S18593 (daily ed. 21 December 1987).
22.   134 Cong. Rec. S682 (daily ed. 4 February 1988).
23.   98 Stat. 1935, 8066 (1984).
24.   Senate Committee on Foreign Relations, 'Security and Development Assistance', 99th Cong., 1st Sess. (1985), pp. 908, 910; House Committee on Appropriations, 'Department of Defense Appropriations for 1986', 99th Cong., 1st Sess. (1985), p. 1092.
25.   Joint Hearings by the Iran–Contra Committees, 'Iran–Contra Investigation' (Vol. 100–7, Part I). 100th Cong., 1st Sess. (1987), p. 180.
26.   *Weekly Compilation of Presidential Documents*, Vol. 22, No. 46, pp. 1559, 1561 (13 November 1986).
27.   Ibid., Vol. 22, No. 47, p. 1584, 19 November 1986.
28.   Ibid., Vol. 23, No. 9, p. 220, 4 March 1987.
29.   Joint Hearings by the Iran–Contra Committees, 'Iran–Contra Investigation' (Vol. 100–8), pp. 158, 290; (Vol. 100–7), p. 207.
30.   Hamilton in Federalist Paper No. 69; Gaillard Hunt, ed., *The Writings of James Madison* (New York: G. P. Putnam's, 1906), Vol. 6, p. 148.
31.   Joint Hearings by the Iran-Contra Committees, 'Iran–Contra Investigation' (Vol. 100–2), 100th Cong., 1st Sess. (1987), p. 280.

6 Ideological Images for a Television Age: Ronald Reagan as Party Leader

Charles W. Dunn and
J. David Woodard

'If I could not go to heaven but with a party', declared Thomas Jefferson in 1789, 'I would not go there at all'. The role of party leader has bedeviled presidents since the beginning of the republic, but history has shown that the greatest among them – Jackson, Wilson, Lincoln and the two Roosevelts – were all skilful party-leaders. 'No matter how fondly or how often we may long for a President who is above the heat of political strife, we must acknowledge resolutely his right and duty to be the leader of his party'.[1]

For all the glib talk about the chief executive as party leader, there are few specific tasks associated with the role; in fact, the job can be broken down into formal and informal categories. The formal responsibilities include appointment of the national chairman and other top officials, the distribution of patronage and an appearance at the party's convention every four years. The president is expected to campaign for aspiring officeholders and provide policies which will enable them to gain election, or re-election.

In the past the primary job of political parties was to nominate candidates, raise the money for their election campaign, organise their followers into a loyal army, and draw together the demands of diverse groups into a coherent party program under which all could unite at election time. Then the parties went to the voters with a program to help the public sort out the issues and encourage the endorsement of the party candidate. The president was expected to lead the party as it performed its various chores.

115

In recent years, the primacy and structure of the political parties has been undermined by a host of changes. Presidential nomination is now determined by direct primaries. Candidates raise their own money and build personal organisations. Party endorsement is frequently an empty ritual. The historic job of dispensing patronage has all but expired in the face of an expanded civil service system. Political machines are a thing of the past, big cities such as Boston and Chicago no longer have a steady infusion of new immigrants to swell the ranks of the party rank and file.

Ask any political observer about the list of formal jobs associated with the president as party leader and you will hear that it does not begin to describe the role he plays as Chief Republican or Chief Democrat. That is because it is the informal powers that matter in day-to-day political leadership. The party apparatus has been displaced into the shadows by modern technology and techniques of politics. Television, not the party, is now the main channel of communication between the leader and his followers. It is the evening news broadcast, and Sunday public affairs shows, that give flesh and blood to party principles. The job of leading mass publics is now symbolic.

What matters in politics today are the personality and image, the gut impressions a viewer receives from a thirty-second campaign spot or a rag-tag interview on the airport tarmac. Presidential campaigns arc superficial, and the links between candidate and party loyalist tenuous, because television is so occupied with the immediate and the visual. When the press examines a politician's performance in detail, few voters bother to read the substance of the critique; but everyone notices the visual gaffe of a television interview. The art of political campaigning has been handed to professional 'media specialists' who work with pollsters to give the best 'spin on an issue' for the candidate.

Governing is also a function of media perceptions. The goal is to control the press agenda by framing the pictures that will be taken and the quotes that will be recorded. Hedrick Smith tells of an interview he had with David Gergen, Reagan's first White House communications director.

> We had a rule in the Nixon operation that before any public event was put on his schedule, you had to know what the headline out of that event was going to be, what the picture was going to be, and what the lead paragraph would be.[2]

The Reagan White House was just as image conscious. There was a public relations script built around the 'story line of the day' (i.e. the message that would appear on the evening television programs and in headlines the next day). To insure that television cameras would record just what was wanted, statements before the White House press corps were limited to 100 written words with only a few select questions.

Ronald Reagan realized, more than most presidents, that party leadership involved rallying the casual television viewer, as well as the ideologically faithful, to the cause. 'Ronald Reagan has championed his party's cause more actively than perhaps any president since Franklin Roosevelt'.[3] The symbolic banner of 'Reaganism' became one under which millions of people could march. His rhetoric was light on substance but quick on slogans (for example, 'Are you better off today than you were four years ago?', 'It's morning in America', and 'Go ahead, make my day'). Reagan knew that the public neither understands the intricacies of issues nor focuses much attention on their resolution. What matters is the short, memorable response that electrifies the viewing audience. Reagan was able to give that response when it was necessary. A discussion of his role as party leader begins with his ideological commitment and the communication skills which he used to perfection.

THE ROOTS OF REAGANISM

Ronald Reagan is unique among modern presidents in the depth and duration of his ideological commitment. In his 1965 autobiographical memoir, *Where's the Rest of Me?*, Reagan documents his involvement in union politics and national political issues, culminating in his conversion to conservatism during the Eisenhower years.[4] Reagan honed his ideas before captive audiences as a business spokesman for General Electric. 'The Speech' he gave emphasized the elimination of government restraint on the free market, the restructuring of power from the federal level to lower jurisdictions, and reduced taxes.

When the GE period ended, Reagan continued speaking before conservative audiences including a national television appearance for Barry Goldwater in 1964. Nearly twenty-five years later he could still remember the emotions of that speech:

Talk about a thrill, that was the speech that I made on behalf of
Barry Goldwater. There was some question on the part of some of
his staff [as to whether the speech should be given]. After I'd done
the speech, I went to bed worrying. But around midnight I got a
call from his campaign manager telling me that the switchboards
were still lighted up.[5]

The values Reagan would carry to the presidency – free enterprise,
less government and appeals to traditional family values – were all
forged on the anvil of Republican adversity in the Democratic
landslide of 1964. In that year Goldwater's ideological followers were
shocked to discover that their candidate could not sell his conservative wares to a skeptical public. But not every conservative lost in
1964. Reagan was involved in both Goldwater's feckless campaign,
and his fellow actor George Murphy's successful run for the US
Senate. Reagan learned that ideological fervor was no substitute for
victory. Political conservatism had to be repackaged. It was difficult
to sell a public accustomed to New Deal-type programs on the virtues
of less government, but a time was coming when New Right ideas
could be marketed in a way that would reinforce, rather than
threaten, American values.

Still, in 1964, a future victory was no consolation for Republican
party conservatives reeling from a landslide defeat. 'Ideologues have
regularly had their supporters in American politics, but to most
observers, the 1964 defeat of an outspoken conservative vindicated
the proposition that realistic American politicians would not choose
true believers (much less noncentrist ones) as presidential nominees'.[6] By the time he ran for governor at the age of 55, Reagan had
sharpened his speaking skills to the point where his conservative
vision would sway grass-roots voters. His approach was to appeal to
the symbolic values of Americanism and emphasize anecdote over
analysis, to be ideological to the party faithful and flexible in practice.
He preferred to give a rhetorical vision on television rather than fill in
the gaps with a detailed policy proposal. Goldwater got into trouble
with the voters by discussing specifics, such as going to St. Peters-
burg, Florida, sometimes called 'the town of the living dead' because
of its large number of social security recipients, to propose abolition
of Social Security and traveling to Tennessee, the state most dependent upon the Tennessee Valley Authority (TVA) for electric power
and other benefits, to advocate the sale of TVA. Reagan preferred
the high road, and instead emphasized the vision of values that have a

base in the collective subconscious of every American. Issues like family, work, neighborhood, peace and freedom became a part of each speech he gave. Such themes would also characterize his presidency.

Could there be a better preparation for the presidency than the round-the-clock regimen of after-dinner speeches Reagan delivered for General Electric? Years on the mashed potato and green pea circuit prepared him for public life and created a core constituency loyal to Reagan the politician. His message had polish, it could reach – and move – even the most casual listener. The new governor knew little about the details of government, instead he delegated the actual activity of ruling to subordinates, while personally attending to the ceremonial and symbolic activities of office. Reagan's style included the regular use of advanced polling techniques geared to media presentations timed to assist in the molding of public opinion. His overall tendency was to act on ideological principles when possible, and compromise when necessary. He governed a state which would have the seventh-largest gross national product in the world were it a country. Two years into his governorship supporters were asking him to seek the presidency.

1980: THE IDEOLOGICAL OPPORTUNITY

Reagan ended his term as governor in 1974 by pointing toward the 1976 election. After a lacklustre start in the New England primaries, he carried North Carolina and a sufficient number of other states, including his own California, to remain in the race until the convention. Reagan might have made a contest of the nomination had John Sears, his campaign manager, not persuaded the candidate to offer the vice-presidential spot to Senator Richard Schweiker of Pennsylvania. The right wing of the Republican Party was furious at the Schweiker selection. Jesse Helms called it the 'shock of my life'.[7]

After the 1976 débâcle, Reagan immediately gathered his staff together and launched another presidential bid. This time his focus was on mending fences with alienated conservatives and expanding his appeal to include disaffected Democrats. The 1980 victory was a result of a three-pronged political strategy. First, Reagan's reconciliation with conservative party loyalists originally energized by Goldwater provided the candidate with a base for all his subsequent campaigns. Second, President Carter's 'malaise' speech and unpopularity with the American people allowed the Reagan coalition to offer an optimistic vision for America. Finally, the emerging independent voters of American politics were making their presence felt at all stages of government, but especially so at the national level.

To restore his standing with dissident conservatives still smarting from the Schweiker move, Reagan made numerous personal appearances, sponsored regular broadcasts on radio and television on a variety of subjects, and authored conservative editorials and newspaper columns on the shortcomings of the new administration. In 1977 Jimmy Carter gave the 'Reaganauts' a perfect issue, the 'loss' of the Panama Canal. Polls showed that 78 per cent of the American public disapproved 'giving up' the canal, and Reagan moved quickly to exploit this sentiment. Soon the conservative arguments were familiar to every television viewer – the Canal was vital to American security and the domestic economy, the withdrawal displayed weakness to the rest of the world and opened the way for communist expansion in the region. After a fierce battle, the canal treaty passed Congress, but all parties to the dispute were aware of the power Ronald Reagan could bring to a political dispute.

In 1978, as the Carter administration worked on the SALT II agreement, Reagan opened an attack on the 'window of vulnerability' such an agreement would leave on the US as a result of neglected defense needs. In such discussions Reagan argued that the mission of the nation was to make itself stronger in the face of communist intrigue and terrorist threats. When the Iranian hostage crisis exposed American vulnerabilities, all the conservative rhetoric looked prophetic, and Ronald Reagan looked to be the champion who could prevent it from happening again.

Still, it was in domestic issues where the Reagan message was most effective. The civil, women's and gay rights movements had alienated the average citizen from government and created a new ruling class of dissident minorities and intellectual activists:

> What had been a relatively isolated position in 1964, when Reagan campaigned for Goldwater, was now the rallying ground for old allies and old foes alike, who found they had much to share in the attack on what they considered Jimmy Carter's 'surrender' of America to foreign intimidation, new-class doubts, and Democratic McGovernites.[8]

Reagan's growing confidence was a distinct contrast to the 'malaise' associated with the administration of Jimmy Carter. After Watergate and Vietnam, the seizure of US embassy personnel in Iran and an inflation rate of 12.7 with 20 per cent interest rates, Carter could only say, 'Government cannot solve our problems. It can't set our goals. It cannot define our vision. Government cannot eliminate poverty or provide a bountiful economy'.[9] It seemed the country was a victim – of the Japanese economy, of the OPEC oil barons, of radical students in Iran, finally, of itself. The curtain was coming down on the 'American Century', as Henry Luce called it, and the citizens were powerless to stop the final act.

In 1979 the Reagan campaign commissioned a poll which found that Americans were despairing about the loss of traditional values and frustrated about their aspirations for the future. A poll found that 68 per cent of the respondents believed that 'families were weaker now than they were several years ago', and half of those surveyed agreed with the statement 'I feel left out of things going on around me'. Seventy-one percent of the American people thought that 'many things our parents stood for are going to ruin right before our eyes'. To a cheering audience of the Republican party faithful in Detroit, Ronald Reagan could rhetorically offer a solution and at the same time ask a question:

Can anyone look at the record of this administration and say, 'Well done'? Can anyone compare the state of our economy when the Carter administration took office with where we are today and say, 'Keep up the good work'? Can anyone look at our reduced standing in the world today and say, 'Let's have four more years of this'?[10]

He promised a new era of national renewal emphasizing traditional values – the dignity of work, love for family and neighborhood, faith in God, belief in peace through strength and a commitment to protect freedom as a legacy unique to America. It was the appropriate prescription for a country losing its self-confidence.

The final part of the Reagan election victory in 1980 was beyond the control of the candidate. For years pollsters, commentators and political scientists had discussed the emergence of the informed ticket-splitter voter. Streams of voters had abandoned the Democratic party, but had not declared their total allegiance to the Republican alternative. At the presidential level there were fully as many Republicans as Democrats. Estimates varied as to the size of the parties, but about thirty to forty percent of the electorate was committed to each one. By the end of the decade, there would be two minority parties, and an amorphous mass of independent voters whose allegiance would be the focus of each one at election time. The present political arrangement is not called 'realignment' to the Republicans, but rather 'dealignment' from the Democrats. At the presidential level, majority party status is now a thing of the past. The party labels still count, and the parties themselves are still made up of solid blocs of voters, but the strategy of a president is to add to his base by appealing to the independent voters who are not party loyalists.[11]

In 1980 the Reagan campaign targeted four groups as likely recruits for a winning coalition: southern whites, blue-collar ethnics, 'born-again' Christians, and Roman Catholics. All but the evangelical Christians had once been strongly supportive of the New Deal Democratic party. In the South, of course, evangelical Christians were in the mainstream of the Democratic Party. Each of these groups was especially plagued with self-doubt in the wake of the Carter presidency, and all were ripe for Ronald Reagan – the new man with the right message at the right time. The GOP was now the party of new ideas and new programs, just at a time when people were asking questions about the old solutions.

Of all the voting shifts that took place during the Reagan presidency the two that are potentially the most long-lasting are the move of white southerners away from the Democratic party, and the allegiance of the very young to the Republican party. In late 1983 three dozen southern Democrats arrived at the White House to renounce their party affiliation and pledge allegiance to the GOP. One of them was Phil Gramm, who subsequently became a United States Senator from Texas and a national spokesman for new conservatives in the Republican Party. Since 1968 no Democrat has carried the vote of southern whites. Even Jimmy Carter twice lost the white Confederate vote. Two scholars examined the emergent voting trends among the southern states in 1987 and concluded:

> The breadth of the Democratic collapse is staggering. It would be difficult to find comparable instances in American political history of such a rapid and comprehensive desertion of an established majority party by an entire region.[12]

Reagan's popularity was especially strong among new voters. In 1984 he would win nearly two-thirds of the vote in the 18 to 24 year old group.[13] On college campuses across the country, where it had once been expected that every student would dabble in some radical cause, it was now the respectable thing to be an 'establishment' Republican.

President Reagan's triumph of symbol over substance dramatically revealed itself in his appeal to religious conservatives, Protestant and Roman Catholic. Unlike President Carter, President Reagan attended church only on the rarest of occasions and certainly never Sunday School and absolutely never with a Bible in his hand. Yet he attained the adoration and accolades of religious conservatives, ironically without achieving much of their agenda. Indeed, the conservative religious and social agenda was put on the 'back burner' of the President's policy agenda during his first administration and never fully recovered from its status as 'second class' citizen. His symbolic and timely identification with the key positions of religious conservatives, such as opposition to abortion and support for school prayer, enabled him to win their support, but without producing very many substantive results.

THE REAGAN RECORD

Like President Franklin D. Roosevelt, one of President Reagan's heroes, Reagan is an impressionist painter both in his administrative style and public policy agenda. He did not get bogged down in either the details of governing or developing his policy ideas. He painted with broad brush-strokes unlike a realistic painter who paints a fine detail on the canvas. Again he contrasted sharply here with President Carter, his predecessor, who was like a realist painter in both his administrative style and public policy agenda. The political skills of an impressionist painter in the Oval Office beautifully coincides with the dictates of the electronic media that rewards style over substance and symbolic impression over substantive impact. That does not mean the Reagan record was without impact, but rather that style and symbol magnified the impact.

Ronald Reagan's election augured well, but history is replete with examples of popular leaders who showed promise but then failed to take advantage of their circumstances. Richard Nixon won a landslide victory, but then resigned after the Watergate scandal. After a similar margin, Lyndon Johnson was a victim of domestic distress and the Vietnam War abroad. Even Presidents Ford and Carter, who suffered no personal humiliation in the office, were described as weak and ineffective as leaders. Before the Reagan presidency the office was a 'single-act tragedy', and some wondered if any future occupant could ever sustain both popular support with the people and an effective working relationship with Congress.[14]

'The Reagan contribution to the Republican resurgence derives mostly from his leadership and the generally positive response it has evoked from the American public'.[15] Ronald Reagan enjoyed a special relationship with the American people. He was the first two-term president since Dwight D. Eisenhower, another Republican who was underestimated by his adversaries, and scored two landslide political victories over the Democrats. Yet it is worth remembering that at one point in 1982 Reagan was as unpopular as Truman, Carter or Ford, and he was well on his way to repeating the 'single-act tragedy' which characterized his predecessors.

Presidents, like students, regularly receive report cards. In the case of the President the score is an 'approval rating', defined as the percentage responding favourably to the question: 'Do you approve/ disapprove of the way President . . . . . . is handling his job as President?' Ronald Reagan enjoyed an average rating of 53.7 per cent well above that of most presidents, and higher than any chief executive in recent memory. His lowest score came during the recession of 1982, which equaled the Truman record. Another decline followed the Iran–Contra scandal in 1987, but was buffeted by the generally positive feelings surrounding the Reagan – Gorbachev summit. On these two occasions the presidency of Ronald Reagan, and the conservative legacy which he embodied, was in jeopardy. Yet, at the end of his presidency, Reagan could stand before the faithful at the Republican Party convention in New Orleans with his approval rating among the American people higher than it was eight years earlier.

The Reagan agenda consisted first of restoring the economy. In his initial inaugural address, 20 January, 1981 he said, 'Our objective must be a healthy, vigorous, growing economy that provides equal opportunities for all Americans, with no barriers born of bigotry or discrimination'.[16] The policies followed the rhetoric Reagan had preached for years – an enhanced, vital, free market, uninhibited by government intrusion, excessive taxes and regulatory burdens. The results were spectacular. After an initial recession, the nation's real gross national product adjusted for inflation increased by almost a quarter. The expansion was helped by reduced inflation and lower interest rates. The picture was not all roses, however. The 19 October, 1987 stock market crash was a jolting reminder that economic growth was not automatic. As the economy grew, new jobs were born. Reagan could boast at the end of his second term that 'nearly seventeen million new jobs' had been created by the booming economy.

The second order of business for the new administration was to shrink the size and scope of the federal government establishment. Again in his 1981 inaugural address Reagan outlined his vision:

> It will be my intention to curb the size and influence of the Federal Establishment and to demand recognition of the distinction between . . . the Federal government . . . the states . . . and the people . . . the Federal government did not create the states; the states created the Federal government.[17]

Reagan instituted commissions and task forces to identify areas of the federal establishment which could be returned to the states, or abolished and replaced by private sector alternatives. The most noteworthy of these groups was the President's Private Sector Survey on Cost Control, better known as the Grace Commission after its chairman, J. Peter Grace. Tax cuts and tax reforms were part of the effort to eliminate the gradual expansion of the federal bureaucracy.

Such reforms had effects that were more symbolic than real, but in the world of media impressions such illusions are often more important than the results. Reagan was seen as a helmsman who was turning the ship of state in a new direction. Even when his changes were shown to be illusory, as they were in the December, 1981 *Atlantic Monthly* article by William Greider, Reagan was seen as an effective leader. Going for tax cuts in the first year of the administration gave the appearance of change. That impression contributed to Reagan's popularity after events like a recession (in 1982) and a scandal in the White House (the Iran–Contra Arms controversy) which had destroyed other administrations.

The third part of the Reagan plan called for an increased commitment to the military and defence needs of the country. 'To those neighbors and allies who share our ideal of freedom, we will strengthen our historic ties and assure them of our support and firm commitment. . . . We will match loyalty with loyalty. . . . We will strive for mutually beneficial relations'.[18] The goals of national security policy involved a commitment to increased defence spending at the expense of domestic programmes, and a long-range commitment to military support. 'Walking tall' meant research on the Strategic Defense Intitiative (SDI) as a basis for approaching the USSR in any discussions of mutually verifiable reductions in US and Soviet nuclear arms. The peace-through-strength approach created a new base for relations with the Soviet Union. Probably Reagan's greatest accomplishment was reducing the likelihood of a nuclear war with the arms limitation agreement with Soviet Premier Gorbachev.

The collective and symbolic efforts of the Reagan presidency were greater than its individual parts. To most Republicans identification with Reagan was equivalent to marrying a popular cause, one which was changing the way Americans thought about their government and its role in their lives. A *Washington Post* polling July of 1988 found that over half – 52 per cent – of the respondents believed the country was better off because of Reagan's presidency, only one-third said they were worse off, and 13 per cent said that his tenure made no difference.[19] The clear implication of such a finding was that Reagan made a difference in the way most Americans thought about the federal government, the Republican party and the conservative political ideology which characterized both those bodies during the 1980s. Republicans had a leader who was both popular and successful, reason enough for disaffected Democrats to change party allegiance at the presidential level. The problem was, however, that the new Republican devotion was first, devotion to a man; second, allegiance to a cause; and only lastly, identification with a political party.

THE NEW REPUBLICAN PARTY

It was an unlikely scenario. An aging outsider, ridiculed by his foes as a B-grade movie actor, rides into town as the new leader. He immediately benefits from a hostage release, wins victories from Congress on taxes, defense and economic policy and succeeds in placing his stamp on history as a strong and successful two-term President. All the while he denigrated the very federal establishment he led. 'Government', Reagan was fond of saying, 'is not the solution to our problem, government is the problem'.

Yet in the wake of his popularity, Ronald Reagan has failed to weld his own popularity to that of the Republican Party. In 1984 a few exuberant party enthusiasts compared the landslide victory to similar gains in 1934 and 1936 after FDR's election. But down the ballot, the Republicans were not doing well. The Democrats regained control of the Senate in 1986, and the President was unable to translate his popularity to candidates at the state and local level. What made the setback all the more painful was that the President had worked hard to garner votes to his party's cause. In the months before the election, Air Force One had traveled to 22 states, logging nearly 25,000 miles and raising over $33 million dollars for aspiring candidates.

Surveys regularly show that party political allegiance tends to ebb and flow with the fortunes of the party controlling the White House. With a popular president in the Oval Office the rolls of the Republican party swelled, but the depth of commitment was often less than desired. Before Reagan's election in 1980 Republican party affiliation stood at 28 per cent, dipping to 23 per cent during the recession of 1982, but then slowly recovered throughout the remainder of his presidency. Shortly before the presidential election of 1984 the Gallup Poll compared the political party affiliation of Americans with responses given seven years earlier. These results are shown in Table 6.1.

In 1977, Democratic President Jimmy Carter was just beginning his term, and the Republicans were wallowing in the mire of the Watergate scandal. The talk was that the Democrats had successfully rebuilt the old New Deal coalition of minorities, urban dwellers, southerners and the middle class. Seven years later Ronald Reagan had effectively destroyed those gains. Table 6.1 shows Republican improvements in practically every classification, especially among the target groups of younger voters, Catholics, blue-collar workers and southerners. With the sole exception of blacks, the GOP averaged about a 15 per cent gain among all parts of the electorate. It is worth remembering that Ronald Reagan, like George Bush, suffered an initial 'gender gap', defined as a lack of support among women. Table 6.1 shows that he was able to overcome this deficiency.

The poll data reveal a numerical increase in voters classifying themselves as Republicans, and also a change in voters' perceptions of the GOP. 'Using a nonverbal scaling device, with the top two positions indicating "highly favourable" ratings, the two parties are

Table 6.1 Change in Republican Party affiliation for select groups: 1977 and 1984

	Year		
	1984 (%)	1977 (%)	Point change
National affiliation	35	20	+15
By sex			
Male	35	19	+16
Female	35	22	+13
By ethnic background			
White	38	22	+16
Black	7	8	− 1
By region			
East	32	23	+ 9
Midwest	34	23	+11
South	36	15	+21
West	40	21	+19
By age			
18–29	36	15	+21
30–49	33	19	+14
50 years plus	37	25	+12
By income			
Upper half	38	22	+16
Lower half	31	19	+12
By religion			
Protestants	38	26	+12
Catholics	32	14	+18
By occupation			
Professional and business	42	27	+15
Clerical and sales	35	18	+17
Blue collar	30	14	+16

about equal' in the strong loyalty they can garner from the electorate. When Ronald Reagan first assumed the presidency, 'the Republican party was given only two-thirds as many highly favorable votes as the Democratic party, 18% and 27% respectively'.[20]

Even with these gains, the Republicans must face the realistic prospect of never gaining control of Congress in the foreseeable future. The Democratic lock on the House of Representatives appears as certain as it has been for 34 straight years. The presidential election victories are personal, not party, triumphs. The task for Republicans is to try and make the popular Reagan message appropriate for Senate, Congressional and statehouse politicians. Kevin Phillips, who first predicted the Republican resurgence in the early 1970s, believes that the cycle of conservative/liberal social and political agendas may have run its course by the early 1990s. His theory dates Republican and conservative ascendancy with Richard Nixon in 1968. He believes the pendulum of national partisan and ideological adjustments may be swinging back after the presidential election of 1988.[21]

While Arthur Schlesinger, Jr, perhaps America's foremost liberal writer, agrees with conservative Kevin Phillips's analysis,[22] neo-conservative Irving Kristol does not. Kristol believes that President Reagan:

has vigorously aligned himself with a basic conservative trend that has established new parameters for American politics, regardless of how people may vote in any particular election. This trend incorporates low marginal tax rates, a slower rate of growth in Government spending, an explicit endorsement of 'traditional values' and a more assertive (as against reactive) foreign policy. No Democratic successor is gong to be able to 'turn the clock back'. Liberal Democrats who indulge in such a fantasy are comparable to conservative Republicans who, for some three decades, dreamed of a repudiation of Franklin D. Roosevelt and his 'abominable' New Deal.[23]

A popular conservative messenger with a popular conservative message has altered the landscape of political debate and public policy. The word *conservative*, no longer anathema in American political discourse, has replaced the word *liberal* as the more popular of the two words, forcing the political opposition to search for other words to describe their ideas, sometimes using the word *conservative* itself. Liberal Democrats are now reacting to the successes of the conservative Reagan agenda rather than conservative Republicans reacting to the successes of liberal New Deal public policies that dominated America's political landscape for three decades.

CONCLUSION

It is impossible to talk about the role of the president as party leader without discussing his image in the media. In a large measure the entire political campaign and act of government is a public relations event. Presidents structure appearances to improve their visibility, they arrange their schedules to conform to media deadlines and constantly seek to fashion a positive perception among the viewing public. No president in modern history has so effectively managed the media as Ronald Reagan.

In the minds of most Americans Ronald Reagan made the Republican Party, not vice versa. Their loyalty to the party is based on Reagan's success. Unlike his predecessors, Reagan was able to maintain his popularity after his election, and re-election. The ideological flag which he hoisted in Washington drew legions of new conservatives to his cause, but the Republican party was unable to capitalize on their enthusiasm to build a party organization. The media presidency does not require that the occupant build close relations with members of Congress, local elected officials or even his own political party. Reagan never tired of telling audiences that he was a follower of Franklin Roosevelt and a registered Democrat for much of his life.

Personal politics means that candidates and elected officials can rely on their image and style to remain popular with the public. Political party organizations are no longer necessary to contact voters and present issues in public debate. Ronald Reagan was an effective leader because he tugged at the grass-root heartstrings of America. The Republican Party benefitted – but only incidentally – from this popularity. Because the affection of voters is primarily personal, we are unlikely to see a major party realignment, like the one which took place in the presidency of FDR in the 1930s, after the Reagan presidency.

Notes

1. C. Rossiter, *The American Presidency* (New York: The New American Library, 1960) p. 28.
2. H. Smith, *The Power Game* (New York: Random House, 1988) p. 405.
3. F. J. Sorauf and P. A. Beck, *Party Politics in America*, Sixth edition (Glenview, Ill.: Scott, Foresman and Co., 1988) pp. 426–7.
4. Ronald Reagan and R. G. Hubler, *Where's the Rest of Me?* (New York: Elsevier-Dutton, 1965).
5. H. Sidey, 'The Presidency', *Time*, 29 August, 1988, p. 29.
6. F. Greenstein (ed.), *The Reagan Presidency: An Early Assessment* (Baltimore: The Johns Hopkins University Press, 1983) p. 5.
7. G. Wills, *Reagan's America* (New York: Viking Penguin Books, 1988) p. 391.
8. Ibid., p. 405.
9. J. K. White, *The New Politics of Old Values* (Hanover: University Press of New England, 1988) pp. 37–55.
10. Ibid., pp. 49–50.
11. The classic work on realignment is V. O. Key, Jr, 'A Theory of Critical Elections', *Journal of Politics*, Vol. 17, 1955, pp. 3–18. See also W. D. Burnham, *Critical Elections and the Mainsprings of American Politics* (New York: Norton, 1970); J. L. Sundquist, *Dynamics of the Party System*, Revised Edition (Washington DC: The Brookings Institution, 1983) pp. 412–50.
12. E. Black and M. Black, *Politics and Society in the South* (Cambridge, Massachusetts: Harvard University Press, 1987) pp. 266–7.
13. White, *The New Politics of Old Values*, pp. 93–6.
14. J. W. Ceaser, 'The Reagan Presidency and American Public Opinion', in C. O. Jones (ed.), *The Reagan Legacy: Promise and Performance* (Chatham, NJ: Chatham House Publishers Inc., 1988) p. 160.
15. P. A. Beck, 'The Reagan Legacy for Parties and Elections', in C. O. Jones (ed.), *The Reagan Legacy*, p. 160.
16. *New York Times*, 21 January, 1981.
17. Ibid.
18. Ibid.
19. *Washington Post*, Weekly edition, 11–17 July, 1988, p. 13.
20. *Gallup Poll*, September, 1984.
21. K. P. Phillips, *The Emerging Republican Majority* (New York: Anchor Books, 1970); *Los Angeles Times*, 9 November, 1986.
22. A. Schlesinger, Jr., 'Are You Ready for the Next Wave of Liberalism?', *The Washington Post National Weekly Edition*, 9–15 May, 1988, pp. 23–4.
23. I. Kristol, 'Don't Count Out Conservatism', *The New York Times Sunday Magazine*, 14 June, 1988, pp. 30–2.

Part III

Policies

7 Reaganomics and Economic Policy

Joseph J. Hogan[1]

THE PROGRAMME FOR ECONOMIC RECOVERY

The Legacy of the 1970s

Reaganomics was a deliberate response to the economic problems of the 1970s. Relative to previous decades in the postwar period, the US economy performed poorly, experiencing unprecedented peacetime inflation rates, high unemployment and slow productivity growth rates. As measured by the Consumer Price Index, the 1982 *Economic Report of the President* calculated that the price level more than doubled during the 1970s. This was about four times as large an increase as occurred during the 1960s. Total output during the 1970s increased by only two-thirds of the rate recorded for the 1960s. The growth in productivity during the 1970s, as measured by the increase in output per hour in the private business sector, fell to less than half the rate obtained in the 1960s. Unemployment rates averaged 6.2 per cent over the 1970s, with the figure hitting over 7 per cent for the second half of the decade. By comparison, unemployment averaged 4.18 per cent in the 1960s.[2] Economic stagnation had brought the postwar boom to an end and made the deterioration of the economy the major public policy issue. Public opinion polls showed that more and more Americans were no longer confident about their economy and were increasingly worried about their prospects for improving their standard of living.

In the 1970s, Washington policymakers found it impossible to tackle successfully an upward rise in stagflation that was largely induced by energy and food supply shocks. During the heyday of the 'New Economics' in the Kennedy–Johnson era, economic policymakers were confident they could manipulate the budget to stabilise the business cycle and avoid high inflation or unemployment. In the 1970s this belief that the budget can direct economic growth gave way to the view that the economy shapes the budget. Economic adversity, as Allen Schick has explained at length, yielded lower receipts and higher expenditures than forecast in the federal budget, leading to larger budget deficits than projected, and a transfer of resources from the private to the public sector.[3] The combination of unemployment and inflation certainly weakened the capacity and the political will of the federal government to deal with the policy problems that seemed to be so strongly and intractably involved in fighting stagflation. If the government went after inflation by restraining the money supply, then unemployment increased before the economy deflated. The rise in unemployment quickly caused political problems, which led the government regularly to switch its policy objective to stimulating the economy at the expense of inflation. The 'stop-go' approach failed therefore to arrest the rise in the 'misery index' during the 1970s.

The advocates of the 'New Economics' had supported a rapid expansion in federal outlays, mainly on economic stabilisation programmes such as unemployment benefits and social policy pro-grammes such as Medicare and Medicaid. In GNP terms, federal spending had risen from 18.2 per cent in the 1955–9 period to 23.4 per cent in fiscal 1980–81. Between 1956 and 1981 the share of federal spending devoted to defence fell from 56.4 per cent to 24.3 per cent. Non-defence spending moved in the opposite direction, with spend-ing on benefit payments and social insurance programmes growing the most in dollar terms. Total tax receipts grew from 17.7 per cent of GNP in 1955–9 to 20.6 per cent by fiscal 1980–81. After inflation began to accelerate during the Vietnam War, Congress passed various tax reductions to counter 'bracket creep' in personal tax payments. However, the reductions overcompensated the lower half of the income distribution for the effects of inflation during the 1970s, but those above the midpoint were forced upwards into higher tax payment brackets. At the same time, inflation hurt business taxation even harder. Depreciation allowances were based on the original cost of an investment. As a result, strong inflation rates eroded the real value of the depreciation regime for businesses. The understatement of depreciation overstated corporate profits, raising the effective rate of corporate taxation above statutory rates. This further discouraged investment, inhibiting improvements in productivity. The rise in spending outstripped, however, the increase in federal tax receipts. As a consequence, the federal deficit followed a strong upward path, rising from 0.5 per cent of GNP in 1955–9 to 2.9 per cent in 1980–81.[4]

Continued economic stagnation, policy failure, fiscal indiscipline and growing public resentment over federal taxation, and a growing concern to increase defence spending created an environment in the late 1970s in which new policy ideas could get a hearing. Around this time a group of predominantly Republican Congressmen and staffers developed what became known as supply-side economics. This theory emphasises the role of relative prices in providing incentives for individuals to work, save and invest. Its advocates believe that a cut in marginal tax rates – the rate at which additions to income are taxed – increases the reward for working or saving. As Paul Craig Roberts, one of the pioneers of supply-side economics, explains, 'Reducing the marginal tax rate lets the income earner keep a larger percentage of any additions to income and therein lies the incentive to generate additional income or GNP'.[5] By the same token, supply-side theorists advocated that more generous depreciation allowances and other tax reductions would similarly provide incentives for greater business investments. A tax-induced rise in savings, investment and work effort is expected to stimulate a higher rate of economic growth and increased productivity. The Revenue Act passed by Congress and signed by President Carter in 1978 represented a departure from previous tax cut legislation by providing one-off cuts for upper income earners and in business and capital gains taxes. The more radical bill proposed first in 1977 by Representative Jack Kemp and Senator William Roth to cut personal income tax rates by 30 per cent over three years was rejected by the Carter administration. The proposal, however, gained growing support among Republicans in Congress, as well as among Democrats, who also noted the success of Proposition 13 in California.

The late 1970s also marked a shift in budget policies. In 1979 President Carter sent Congress a budget designed to fight inflation that was billed as an austerity budget. Fiscal 1980 included what then seemed to be unusually large cuts in domestic spending to reduce the deficit to $30 billion; the budget proposed to increase defence spending. The administration succeeded in initiating a defence build-up, but failed to obtain its domestic spending reductions. In 1980 the administration sent Congress an election-year budget that abandoned the austerity theme and sought to offend no important constituency. The budget was received with scepticism and was replaced by one negotiated with leaders of the Democrat-controlled Congress. The new budget blueprint would raise taxes by over $4 billion and reduce domestic spending by over $6 billion to achieve a balanced budget. At this point Congress utilised, for the first time since the establishment by the 1974 Congressional Budget and Impoundment Control Act of new budget procedures, a mechanism known as reconciliation.

Using this device facilitated cuts of $4.6 billion in domestic spending. The tax cuts amounted to $3.8 billion. The combination was patently inadequate to balance the budget. However, the fiscal battles of the 96th Congress did succeed in reducing the rate of growth in federal spending and managed to redirect federal spending priorities, thereby marking a significant policy transition.

Perhaps the shift of greatest long-term importance took place in October of 1979 when the Federal Reserve Board, acting under the leadership of its new chairman, Paul Volcker, abandoned its policy of manipulating interest rates to tackle inflation and announced the introduction of a regime of strict restraint in the supply of money and credit. This change, along with the growing pressure for a supply-side tax regime and the alterations in budget policies, indicated an important transformation in economic policies by the time of the presidential and congressional elections of 1980. During the course of the campaign season and the five months following his election in November, Ronald Reagan and his advisers developed an economic plan that built upon these changes, but moved in more radical directions.

Making 'The Economic Recovery Program'

The economic budget and political legacies of the 1970s did provide some justification for the major elements of what became the Reagan administration's economic strategy. In the 1980 presidential election, candidate Ronald Reagan persistently argued that Keynesian proposals to tackle stagflation had failed because, as he later put it in his inaugural address, 'Government is not the solution to our problem; government is the problem'. In line with this conviction, Ronald Reagan argued that the federal government – its tax and spending policies, its regulation of the economy and of state and local governments – was an engine of economic disorder, and promised to bring lasting economic growth by switching resources to the private sector. The various strands of what came to comprise President Reagan's *Program for Economic Recovery* were, however, adopted at different stages during the period between the campaign and the first months of his first term. Piecemeal policy development was responsible for injecting flaws and contradictions into the Reagan administration's economic strategy.

Because presidential campaigns are synthesising processes it is not surprising that the main components of the strategy were put together on the election trail. The broad policy architecture was laid down in a speech Ronald Reagan delivered in Chicago on 9 September. The Republican candidate rejected demand management as fighting inflation with unemployment and unemployment with inflation. Instead, reliance would be placed on improving incentives on the supply side. Reagan thus confirmed that he would support the Kemp–Roth formula for reducing personal taxes and would also cut deeply business taxes. At the same time, he promised that he would expand greatly the Pentagon budget, curtail wasteful federal spending, and yet balance the federal budget by fiscal year 1983 (1 October 1982, to 30 September 1983). In unambiguous terms, Reagan stated that domestic government spending would be cut only by a 'comprehensive assault on waste and inefficiency', and emphasised that this would not require drastic cuts in existing domestic spending programmes.[6] Ronald Reagan also announced he would abandon a stop-go monetary policy and in its place support a steady, moderate and predictable rate of growth in the money supply. The overall package endorsed the view that the economy can enjoy a rise in real GNP while inflation declines. Monetary policy would first stabilise and then control inflation, while the tax cuts would provide liquidity as well as incentives and prevent the slower money growth from causing a recession.

Unlike many of his predecessors, president-elect Reagan decided not to downplay his campaign pledges once he had defeated Jimmy Carter, but chose instead to place them at the top of his initial governing agenda. The reasons for this choice were strongly influenced by political considerations. The president-elect and his advisers knew that polling analyses attributed Reagan's victory more to a firm rejection of President Carter's leadership and his policies than to a *mandate* for Reagan's policies or political *realignment* in favour of the Republicans.[7] None the less, Reagan's inner circle decided shortly after the November elections to capitalise upon the defeat of Carter by 489 electoral votes to 49 and upon congressional election results that gave the Republicans control of the Senate for the first time since 1954 and increased representation in the House of Representatives by taking quick and decisive action. This was achieved by behaving as if the incoming administration had won a convincing mandate to implement Reagan's campaign promises. In so reasoning, they recognised that 'Electoral mandates are made, not born',[8] and that what an incoming administration does during the first few months in office can go a long way to set the tone for the rest of its term. Hence, the administration decided to capitalise upon this initial political momentum by attempting to enact Reagan's economic policies quickly, thereby hoping to create a positive public perception of him as an effective leader during the early months of his administration.

The decision meant that the task of the president-elect's economic advisers was to implement rather than determine his economic policy objectives. During November, however, Reagan's economic advisers encountered difficulties in converting the 'Chicago statement' into firm policies. After the elections the Federal Reserve Board had imposed tight controls upon the growth of the money supply. It was feared this action would inflate interest rates and induce a recession. It was felt that the onset of recession would impede enactment of the president's fiscal objectives, particularly the tax cuts which would enlarge the deficit. It was during this impasse in late November that David Stockman prepared for Jack Kemp, who was to be present at an economic strategy session of Reagan's advisers, a 23 page memorandum. Entitled *Avoiding a GOP Economic Dunkirk,* the document served several functions. From Stockman's viewpoint, the memo was first and foremost a lobbying tool intended to persuade Reagan's inner circle that the 34-year-old Republican Representative, who had just been elected to a third term, had the qualities to become Director of the Office of Management and Budget (OMB).

In particular, Stockman claimed to have answers to the problems confronting Reagan's economic team. As he put it:

> *The preeminent danger is that an initial economic package that includes the tax cuts but does not contain decisive, credible elements* on matters of policy control, future budget authority reduction and a believable plan for curtailing the federal government's massive direct and indirect credit absorption will generate pervasive expectations of a continuing *'Reagan inflation'.* Such a development would almost insure that high interest rates would hang over the economy well into the first year, deadening housing and durable markets and thwarting the industrial spending boom required to promote sustained economic boom.[9]

In essence, Stockman argued that adopting an extensive package of reductions in non-defence spending would provide a better solution to the three-sided dilemma of how to cut taxes, increase defence spending and yet balance the budget than did the earlier dependence on a campaign against 'fraud, waste and abuse' in federal welfare benefits. He further argued that these cuts should be pursued rapidly as part of a comprehensive economic plan to tackle stagflation, which would thus reverse market expectations of continued stop-go policies. The Dunkirk memo was well-received by Reagan and his transition advisers because it offered solutions to the complex economic and political problems that they confronted. The assault on domestic spending was simply adopted as an enabling amendment to the Chicago speech. Furthermore, recommending that the revised economic plan be pressed quickly in order to push market psychology in a favourable direction dovetailed with the choice of legislative strategy for the new administration. Stockman was rewarded with the post he had sought, and began putting together the fiscal policy components of the administration's economic plan.

The appointment of David Stockman exposed divisions within the president's economic team over economic policy objectives. The fight began during the course of work in early 1981 to determine the economic assumptions and budgetary implications of the Reagan economic programme, which became a vehicle for jockeying over policy priorities. The supporters of supply-side policies, which included Paul Craig Roberts as Assistant Secretary of the Treasury for economic policy and Norman Ture as Treasury Under-Secretary, largely joined with the advocates of monetarism, led by Beryl Sprinkel as the Treasury's Under-Secretary for monetary policy, in supporting a steady reduction in the money supply to squeeze inflation. The supply-siders wanted quick and deep tax reductions to fund growth and thus prevent the diminished money supply from promoting a recession. The two groups thus supported an economic forecast that projected a decline in inflation, an increase in savings and an increase in real economic growth. Supply-siders treated the budget deficit as 'a residual of the economy's performance. It would gradually be eliminated by economic growth'.[10] They argued that Reagan's campaign statement that he would balance the budget meant that 'a balanced budget would be a result of a program of economic growth designed to restore economic prosperity and self-reliance. He did not mean that a balanced budget was his principal aim or a constraint that would dictate his economic policy'.[11]

By comparison, Stockman focused on the budget deficit. He argued that the tax cuts and the defence increase would deeply enlarge the deficit. Financing the deficit would raise interest rates, 'crowd out' investment and threaten a recession, which would stiffen political opposition to the economic strategy of the Reagan administration. This position led Stockman to argue for deeper budget cuts than he originally anticipated, to support revisions in the schedule for reducing taxes, and to favour an economic forecast that would inflate revenues and deflate spending and thus reduce the projected deficit. Ture and Roberts dismissed Stockman's proposals as traditional Republican budget-balancing, which was also largely favoured by Donald Regan – their boss as Treasury Secretary – as largely inconsequential to solving America's economic problems. They argued strongly that the tax cuts should be pressed quickly and in their entirety to promote growth while Volcker's monetary regime was deflating the economy.

By comparison Murray Weidenbaum, Reagan's designated Chairman of the Council of Economic Advisers had no special theoretical axe to grind. He was none the less unhappy that the participants in the debate wanted to set strongly positive economic forecasts to justify their particular policy objectives. Weidenbaum pushed the debate to a resolution on 7 February by disclaiming the forecast of very low inflation rates sought by the monetarists and supply-siders as impossibly low. Instead, Weidenbaum forecast an inflation rate for fiscal 1982 of 7.7 per cent and 5.2 per cent real economic growth. The combination added, according to figures provided by Stockman, nearly $700 billion in money GNP over fiscal 1982–6. This provided nearly $200 billion in additional revenues that were thereby used to reduce the size of the deficit.[12]

Because the Reagan administration was committed to sending a full-blown package of economic proposals to Congress on 18 February there was little opportunity for a protracted policy debate within the administration. Consequently, the debate was resolved on 7 February by simply giving each participant a significant portion of what they wanted. The supply siders got a programme of tax cuts and a forecast – 5.2 per cent – of high economic growth. The monetarists were appeased by the adoption of their policy instruments and a forecast of a sharp reduction in inflation. The Stockmanites were given a forecast of declining deficits. In effect, the administration had three economic theories, with each focusing on a single aspect of economic behaviour. The disputants resolved their conflicts by compartmentalising policy areas. Each participant merely focused on getting their desired policy instruments and objectives included within the president's economic strategy. It was for this reason that, as Stockman later put it, 'the pieces were moving on independent tracks'.[13] In practice, no one got all they wanted, or succeeded in protecting their policy objectives from revision. Stockman did manage to have the proposed date for implementing the cuts in individual taxes delayed from 1 January 1981 to 1 July 1981 in order to lower the deficit. Stockman would later be instrumental in pegging the start back to 1 October, with the first tranche cut in half. The advocates of supply-side policies would later charge that these decisions meant that the tax cuts were delayed until after a recession had been started by Volcker's squeeze, which thus meant the administration had no means to avoid a deep recession. The supporters of budget-balancing obtained less spending cuts than they desired because they failed to carry the support of supply-siders, while the monetarists received mixed support, with the White House both attacking and supporting Volcker's squeeze.[14]

The delay in determining the administration's economic forecast meant that Stockman's budgeteers had to do most of their work in putting together the spending side of the president's budget plan without the benefit of a firm budget baseline, at least until late in the exercise. This severely complicated the task of cutting spending as it made it nigh impossible to cost the amount of supposed reductions accurately. Stockman had obtained the President's approval in early January to cut $40 billion from Carter's outgoing fiscal 1982 budget proposals. The President attached certain conditions. Most of the spending on what Reagan called the 'social safety net', welfare benefits primarily for the middle class – accounting for 48 per cent of all federal spending – was declared immune from reductions. National defence spending, which was scheduled to grow from around 25 per cent to over 30 per cent, was also exempt. Interest payments on the national debt accounted for 10 per cent of federal spending, and could not be forestalled. Stockman therefore had to raise the majority of the cuts from the remaining 17 per cent, which financed the traditional operations of the federal government and a host of federal grant programmes such as financing and running the FBI and the payment of grants to state and local governments for building highways and for funding many programmes designed to benefit the poor. In effect, Stockman had to raise a large amount of cuts from a limited portion of federal spending, and do so without a firm base to guide the exercise. The President's budgeteer also had to make the cuts by 18 February for presentation to Congress.

Because of this very tight schedule it was not possible to go through the normal routines of 'bottom-up' budgeting under which OMB requested each spending department and agency to compile and submit its spending bids for consideration and review by OMB, which would then be followed by an appeals process that saw the thorniest conflicts settled in the Oval office. The executive budget process was therefore both dramatically truncated and centralised under the control of Stockman and the leading White House aides. Stockman and his aides in OMB simply started with the fiscal 1981 and 1982 budgets fashioned by the Carter administration, and then made changes to accord with the new administration's plans. Centralised budgeting was facilitated by the fact that many cabinet officers were unfamiliar with their departments and were thus limited in their capacity to defend their turf. Many cabinet and subcabinet posts were slow in being filled which meant that resistance to spending cuts within the executive branch was further reduced. Those who were appointed were also expected to be loyal defenders of Reagan's governing agenda. Despite these supports for centralised budgeting, the administration needed to adopt other short-cuts. This included giving cabinet heads only 48 hours to review proposed cuts in their department's budget. Any protests were heard by a 'budget review group'. This innovation in executive budgeting consisted of the leading defenders of Reagan's governing agenda, and was thus something of a 'Star Chamber' because it was stacked heavily against appellants.

High-speed, centralised budgeting enabled Stockman to trim around $49 billion from the spending outlays projected in Carter's fiscal 1981–2 budgets, with most of the reductions affecting programmes for the poor. Even so, Stockman found these cuts were insufficient to balance the budget in two years. His proposals to enact further cuts were rejected. Instead, the 'solution' – jointly devised by Weidenbaum and Stockman – was found on 16 February by resort to budgetary sleight-of-hand. This came in the form of the 'magic asterisk' ploy, under which the Reagan administration's first budget incorporated 'unidentified spending reductions' amounting to $74 billion over fiscal 1983–4. In essence, the Reagan administration was promising to come up with more spending cuts in the future, which amounted to an admission that the administration had not completed its budgeting on schedule.[15]

None the less, President Reagan presented his economic strategy – the appealingly titled *Program for Economic Recovery* – to a meeting of both houses of Congress on 18 February 1981. The President claimed:

> The most important cause of our economic problems has been the government itself. The Federal Government, through tax, spending, regulatory, and monetary policies, has sacrificed long-term growth and price stability for ephemeral short-term goals. In particular, excessive government spending and overly accommodative monetary policies have combined to give us a climate of continuing inflation. That inflation itself has helped to sap our prospects for growth. In addition, the growing weight of haphazard and inefficient regulation has weakened our productivity growth. High marginal tax rates on business and individuals discourage work, innovation and the incentive necessary to improve productivity and long-run growth. Finally, the resulting stagnant growth contributes further to inflation in a vicious cycle that can only be broken with a plan that attacks broadly on all fronts.[16]

The plan consisted of four parts – a multi-year budget programme that provided for a 'substantial reduction in the growth of federal expenditures', a 'significant reduction' in federal tax rates, 'prudent relief' of federal regulation of industry and state and local governments, and restraint of the supply of money to levels consistent with a non-inflationary expansion of the economy. Far from being a late addition to Reagan's economic strategy, the plan states, 'The leading edge of our program is the comprehensive reduction in the rapid growth of federal spending'. The document sought $197 billion in spending reductions over the fiscal 1982–4 period, including the as yet unidentified savings covered by the 'magic asterisk'; specifically, savings of $49.1 billion, including $5.7 billion in off-budget outlays, were sought for fiscal 1981. The document claimed this restraint would lower budget outlays from 23 per cent of GNP in fiscal 1981 to 19 per cent in fiscal 1986. The plan stated this course would lead to a small budget surplus in fiscal 1984 and an even bigger surplus in fiscal 1986. The budget provided for a growth in defence outlays from 24.1 per cent of all outlays in fiscal 1981 to 32.4 per cent of all outlays in fiscal 1984. The economic blueprint proposed to reduce taxes by implementing the Kemp–Roth 10–10–10 formula over three years, with the first tranche of reductions taking place on 1 July 1981. The plan incorporated a schedule of increased reductions for business investment in machinery and equipment. The reductions totalled

$720 billion over the fiscal 1981–6 period, with the reductions in personal income taxes accounting for $555 billion of the total package. A rapid and excessive growth in federal regulation was blamed for retarding economic growth and for contributing to inflationary pressures. The administration thus justified a five-point programme to reduce federal regulation. The final strand pledged the administration to a consistent, steady and gradual reduction in the money supply.

The proposal argued that all components should be enacted simultaneously and cover a five-year budget period to tackle and reverse the economic decline experienced during the 1970s. Simultaneous enactment would, it was claimed, create a new environment, one which ensures efficient and stable incentives for work, saving and investment. The plan claimed this would provide for real economic growth rates of between 4 to 5 per cent annual growth through 1986, with inflation declining from double-digit levels to less than 5 per cent annually by 1986. The authors even suggested these growth rates might be exceeded because of the combination of a stable monetary policy and supply-oriented tax and regulatory policies. Such strong optimism failed, however, to mask the fact that the president's economic strategy contained severe contradictions. Monetary restraint clashed with stimulative fiscal policies, producing the likelihood – which Stockman feared – of high real interest rates and a subsequent recession. The conflict between monetary and fiscal policies made the administration's optimistic economic forecasts unachievable. This meant that the administration's deficit targets could not be realised. Delaying the tax cuts meant they would be overtaken by the recession provoked by Volcker's monetary squeeze. In turn, this meant there would be larger recessionary deficits prior to the loss of revenue from the tax cuts.

REAGANOMICS: IMPACT, 1981–8

Enacting 'The Program for Economic Recovery'

Despite these policy flaws, the President's economic plan was enacted by mid-summer. This achievement defied the conventional wisdom of the 1970s, which claimed that presidents could no longer be effective legislative leaders. In part, this surprising success must be attributed to the political attractiveness of the Reagan administration's proposals. Deep reductions in personal and business taxes were popular with voters and most Congressmen. The administration's endorsement of tax-induced growthmanship offered the vision of economic growth without the pain associated with either traditional Republican budget-balancing or monetarist strategies for managing the economy. As Hugh Heclo and Rudolph Penner have noted,

> As far as treating an ailing economy was concerned, supply-side theory was the equivalent of laughing gas when compared to the monetarists' and orthodox conservatives' devotion to chemotherapy. It is not difficult to convince people that the world would be a better place if their taxes were cut.[17]

Just as importantly, the administration had a detailed political strategy for implementing its economic agenda. The strategy was predicated upon controlling the legislative agenda of Congress. The President's legislative liaison team reasoned this could best be done by separating the economic plan into its spending and taxing components, and spacing them apart to permit the administration to concentrate its efforts upon building a bipartisan and conservative coalition in the House of Representatives. In effect, this meant obtaining the support of at least 26 Democrats and maintaining Republican unity to thus fashion a majority, and then putting them to the test in only a handful of votes to enact the president's entire economic strategy. The administration used Republican control of the Senate for the first time since 1954 to facilitate courting the House. This required putting its economic legislation on a 'fast track' in the Senate. The administration bowed, however, to David Stockman by pressing its proposal to cut domestic spending first. The proposal was solidly supported by Republicans and fiscal conservatives in the ranks of the Democrats, and was passed in early April. Later in the month the Senate adopted a first budget resolution that endorsed the president's budget blueprint.

The initial budget battle of 1981 was fought over the first budget resolution in the House. Early in April the House Budget Committee reported a resolution that acceded to the main outlines of the president's proposals, but differed in important ways. The Democrats contended that Reagan's policy of cutting taxes more than spending would increase the deficit rather than balance the budget. Therefore, they proposed a one-year tax cut along different lines from the administration's request, and increased the amount of spending reductions to lower the projected deficit for fiscal 1982 to $25.6 billion as opposed to the administration's forecast of $42 billion. The Democrat's budget was challenged and defeated on the floor of the House by a first budget resolution, known as Gramm–Latta I, that was agreed with the administration and was co-sponsored by Phil Gramm, a leader of the House Conservative Democratic Forum, and Delbert Latta, the leading Republican on the House Budget Committee. The budget resolution included a reconciliation measure that instructed fourteen Senate and fifteen House committees to rewrite existing laws to mandate lower spending on over 200 domestic spending programmes by $136 billion over fiscal 1982–4. The affected committees had only 30 days to comply with their reconciliation instructions. The changes were to be packaged into one single bill. This meant that members had to vote for or against the president's programme of spending reductions, not for or against particular cutbacks. In effect, the administration controlled not only the legislative calendar, but also forced Congress to legislate on terms favourable to the administration.

The second budget battle was also fought in the House. The Democrats produced a reconciliation bill that cut spending on 250 different programmes. The package failed to satisfy the administration, which again put together an alternative bill in conjunction with conservative Democrats and Republican members. The House Democrats, chastened by the experience of Gramm–Latta I, brought their bill to the floor under a rule that provided for separate votes on each of the six parts of the reconciliation bill. The Democrats anticipated that Republicans and conservative Democrats would not want to be recorded as voting for increased cuts in domestic policies to match the cuts sought by the White House. The Democrats' rule also precluded a vote on the administration's alternative bill, known as Gramm–Latta II. The administration's counter-strategy won the day. President Reagan effectively courted the Democrats who had supported him earlier, providing them with spending concessions on projects favouring their constituencies such as increased farm supports. By a six-vote margin the conservative coalition overturned the Democrats' rule and substituted Gramm–Latta II, and then adopted a rule, again by a six-vote margin, through which members were allowed only one vote – for or against – on the entire package of spending cuts, affecting hundreds of federal policies, contained in Gramm–Latta II. The rule adopted for debating the bill contravened most of the legislative procedures of the House, which led Leon

Pannetta, chairman of the House Reconciliation task force to lament, 'We are dealing with over 250 programs with no committee consideration, no committee hearings, no debate and no opportunity to offer amendments'. To complicate the situation, the draft of Gramm–Latta II only arrived on Capitol Hill on the morning of the floor debate, was poorly drafted and contained numerous errors. After several days of acrimonious and confused floor debate, the Omnibus Reconciliation Act of 1981 was passed.

Meanwhile, its companion legislation, the Economic Recovery Tax Act of 1981, was making its way through Congress. Legislative action on the tax package followed now familiar lines: the Senate had quickly endorsed the package, but had lowered the president's 30 per cent across-the-board cut in personal income taxes to 25 per cent and backdated the first tranche to 1 October 1981, while the House Democrats compiled an alternative bill that the White House sought to counter by offering tax concessions to swing Democrats. But this time the Democratic leadership regarded the measure as a test of who controlled the House and offered even more concessions to waverers in order to record a victory against the administration on economic legislation. The administration responded in kind, leading to a tax auction on Capitol Hill. David Stockman described the ensuing scramble as one in which 'the hogs were really feeding. The greed level, the level of opportunism, just got out of control'. In the end, the administration's measure, which had been reshaped several times to attract majority support, passed on the back of the conservative coalition.

Within less than five months the Congress had enacted the main outlines of the president's economic strategy. The political attractiveness of his programme was complemented by an astute political strategy. The reconciliation procedure offered the administration an integrated and expedited means to enforce Congress to consider the President's spending reductions as a package and on his terms. The administration maintained impressive unity among the ranks of the Republicans in both houses. The key to the administration's victory lies in the fact that the House Democrats enjoyed a majority of 51 seats, which required the White House to gain only 26 defections. The President's legislative strategists concentrated their efforts upon conservative Democrats, mainly from the South and the West, and freely dispensed concessions. As Representative John Breaux commented, his vote could not be bought but it could be 'rented'. President Reagan skillfully used the media to mount a grass-roots lobby for his policies and capitalised upon the second honeymoon effect created by an attempted assassination on his life to convert the nominal Democratic majority in the House into a minority on economic policy votes.[18]

The Budget and Trade Deficits, 1981–8

Undoubtedly, the carrot of economic recovery heavily influenced the public and Congressmen to support President Reagan's economic policies. But instead of buoying the US economy into recovery on a tidal wave of tax-induced industrial investment and consumer spending the Reagan plan led initially to the deepest recession since the 'Great Depression'. The administration was clearly most optimistic in claiming its fiscal and monetary policies would enable it to tame inflation and promote growth without incurring an intervening period of recession. While a major contraction was by no means inevitable, it was difficult to reason that inflation could be reduced without a period of at least sluggish economic growth. In the event, the Reagan administration experienced a sharper contraction in the rate of growth in the supply of money than it recommended in its economic plan. Indeed, throughout 1981 the rate of growth in the monetary aggregate M1 B remained significantly below the target growth rates set by the Federal Reserve Board and below those incorporated in the administration's economic strategy. Because this aggregate measures the balances held for financing market transactions, it clearly indicated that monetary policy was most restrictive.[19]

This policy of the Federal Reserve prompted a desired decrease in inflation. But it also led to a slowdown in credit supplied relative to demand. The combination led to a sharp increase in real interest rates – nominal interest rates minus some measure of inflation. This especially hurt industries that are sensitive to long-term real rates of interest, either because their retailers borrow to purchase stock, as is the case with both farm machinery and car sales, or because the product is bought with borrowed money that is repaid over the long term, as with the entire construction industry. In the fourth quarter of 1981 real interest rates hit double figures as opposed to an average of 1.77 per cent throughout 1980. The pressure on credit fostered a sharp contraction in interest-sensitive industries, which hit their suppliers, leading to a chain reaction of lowered sales, production and labour-shedding that eventually spread to other sectors of the economy, particularly medium and small-sized businesses, throughout 1982. As a result, unemployment hit close on 13 per cent, the highest level since the economic collapse of the 1930s.

The administration's economic strategy was derailed in other ways. The advocates of supply-side economics argue that the magnitude of the recession could have been moderated significantly if the Reagan administration had stuck with the 'Chicago statement'. The original plan would have implemented the first tranche of 10 per cent reductions in individual income taxes with effect from early 1981. The supply-siders claim this action would have injected growth while the economy was being deflated, and thus at least moderate if not avoid a recession. These advocates therefore regarded Stockman's success in forestalling the first tax cut to 1 October and reducing it to 5 per cent as, along with Volcker's tighter than forecast restriction of the money-supply, as economic sabotage.[20]

The legislative debate further changed the administration's tax policies. In order to obtain enough support to enact the Economic Recovery Tax legislation the administration agreed to index the individual tax structure after 1985 and granted much more generous reductions to business. The consequence was to reduce revenues much more than planned. Indeed, it has been estimated by OMB that the legislation reduced federal revenues by $963 billion over the fiscal 1981–7 period, whereas the Congressional Budget Office (CBO) projects the loss over the same period as $1041 billion.[21] Volcker's squeeze on inflation further depressed total revenues. The cuts in tax rates were not offset by bracket creep to the degree that was anticipated when the Reagan administration determined its fiscal arithmetic. Similarly, the reductions in business taxes were more generous than expected because the real value of the new depreciation deductions for investing in new plant and equipment was eroded less by inflation than originally projected. In effect, deflation diminished the planned amount of federal revenues much more than expected.[22]

The administration similarly failed to obtain its proposed reductions in domestic spending. While the administration sought cuts of $40 billion for fiscal 1982 and Congress claimed to have cut nearly $33 billion, the actual reductions amounted to only $12–15 billion. Precise estimates are difficult to calculate because the cuts are made from different spending baselines and reflect different economic forecasts, which have the net effect of overestimating reductions. Congress also claimed savings by budgetary legerdemain, such as shifting $685 million in Medicare payments from the first month of fiscal 1982 to the last month of fiscal 1981 to claim non-existent reductions in spending.[23] The combination of Volcker's squeeze, and the taxing and spending policies put in place in 1981 altered significantly the prevailing economic and budget circumstances. Monetary restraint promoted a recession that led to increased federal spending on unemployment and related benefits. Economic contraction further lowered federal revenues. The recession led to a decline in inflation. But this seemingly good outcome also had the 'negative' effect of eliminating bracket creep and thus further depressed revenues. The economic stabilization measures triggered by the advent of recession in mid-1984 contributed significantly to increasing the deficit from the $45 billion forecast for fiscal 1982 to an actual figure of $128 billion. Economic analysis suggests that two-thirds of this deficit figure is accounted for by cyclical deficit spending. The cyclical component of the deficit declined progressively to account for around one-third of the actual deficit of $185 billion for fiscal 1984. The Reagan administration thus evidently failed to balance the budget in fiscal 1984.

When the US economy was in recession, economic stimulus in the form of deficit spending was welcome. However, the policy decisions taken in 1981 created a severe imbalance in federal spending and revenues. This imbalance persists even when the economy has recovered – 'full employment' is measured at 6 per cent unemployment – and is termed the 'structural deficit'. Most economists outside the Reagan administration believed that the persistent imbalance in federal spending and revenues has several risky and negative economic consequences. The federal deficit is financed by borrowing funds, which brings the federal government into competition with other borrowers for credit. With a higher demand for credit, interest rates are driven upwards. High interest rates discourage consumer purchases and investment for consumers who cannot afford to pay prevailing rates, thus depressing economic activity. Similarly, high interest rates increase the level of consumer debt for those who borrow to spend, which eventually also dampens economic activity. High interest rates further increase government payments for servicing its debt, which thus increases the deficit. Financing the deficit also means a lower standard of living in the future because future generations must finance the deficit.

The high budget deficit is also related to the growth of the high trade deficit. The two are linked via interest rates, exchange rates and capital flows. Financing the deficit placed upward pressure on US interest rates in the first term in order, in significant part, to make US rates more attractive than those abroad and thus encourage an inflow of capital. The result, along with a restrictive, anti-inflationary monetary policy, was to attract great capital inflows, especially from Japan, the Middle East and West Germany. These inflows sharply increased demand for US dollars and, therefore, their value. Dollar appreciation priced many goods made in the United States out of markets at home and abroad. This made US exports much less competitive, and also made foreign imports more attractively-priced to consumers. The overall combination led to a rapid deterioration in the external account of the United States, producing a marked trade imbalance. The trade deficit thus exerts great pressure on US economic growth because domestic demand and funds are drained abroad.[24]

The budget and trade deficits have dominated the economic agenda since late 1981. Because the budget deficit was more evident and severe during the first term, the red-ink budget initially gained more prominence. This attention did not, however, lead to extensive presidential actions to eliminate the structural deficit. David Stockman has claimed in his study of economic policymaking in the Reagan White House,[25] that he sought repeatedly during the legislative battles of 1981 and thereafter to persuade President Reagan to recalibrate his fiscal policies. Stockman professes that Defence Secretary Caspar Weinberger succeeded in not only protecting his turf from reductions but also obtained a five-year defence budget that greatly exceeded planned levels. Reagan's first budget director further claims that his attempts to diminish the planned revenue losses through income tax reductions were also rebuffed. Stockman makes it clear that he was persistently opposed by Cabinet Secretaries who were evidently upset by the way their budgets had been cut in 1981. Stockman's proposals also lacked support from Reagan's senior White House aides, primarily because the President remained opposed to altering his tax and defence policies. As a result, the President persistently instructed Stockman to seek further reductions in domestic spending programmes that primarily benefited the poor to reduce the deficit. President Reagan knew well that Congress would reject these proposals. Reagan's choice of tactics contained political advantages. It enabled the administration to protect the President's tax and defence policies from revision. It also meant that the political initiative for reducing the deficit was ceded to lawmakers on Capitol Hill. This both let the President blame Congress for the deficit, and to assess the political momentum of any proposals developed by Congress to lower the deficit.

The Republican-controlled Senate of 1982–6 attempted to fill the political vacuum. In 1982 it passed a budget that called for lowered defence spending and a tax increase that President Reagan had strongly opposed. Republican leaders in the Senate signalled they were also prepared to delay and or reduce the third tranche of income tax reductions, which forced the administration to return to the negotiating table. The administration agreed a proposal that left the tax cuts alone, but reduced defence spending by $22 billion, cut domestic spending by close to $30 billion and raised $97 billion in new taxes over three years. The President also had, however, to take political responsibility for the package in order to obtain the support of the Democrat-controlled House. Late in 1982, Congress and the administration worked together to enact in 1983 a reform of the social security system that raised social security taxes and reduced future benefits; the package therefore reduced future deficits from their projected levels. In 1983 Congress initiated an energy tax increase and in 1984 passed another significant tax increase, which the President again belatedly signed.[26]

The measures succeeded in lowering the deficit from forecasts of $300 billion to a record deficit of $208 billion in fiscal 1983 as compared to $59 billion in fiscal 1980. This drove up the deficit from 2.3 per cent of GNP in fiscal 1980 to 6.4 per cent in fiscal 1983. This rapid growth increased interest payments on the national debt from 9 per cent of total federal spending in 1980 to close to 14 per cent in fiscal 1983. Sustained deficit spending doubled the national debt during President Reagan's first term. From the organisation of the US federal government in 1789 to the end of 1980, the national debt grew to a total of around $900 billion. The total national debt then hit $1746 billion in 1985. These unprecedentedly high levels of deficit spending injected massive stimulus into the economy, which sharply rebounded after the recession of 1981–2. As one report in August of 1984 noted of the US economy:

> After declining 3 per cent from the third quarter of 1981 to the third quarter of 1982, real GNP has increased 11 per cent as of the second quarter of 1984. The decline was the second most severe of the postwar period (1973–75 saw a steeper decline); the recovery is the second fastest (with the most rapid being that of 1949–51

including the beginning of the Korean War). Unemployment rose to a postwar record high of 10.7 per cent at the end of 1982 and has now declined to 7 per cent, the sharpest postwar recovery except for 1949–51. Inflation as measured by the GNP deflator was reduced from 10.2 per cent during 1980 to 3.8 per cent during 1983, and in the second quarter of 1984 the deflator continued at 3.8 per cent above a year earlier.[27]

The combination of reduced inflation and increased employment buoyed public support for President Reagan, who enjoyed a landslide re-election in 1984 and also managed to retain Republican control of the Senate.

Early in the second term, frustration grew strongly among congressmen over President Reagan's continuing refusal to come to the negotiating table to agree measures to restrain the budget deficit. As a result, a group of conservative Republicans developed a proposal that set maximum allowable annual federal deficits for fiscal 1986 to 1991 in order to lower the deficit each year by tranches of $36 billion until it was thereby eliminated in fiscal 1991. Failure of Congress and the administration to agree deficit reductions would trigger automatic reductions, drawn in roughly equal amounts from defence and domestic spending. The measure thus promised a way forward from fiscal deadlock and consequently spread like a prairie fire in Congress, quickly proved popular with the public and was soon endorsed by President Reagan. This widespread support led to the passage of the Balanced Budget and Emergency Deficit Control Act in the autumn of 1985 (the Gramm–Rudman–Hollings bill, popularly known as Gramm–Rudman).[28]

The measure is an added force for restraint on federal spending, but can not by itself substitute for the lack of political agreement between lawmakers on how to reduce the deficit. Indeed, failure to agree such measures led in 1987 to the deadline for eliminating the deficit being extended by another two years. Faced with the difficult problems involved in meeting predetermined deficit targets in the absence of a political consensus on reductions, lawmakers have regularly utilised budgetary sleight-of-hand. This has included, for example, both postponing and bringing forward federal spending on specified programmes to thereby claim reduced spending levels. Congress also claimed reductions of $11 billion in fiscal 1987 by drawing a 'tax windfall' from the Tax Reform Act of 1986 even though this artifice increased the projected deficit for the next two fiscal years. Substantive reductions have been made by measures taken to curtail President Reagan's build-up in defence spending in 1985 and 1986. Spending on domestic discretionary programmes has similarly been cut back in the second term. Along with lower interest payments due to faster than expected declines in interest rates, a comparable reduction in anticipated inflation rates that had – especially in fiscal 1987 – the effect of reducing outlays, these various measures combined to lower the deficit from a record level of $221 billion in fiscal 1986 to $170 billion in fiscal 1987, to $155 billion for fiscal 1988. The massive government deficit has provided an unprecedentedly large fiscal stimulus to the domestic economy, with the budget deficit accounting each year for 2.9 per cent of GNP, on average, during the Reagan administration. As a result, the national debt has tripled during the Reagan era.[29]

After 1982, monetary policy also turned expansive, with the greatest growth rates taking place during the second term. In 1986, the monetary supply grew extremely rapidly, and continued to do so well into 1987. Indeed, this sustained rate of growth in the money supply has meant that the real money supply has increased six times as much in the Reagan period as in the previous twenty years. Over the period since 1982, interest rates have declined, with the greatest reductions also occurring in the second term. In 1987, the discount rate was reduced four times. Monetary expansionism and attractive interest rates supported a continued consumer boom during the second term. Much of these funds were spent on imported goods and services. This fuelled the growth of the trade deficit. Imports exceeded exports by, on average, 1.8 per cent of GNP during the Reagan administration. This led to the huge trade deficit of over $170 billion in 1986. The advent of the trade deficit marked the transition of the United States during the Reagan administration from a net creditor to the world's largest debtor nation. Much of the budget and the trade deficit is financed with capital provided by the rest of the world. Net investment by foreigners in the US amounted to a cumulative total of over $600 billion during the Reagan era. By contrast, the cumulative total from 1948 to 1980 amounted to $95 billion. The sustained excess of imports over exports, and the corresponding flow of foreign investment into the US is thus the most unique consequence of the Reagan administration's programme for economic recovery.[30]

CONCLUSION

Governor Ronald Reagan campaigned in 1980 on an economic policy platform that proclaimed the federal government was responsible for the economic problems of the United States. He proposed to solve these problems by diminishing the role of the federal government in the economy to foster a recovery led by the private sector. To do so, Reagan proposed to cut taxes, to cut public spending, to curtail public interference and thus promote economic growth, which he claimed would eventually lead to a balanced budget. The process of formulating the President's *Program for Economic Recovery* did reflect a greater concern for moderating the more exaggerated claims made by the administration's supply-siders, but none the less resulted in an economic plan that still proposed an ambitious programme for economic growth led by the private sector. The process of policy implementation led to further changes in the President's initial economic game-plan, but these were accepted by the administration as a price worth paying for initiating a programme led by the private sector which Reagan claimed would promote economic recovery.

While consistently disavowing government interventionism and proclaiming the virtues of a free market economy, the Reagan administration continually pursued expansionist economic policies based upon massive government deficits, periods of sustained monetary expansionism and unprecedentedly high levels of international borrowing. This programme of fiscal and monetary stimulus had more in common with 'left wing' interventionism than with 'right wing' free market models of economic management. The Reagan administration did stimulate employment, with unemployment falling to 5.4 per cent in the autumn of 1988. Most of the new jobs created during the Reagan era were, however, located in the low productivity, low export service economy. The rate of inflation also fell in the US after Volcker's squeeze, but it also fell in other OECD countries because they similarly benefited from deflation in energy and food prices after the supply shocks of the 1970s. The rate of US economic growth was virtually the same, from 1981 to 1988, as the average rate for OECD countries, and the growth of productivity was much less. The US share of total exports fell sharply, as the US external deficit increased greatly. The overall economic performance of the United States during the Reagan era was thus a little more than average for OECD countries, while the claim that this performance was the product of free market policies is untenable.

The great federal budget deficits, the large trade deficits and their impact in converting the US into the world's leading debtor nation are the prime legacies of the Reagan era. Confronting these economic problems will intimidate any succeeding administration as dealing with them involves making politically painful economic choices. In addition, lawmakers must be careful not to attempt to reduce the deficit at the expense of creating a recession nor take difficult steps that might lead creditors to conclude that their funds are better invested in other countries. In sum, the process of making a necessary transition from the economic legacy of the Reagan administration is likely to be a complex, difficult and protracted adjustment.

Notes

1. The author wishes to acknowledge that the research for this chapter was funded in large part by research grants from the Nuffield Foundation, the United States Information Service of the US Embassy, London, and the Political Studies Association of the United Kingdom.
2. I. Sawhill, 'Economic Policy', in J. Palmer and I. Sawhill (eds), *The Reagan Experiment: An Examination of Economic and Social Policies under the Reagan Administration* (Washington DC: The Urban Institute Press, 1982) p. 33.
3. A. Schick, *Congress and Money: Budgeting, Taxing and Spending* (Washington DC: The Urban Institute Press, 1981).
4. H. Heclo and R. Penner, 'Fiscal and Political Strategy in the Reagan Administration', in F. Greenstein (ed.), *The Reagan Presidency: An Early Assessment* (Baltimore, Maryland: The Johns Hopkins University Press, 1983) pp. 22–4.
5. P. Roberts, *The Supply-Side Revolution: An Insider's Account of Policymaking in Washington* (Cambridge, Mass.: Harvard University Press, 1984) p. 13.
6. L. Barrett, *Gambling With History: Reagan in the White House* (Harrisonburg, Va.: R. R. Donnelley and Sons, 1984) pp. 133–4.
7. A. Ranney, *The American Elections of 1980* (Washington DC: The American Enterprise Institute, 1981); E. Sandoz and C. Crabb, Jnr, *A Tide of Discontent: The 1980 Elections and their Meaning*, (Washington DC: Congressional Quarterly Press, 1981).
8. J. Pfiffner, 'The Carter–Reagan Transition: Hitting the Ground Running', *Presidential Studies Quarterly,* Vol. XIII, 1983, p. 623.
9. W. Greider, *The Education of David Stockman and Other Americans* (New York: E. P. Dutton, 1982) p. 140.
10. Roberts, *The Supply-Side Revolution*, p. 95.
11. Ibid., p. 90.

12. D. Stockman, *The Triumph of Politics* (New York: Harper & Row, 1986) p. 102.
13. A. Schick, 'How the Budget Was Won and Lost', in N. Ornstein (ed.), *President and Congress: Assessing Reagan's First Year* (Washington DC: The American Enterprise Institute, 1982) p. 40.
14. Heclo and Penner, 'Fiscal and Political Strategy in the Reagan Administration'; Schick, ibid.; Stockman, *The Triumph of Politics*; Roberts, *The Supply-Side Revolution*.
15. Barrett, *Gambling with History*; Heclo and Penner, ibid.; Stockman, ibid.
16. Council of Economic Advisers, *The Program for Economic Recovery* (Washington DC: US Government Printing Office, 1981) p. 4.
17. Heclo and Penner, 'Fiscal and Political Strategy in the Reagan Administration', p. 27.
18. L. LeLoup, 'After the Blitz; Reagan and the US Congressional Budget Process', *Legislative Studies Quarterly*, Vol. 7, 1982; Schick, 'How the Budget Was Won and Lost'; S. Wayne, 'Congressional Liaison in the Reagan White House: A Preliminary Assessment of the First Year', in N. Ornstein, *President and Congress*, pp. 44–65.
19. Congressional Budget Office, *The Prospects for Economic Recovery* (Washington DC: Congressional Budget Office, 1982) pp. 39–49.
20. Roberts, *The Supply-Side Revolution*.
21. J. Hulton and J. O'Neill, 'Tax Policy', in J. Palmer and I. Sawhill (eds), *The Reagan Experiment: An Examination of Economic and Social Policies under the Reagan Administration* (Washington DC: The Urban Institute Press, 1982).
22. Heclo and Penner, 'Fiscal and Political Strategy in the Reagan Administration', pp. 31–2.
23. J. Palmer and G. Mills, 'Budget Policy', in J. Palmer and I. Sawhill (eds), *The Reagan Experiment*.
24. P. Cagan (ed.), *Essays in Contemporary Economic Problems: The Economy in Deficit* (Washington DC: The American Enterprise Institute, 1985); and P. Cagan (ed.), *Essays in Contemporary Economic Problems: The Impact of the Reagan Program* (Washington DC: The American Enterprise Institute, 1986).
25. D. Stockman, *The Triumph of Politics*.
26. N. Ornstein, 'The Politics of the Deficit', in P. Cagan (ed.), *Essays in Contemporary Economic Problems*.
27. House Budget Committee, *A Review of President Reagan's Budget Recommendations, 1981–1985* (Washington DC: House Budget Committee, 1984).
28. J. Hoadley, 'Easy Riders: Gramm–Rudman–Hollings and the Legislative Fast Track', *Political Science*, Winter, 1986, pp. 30–36.
29. Congressional Budget Office, *An Analysis of the President's Budget Proposals for Fiscal Year 1989* (Washington DC: Congressional Budget Office, 1988; W. Cox, *Budget Cuts: Updated Projections and Gramm–Rudman–Hollings* (Washington DC: Congressional Research Service, 1987).

30.   Council of Economic Advisers, *Economic Report of the President, Transmitted to the Congress, February 1988, Together with The Annual Report of the Council of Economic Advisers* (Washington DC: US Government Printing Office, 1988); Office of Management and Budget, *Budget of the United States Government: Fiscal Year 1989* (Washington DC: US Government Printing Office, 1988).

8 Domestic Policy in an Era of 'Negative' Government

Dilys M. Hill

The administration has heightened public awareness of a tension among political values that decades of economic prosperity had obscured, namely, the tensions among economic efficiency, social justice, and individual liberty – the reconciliation of which John Maynard Keynes identified as 'the political problem of mankind'.[1]

A NEW BEGINNING

President Reagan's domestic policy record throws into sharp relief the dilemmas and contradictions of style and substance. In order to see why this was so, it is necessary to take a broad range of issues and programmes into account in order to understand how domestic policy came to be subsumed under economic policy, with budget and tax changes as Reagan's major impact on domestic affairs.

The agenda of the incoming administration, influenced as it was by new right thinking and by Ronald Reagan's experience as governor of California with welfare problems, promised a radical approach to social policy. Social Security benefits – the entitlement programmes of pensions, unemployment insurance, medical services for the elderly, together with civil service and military pensions – were the only programmes guaranteed immunity; everything else was subject to reappraisal with a view to reversing the trends of the previous twenty years. The new right approach was a brand of radical conservatism which aimed to reduce collectivism and state intervention in economic matters while strengthening it in social and moral affairs.[2] From the new right perspective of the Reagan administration reduced domestic spending was more than a regrettable corollary to a strong defence policy and a balanced budget. Reduced welfare spending was essential in its own right, to reduce dependency, increase personal and familial responsibility, and enhance incentives

161

to work. The aims were twofold: to reduce dependence on the state and liberate the innovative and entrepreneurial powers of individuals and groups; and to reduce, through the 'New Federalism' initiative, the role of federal government. This promise was not fulfilled; after initial cuts, domestic programmes were protected by Congress from wholesale erosion and the New Federalism proposals were effectively abandoned. Reagan's domestic agenda, however, was not solely concerned with the role of the federal government or with cutting domestic expenditure and reducing welfare 'dependency'. The new right, including influential Reagan supporters, had championed the causes of the moral social agenda: abortion, school prayer, the family. It saw the Reagan administration as the means of achieving substantial reversals of existing policy. The advocates of the moral agenda also suffered major disappointment at the lack of progress made.

It would be wrong, however to judge the record a failure from the administration's perspective (David Stockman's criticisms not-withstanding) or to believe that the territory of domestic policy has remained unchanged. The major achievement of the Reagan presidency has been to alter the terms and nature of the debate about domestic issues and thus the political agenda itself. As in Britain, political discourse was influenced by the new right perspective: liberty, the market, the moral and social evils of dependency, the obligation to work for benefits ('Workfare'). The success of the new right in shaping the policy agenda by its influence on the terms of political discourse was further revealed by the defeat of the previously dominant problem-solving approach. The expert was in retreat; the claim to solve problems by the application of rational analysis followed by collective societal solutions had failed. Problem-solving was the hallmark of the 1960s and 1970s: the result had been the 'welfare mess', rising crime and a permissive culture. The Reagan administration did not need to be told by professionals or sectional interests what policies should be followed since the new policies had already been determined by belief in the market and in the reduced role of the state. What was needed was determined implementation.

Changing the climate of political discourse was not the only evidence of a new era. Substantial changes were made in the extent of social provision for the least well-off in society, most notably by altering the eligibility criteria and thus reducing the numbers of claimants and the amounts they received. Allied to this was the impact on states and localities of the failure of the federal government to maintain benefit levels and of the fall in general grant aid. The outcome was the need for enhanced activity by state and city governments, particularly in the area of the economic regeneration of the cities.

THE DOMESTIC STRATEGY

Domestic strategy rested on control of the appointment of key personnel by the White House and the co-ordination of policy through the Cabinet Councils system. Members of the Cabinet did not have authority to appoint staff unilaterally, and the Office of Presidential Personnel (OPP) under Pendleton James was a prime factor in assuring the ideological and personal loyalty of subordinate personnel to President Reagan. The result was a more effective degree of loyalty and coherence in the bureaucracy than previous presidents had achieved. To co-ordinate policy and prevent Cabinet members becoming absorbed into the bureaucracy's perspective, a system of five Cabinet Councils, proposed by Counselor Edwin Meese III, was set up in February 1981 under the aegis of the Office of Policy Development.[3] The Cabinet Council system under Meese was seen as responsible for longer-term strategy; its numbers grew to seven in 1982 (Economic Affairs, Commerce and Trade, Human Resources, Natural Resources and Energy, Food and Agriculture, Legal Policy, Management and Administration). Each Council brought together six to ten Cabinet Secretaries, with the President presiding as chairman of each Council: a mechanism which involved President Reagan with Cabinet members on a regular basis, even though this decreased over time. The Council for Economic Affairs was by far the most active of the Councils, but in practice the system dealt with secondary policy issues and with implementation, and never had the dominant place which Meese had hoped for. Within the system, the Office of Policy Development, although never as powerful as Carter's Domestic Policy Staff under Stuart Eisenstat, initially played a major role in promoting policy proposals.[4] The Office of Policy Development was responsible for short-term policy execution; its role was undermined, however, by the rapid turnover in Directors and a weakening of its independent role. Far more important was the dominance of the Office of Management and

Budget under David Stockman's Directorship. This activity included clearing agency testimony, and blocking draft legislation, in Congress, and controlling agency rulemaking. The outcome of the new system in domestic affairs was that, in Heclo's view, the White House commanded strategic decision making and ensured its implementation.[5]

The second term brought major changes. In April 1985 the seven Councils were reorganised into two policy councils: the Domestic Policy Council chaired by Edwin Meese (then Attorney-General designate), and the Economic Policy Council (chaired by James Baker, Secretary of the Treasury). The result was even further centralisation of power in the White House. At the same time, Cabinet members increasingly ignored the Cabinet Council system and reverted to a more traditional and individual role.

The use of the appointments system to secure ideological and personal loyalty was judged a success, as was the attempt to reduce civil service establishments. But the campaign commitment to eliminate the Carter innovations of the Departments of Energy and Education – the first on grounds of relying on market forces, the second on turning back the power the federal government had usurped to the states – both failed, as Congress questioned the savings to be made and declined to engage in the politics of interest group intransigence which abolition would entail.

THE POLICY PROCESS: INSTITUTIONALISED INERTIA

President Reagan's domestic policy agenda implied a deliberate strategy of inaction and withdrawal. As Heclo has put it, the dominant philosophy was:

> Doing less through government is consistent with doing less and knowing less in the White House. As opposed to the hyperactivity of Democratic presidents and the mushrooming expectations placed upon them, President Reagan can work at his domestic priority (limiting domestic government) by not becoming involved, by not thinking up new things to do, by not claiming to solve other people's problems.[6]

This philosophy shaped a policy process dominated by inertia and by fiscal techniques to rein back domestic spending. The result was a fundamental change in that the 'Great Society' era inaugurated by President Johnson has ended. This was apparent in two main ways. First, the incremental approach to programme and expenditure growth, that is of additional services, to more groups, with expanded budgets, was rejected. Fiscal restraint, not expert analysis and promotion of right solutions, was the favoured approach. Reagan specifically disavowed social engineering; his success was in appearing to capture and promote the public mood. Secondly, the prevailing value system, while acknowledging the need for basic support for the elderly and unemployed, came to emphasise the personal characteristics of non-dependency and moral worth rather than of the rights-claiming citizen.

In 1981 the administration put forward proposals for changes in the Social Security system to meet the crisis in its funding. The administration suffered a major defeat when these proposals were roundly rejected by Congress. In December 1981 the National Commission on Social Security Reform was set up on a bipartisan basis and a compromise solution – which pushed back the implementation of the change in the retirement age from 65 to 67 to the next century – was finally agreed early in 1983. One of the reasons that social insurance enjoys a privileged position is that authorisations for these entitlement programmes constitute a binding obligation on the Federal government and spending takes place automatically. To change policy, Congressional committees must take positive action to change the law. The result is that in theory authorizing committees (which traditionally are viewed as advocates of programmes they oversee) can protect programmes by not acting on proposals for change. In practice this inertia will only protect those programmes which are index-linked: Social Security and Medicare, but not AFDC. Nevertheless, Congress's behaviour is characterised by legislative inertia in a system riddled with veto points.[7]

In spite of this institutionalised inertia, cuts in expenditure were made. The bulk of the cutbacks in domestic spending took place early in the first Reagan term with the passage of the Omnibus Budget and Reconciliation Act (OBRA) of 1981 which imposed cuts in domestic programmes. President Reagan and his Budget Director David Stockman secured a masterly victory in forcing the budget through Congress by use of the reconciliation procedure (see above, Joseph J. Hogan, Chapter 7, 'Reaganomics and Economic Policy'). The major achievement for the Reagan administration was that it was able to effect the cuts mainly through budgetary and administrative means, by reducing benefit levels and, above all, altering the criteria of eligibility so that fewer people qualified to receive benefits. As a result of tightened criteria of eligibility, some half a million AFDC families and a million potential Food Stamp beneficiaries were totally excluded from benefit, and benefits for others were reduced.[8]

Ronald Reagan had claimed, in the 1982 State of the Union address, that benefits often went to 'the greedy rather than the needy'. This, and the problems of waste and fraud which were seen as endemic in the programmes, were to be the administration's main targets for reform. Help would be targeted on the truly needy, the work ethic firmly endorsed, and management improved. Economic recovery (Reagan's 'a rising tide lifts all boats') would be the key element in improving help for the poor, not expanded welfare programmes.

The impact of the changes in domestic spending, however, lies as much in their signalling of a philosophy as in their real effects. The Reagan cuts did reduce the growth rate of the programmes and took benefit levels back to what they had been in the mid-1970s. This signalled a major and principled change in direction:

> the long cycle of dramatic growth in the social activism of the national government that began with President Roosevelt's New Deal has ended. President Reagan has shifted the national social policy agenda from problem solving to budget cutting; and as long as the federal deficit remains a serious problem . . . there is little room for the agenda to shift back.[9]

The tax cuts of 1981 and the indexation of tax rates in 1985 permanently depleted revenues. This, and the continuing federal deficit effectively amounted, in Heclo's words 'to a kind of institutionalised "no" in the political system. By denying liberals the resources to finance new activities, both tax cut entitlements and deficits created a presumption for negative government'.[10]

SOCIAL PROGRAMMES

Ronald Reagan's first Domestic Policy Adviser Martin Anderson drew attention to what he called the 'new caste' of 'Dependent Americans' for whom the reliance on welfare programmes was a powerful disincentive to work.[11] This 'dependent caste' belief coloured the administration's whole approach to social programmes.

Politicians and the public generally define welfare as that system which provides cash and in-kind assistance to the poor. A more realistic assessment covers both the major entitlement programmes: old-age pensions, disability and unemployment benefits (Social Security); veterans and civil service pensions; and health care for the elderly (Medicare); as well as the means-tested programmes of Aid to Families with Dependent Children (AFDC); Food Stamps, and health coverage for the poor (Medicaid). In the Reagan years the officially defined poor increased from 11.7 per cent of the population in 1979 to a high of 15 per cent in 1982, falling back to 13.5 per cent thereafter. The majority of the poor were black and female; the 'feminization' of poverty reflects the rapid rise in the number of households headed by women and the fact that about 80 per cent of the AFDC caseload consists of female-headed households. Around 3.7 million *families* receive AFDC; just under 20 million people participate in the Food Stamps programme and some 21.6 receive Medicaid. The significance of these figures is that while the entitlement (pensions; Medicare) programmes are far larger, the sheer number of people receiving means-tested welfare benefits marks them out for debate. AFDC raises other fears. It is the basic programme for the destitute, it covers a substantial proportion (about a fifth) of the black population and is the main support for a large part of the population of inner cities. As such, it gives rise to fears that individuals will not be integrated into work and family life and will hand on their dependency to their children.[12]

Commentators disagree about the impact and meaning of the changes in expenditure in the Reagan years, given that benefit levels had been declining in real terms throughout the 1970s. Krieger, however, takes the view that, compared with projections of necessary expenditure based on the provisions of existing legislation, the 1981 Omnibus Budget and Reconciliation Act (OBRA) cut AFDC and Food Stamps by almost 13 per cent for 1982–5; child nutrition programmes by 28 per cent and Medicaid by 5 per cent. The totality of means-tested programmes were cut by about 8 per cent overall, while the non-means tested entitlements were cut by only half this amount.[13] The Brookings analysis puts the 1981 reductions on the 1982 budget of $27.1 billion in outlays, out of a budget of $725 billion.[14] By contrast, Senator Pete Domenici (New Mexico), the senior Republican member of the Senate Budget Committee, stressed that Medicaid, Food Stamps, and AFDC spending had all increased in dollar terms in the Reagan years even after allowing for inflation.[15] But this is not the same as what would have been spent on social programmes if existing criteria had been used. That is, in the Reagan years, while needs and social demands rose, the trend of incremental spending based on those needs and demands was reversed. Other estimates of effective cutbacks range between 7 and 10 per cent in budget authority cuts and 3–7 per cent cuts in actual outlays. But these total cuts of around 4 per cent of the federal budget fell disproportionately on AFDC, Food Stamps and Medicaid and were a large proportion of their expenditure. That is, the poor were the worst affected.

In the eyes of new right commentators and of many members of the Reagan administration, this concern with relative expenditures was beside the point. From their perspective the major welfare problem was the massive and debilitating change in family structures which had occurred over the previous twenty years and which had shifted responsibility from the individual to the state. Thirty per cent of the total numbers in poverty are single mothers and their children; in black poverty areas single parent families outnumber married couple families by three to one, and the illegitimacy rates in some poverty tracts are over 80 per cent.[16]

The outcome for different groups reflects both these structural changes and dominant American values. The largest demand on the federal budget in the domestic field is for entitlement programmes, amounting to some 48.5 per cent of all federal outlays. In 1985 Social Security cost $180 billion, which was about 20 per cent of the federal budget and the largest of all the non-means-tested entitlements. The next largest was Medicare at about $50 billion. Among the means-tested programmes, Medicaid was the largest at around $18 billion, Food Stamps was $10 billion and AFDC $8 billion. Between 1980 and 1984 the real disposable income of the poorest one-fifth of all families declined by nearly 8 per cent while that of the top fifth rose by almost 9 per cent. The incomes of the elderly rose; female-headed and black families were the major losers.[17] This was not fortuitous. Reagan had an ideological commitment to reversing the policy trend of the previous twenty years; if he had obtained all the cuts he had called for, social insurance programmes would have shrunk 'to a scope more nearly approximating their New Deal origins'.[18]

While the two decades after 1965 had significantly reduced elderly poverty through the entitlement programmes, public assistance programmes did not eliminate poverty among the rest of the population.

The reasons were based in American traditions of the ethical claims to help by the poor, that is, on their deserving or undeserving nature. Although AFDC is small compared with Social Security and Medicare, it covers about a fifth of the black population and is the main means of support for the inner city poor. The conclusion must be that the Reagan administration was not interested in analysing the effects of welfare but was concerned rather to ensure that welfare should be so limited that it deterred applicants, even if working paid less. President Reagan, in his 1986 State of the Union address, said that the success of welfare was to be judged by how many recipients became independent of welfare. By contrast, Social Security and Medicare experienced real growth.

NEW FEDERALISM

Targeting help on the poorest, cutting taxes and rejecting new programmes or programme expansion, were originally accompanied by proposals for a major shift in the role of the federal government. The New Federalism, which attempted to reduce federal government involvement in welfare state provisions and to allow states decide the form – and level – of welfare, had its roots in California's Welfare Reform Act of 1971 passed under Ronald Reagan's governorship. Under this legislation, California increased its own control over welfare *vis-à-vis* federal provisions, such that eligibility was tightened and the numbers receiving benefit fell markedly (while the remaining beneficiaries received increased payments). Reagan's first inaugural address in 1981 stated: 'It is my intention to curb the size and influence of the federal establishment and to demand recognition of the distinction between the powers granted to the federal government and those reserved to the states or to the people'.[19] On 8 April 1981 the President established two potentially high-powered committees: the Presidential Advisory Committee on Federalism (70 per cent Republican and overwhelmingly conservative), and the Coordinating Task Force on Federalism (which included Meese, Baker, Stockman, Anderson, Robert Carleson, special assistant to the President for policy development, and Rich Williamson, assistant to the President for intergovernmental affairs). Both committees were chaired by Senator Paul Laxalt (R–Nev.), a close friend and adviser to the President.[20] In his 1982 State of the Union message, Reagan put forward a ten-year 'New Federalism' plan which would devolve power to the states and reallocate certain responsibilities. The federal government would take over responsibility for Medicaid, while Food Stamps and AFDC, the main 'welfare' provisions, would become the sole responsibility of the states. It was this last provision that Reagan felt most strongly about; since his days as Governor of California he had argued that welfare should be localised, not nationalised.

The aim of new Federalism was two-fold. First, there was the need to reduce domestic expenditure. This could be achieved by restructuring and reducing federal grants in aid and pursuading states and localities to resist the inbuilt bias towards incremental spending which existed throughout the public sector. If the proposals had been implemented, the result at the end of the ten-year plan period would have been to return American federal involvement in domestic policy to what it was at the start of the New Deal, with federal grants providing only some 4 per cent of state and local budgets. The second aim was the more general one of devolving domestic policy to what the President saw as its rightful place: Reagan had campaigned on the basis of 'bringing government closer to the people' and allowing states their proper freedom to pursue their own policy goals. The main tool here was the block grant provisions. Reagan called for block grants, together with cuts in funding, in education, health and social services, and community development. Enhanced state freedom would also include regulatory responsibility, as part of the Reagan plans for deregulation. These proposals, though clearly rooted in new right thinking, also emerged against a background of debate on government 'overload' and of the vast apparatus of federal bureaucracy which many saw an inimical to flexible and efficient policy making. In that sense the election of 1980, in Theodore White's view, marked the end of an era: 'What had come to issue was the nature of the federal government's power'.[21]

Richard Nixon's New Federalism proposals of the early 1970s had also aimed to consolidate categorical grants into block grants and introduced a system of general revenue sharing, in order to simplify the system and rein back its propensity to rapid incremental growth. But these moves were based on the financial inducement of increased money that the general revenue sharing provided, in contrast to the reduced federal spending of the Reagan plan. General revenue-sharing was enacted in 1972, but except for some law enforcement and manpower training block grants, Congress rejected Nixon's proposals. Reagan's aims were more fundamental and ideological in that they sought to challenge the existing federal settlement by returning power to the people and cut the public sector. This was closer to the tradition of the pre-Roosevelt 'dual federalism' doctrine which separated federal and state functions.

The administration's goals were in part achieved in 1981-2 when the budget cuts identified grants in aid as the most effective way of reducing domestic spending.[22] At the same time the principles of block grants were introduced as part of the New Federalism package. This move sought to restore power to the states by making them, not the localities, the main recipient of federal aid and giving them maximum discretion over those funds (though in fact at least one-fifth of federal aid was still going to local units up until the final abolition of General Revenue Sharing in 1986). In 1982, Congress approved the consolidation of some 76 categorical grants into nine block grants, primarily in the areas of health and social services. The amount of consolidation was, however, much less than had been hoped for, and represented around only one-fifth of all federal grant monies. Further proposals for grant consolidation put forward in 1983 were not proceeded with by Congress. But the administration did succeed in reducing expenditure – though states tried to replace lost grant revenues from their own funds they were not able to do so completely, and again the effect was to halt that incremental growth which had marked domestic policy in the previous twenty years. The administration was equally successful in curtailing the matching provisions of categorical grants and thus reduced part of the impetus to public sector spending.

The New Federalism proposals were never accepted by Congress; many politicians, including the state Governors, were suspicious of what was seen as devolved powers accompanied by substantially reduced federal funding. The National Governors' Association concluded that the budget proposals would mean a 'substantial cutback on the federal involvement in intergovernmental domestic programs in both the near and long term'.[23] As Beam puts it, 'The impression was created that *federalism* was nothing more than a code word for stringent expenditure cuts'.[24] Devolved welfare spending would fall below acceptable standards under local pressures and the absence of enhanced matching grants in poor states. In addition, the New Federalism proposals put the onus on states not merely to choose whether to provide a whole range of services but to raise the taxes needed to do so, even though the cushion of an interim trust fund was promised.

Although New Federalism as such was not implemented, the

administration did succeed in cutting grants to states and localities substantially, particularly in the first year. Reagan's achievement was thus to promote a 'fiscal new federalism' which permanently reduced the federal government's role by reducing the revenue base. It can also be judged a success in that it meant the federal government was able to resist demands for new services and initiatives. As Peterson puts it, 'over the long run, the fundamental expression of Reagan's views on federalism may be his tax and budget policy'.[25] That is, tax and expenditure cuts reduce the likelihood that demands from the states and localities will result in an expansion of the federal role. Categorical grants have had their matching-grant incentives removed which depresses spending further. The overall result was to reduce expectations that the federal government would ensure national uniform standards for services.

WORKFARE

The dominant anti-dependency thrust of domestic policy was highlighted by the Workfare debate. In 1981 the Reagan administration tried to strengthen work-related obligations, particularly through the use of Workfare. The 1981 OBRA, which limited eligibility for AFDC, also allowed states to require welfare recipients to do community service work in exchange for benefits. An element of work requirement as a condition of welfare has been a part of the system for over twenty years, since the Community Work and Training Programme of 1962. The Work Incentive scheme (WIN) set up as part of the Social Security Amendments of 1967, extended these projects and made them permanent. In the post-1981 period, the requirements have become more stringent in the sense that refusal to take part in them can lead to a reduction or denial of welfare benefits. The states experimented with a variety of programmes and by January 1987 42 states were operating one or more of the optional programmes, though the majority of states have not made workfare mandatory and registration, and participation in job search are the most that have been required.[26]

Questions about the ethics and efficacy of Workfare, and the effects on wage rates and worker displacement, have also to recognise a more fundamental issue. This is the apparent wish to distinguish between the citizen, who has rights, and the suppliant, whose request for assistance is *thereby* regarded as dependency. The explicit assertion is that public assistance creates dependency, that this dependency gives rise to a deviant subculture or underclass, particularly in the urban ghettos, and that these undesirable features of American life must be tackled by something more than state handouts. The Reagan administration saw the major welfare problem as long-term dependency, whose prime cause is changing family structures and behavioural characteristics of individuals, manifested in high illegitimacy rates, the feminisation of poverty, male black youth unemployment, and crime. For the leading figures in the debate, such as Charles Murray and Lawrence Mead, welfare is seen not as the solution but the problem, exacerbating dependency and inappropriate behavioural characteristics.[27] These perspectives were a major influence on the welfare/workfare debate, but the stringent implementation of Workfare was never accomplished because although the Reagan administration was enthusiastic, the states responsible for welfare programmes proceeded cautiously and incrementally.

URBAN POLICY

President Reagan, unlike President Carter who had launched a major urban programme (little of which was implemented) had no proposals for an urban policy. The requirement laid down by Congress, however, that presidents present a biennial Urban Policy Report, the next of which would fall due in the late summer of 1982, meant that policy positions were put forward. In the field of urban affairs, as in domestic policy generally, the driving force of Reagan's agenda came from the new right commitment to reduced state intervention and increased reliance on private initiatives. The new approach to urban problems was laid out clearly in the President's first National Urban Policy Report. The foundation of urban policy was the supply-side approach of Reaganomics as emplified by the Economic Recovery Act of 1981: tax cuts; reductions in the rate of government spending; removal of regulations; monetary restraint. As the Report stated: 'Implementation of the Administration's Economic Recovery Program is a major element of a new urban policy – economic recovery will directly strengthen the economy of cities and thereby cure many related problems'.[28] Above all, the new philosophy demanded a disengagement of the central government: 'Individuals, firms, and state and local governments, properly unfettered, will make better decisions than the Federal Government acting for them'.[29] Ideologically, this was a major change: no previous administration had had, as its main intergovernmental policy goal, large-scale cuts in federal help to states and localities.

For twenty years, economic regeneration had been a key element of urban policy. But the Reagan administration was critical of federal involvement in urban regeneration programmes, particularly of the Urban Development Action Grant (UDAG), though it did not succeed in abolishing UDAG until September 1988. In addition, there was a commitment to business deregulation and to the belief that the promotion, rather than control of, development was crucial. In 1981 the President's Task Force on Private Sector Initiatives emphasised the changed approach, in which the federal role would be severely reduced. The biennial President's National Urban Policy Reports published in the Reagan years stress private sector initiatives and a move away from proposals for new policies to solve social problems.

In practice the main effort continued to come from public–private partnerships in which public funds played a major role: Community Development Block Grants (CDBG); the 1982 Job Training and Partnership Act (JTPA); HUD Section 8 housing programmes; Urban Development Action Grants (UDAG); grants and loans through the Economic Development Administration; Small Business Administration programmes; enterprise zones; state and local economic development programmes. At the same time the Reagan administration ended the provision of public sector jobs through the Comprehensive Employment and Training Act, CETA, projects. Instead, the Job Training and Partnership Act, JTPA of 1982 promoted private sector involvement in training; the main outcome was, as in other areas of domestic policy, a shift away from federal involvement in order to devolve the onus for action onto state and local initiatives drawing on private sector collaboration.

President Reagan's 1984 urban policy *Report* revealed his confidence that his economic growth aided urban well-being: there was sustained non-inflationary economic growth after 1981–2; states had taken greater responsibility for the problems of the localities; public–private social and economic initiatives for the inner cities had grown. Subsequent *Reports* largely repeated these convictions, but added as a policy goal the need to encourage self-sufficiency – which meant in practice support for the Workfare concept. There was in effect a state of urban policy inertia, with no new major proposals and with Congress able to defend previous programmes such as CDBG, UDAG, and the work of the Economic Development Administration and the Small Business Administration, albeit at reduced levels (CDBG was cut by 34 per cent in real terms between 1981 and 1987).

Policy inertia led to some harsh outcomes. Downs takes the view that major cutbacks, justified on the basis that many social programmes 'don't work', resulted in 'a social policy that preserves the inequality of opportunities that so blatantly marks most U.S. minority group communities across the nation'.[30]

CONCLUSION

President Reagan never revised his view, expressed in his 1983 State of the Union Address that: 'The fact is, our deficits come from the uncontrolled growth of the budget for domestic spending'. From this perspective, domestic policy was a failure since the President's agenda was defeated by congressional defence of domestic programmes. This was true across the spectrum of domestic programmes. Failure of farm policy – spending for farm income and price supports was the most rapidly growing element in the budget – arose from the crisis in the industry which made the President reluctant to oppose Congress's Food Security Act of 1985. In transportation, the administration was more successful in achieving cuts, though it failed to eliminate federal highway aid as part of its 'New Federalism' proposals. Similarly, the President's desire to remove what he saw as inappropriate federal involvement in education and energy matters by closing down the Departments of Energy and Education which President Carter had established, came to nothing.

In terms of broader goals of the Reagan agenda, two conclusions may be drawn. First, in spite of the rhetoric of neo-liberalism, policy has in practice been dominated by institutionalised inertia and by the fiscal consequences of the tax changes of 1981 and the burgeoning budget deficit thereafter, rather than by the demands of the new right. The expenditure cuts of the first term did constitute an important change in direction since they ended a long period of growth in domestic spending and of proactive, problem-solving behaviour by the federal government. But it is the fiscal consequences of deficits and tax cuts which will be Ronald Reagan's most lasting success: curtailing domestic expenditure growth not through debilitating confrontation with Congress over changes in the law or in the fundamental nature of domestic programmes, but by a stringent cutback of available revenues through lowered tax rates. The changes reflected a fundamental redirection in American domestic policy thinking from problem solving to budget cutting. Nor does domestic policy appear likely to change course in the immediate future. Tax reforms which increase tax rates are difficult to envisage. And reducing the Budget deficit, even if Congress becomes more determined to curtail defence spending, offers little prospect of substantial increases for welfare aid programmes aimed at the very poor, in spite of President Bush's proclaimed belief in a 'kinder, gentler' approach (which appears to be directed primarily at crime reduction, drug abuse, child care, and education).

The second conclusion is that, while the 1980s has seen something of a demonology of new right philosophy the reality has been rather different. It is true that there are widening gaps between rich and poor but the basic programmes of transfer payments for the retired and unemployed remain in place. What Reagan accomplished was a shift in budget priorities, not an overall reduction. Furthermore, the 1981 across-the-board tax cuts brought tax burdens back to the pre-inflation levels of the mid-1970s and later tax increases reclaimed about one-third of that original tax cut. On social and moral issues, President Reagan abandoned many of his pre-1980 positions in the face of Congressional opposition or inaction.

The impact of the Reagan era on domestic policy was a vigorous assertion of a new policy perspective which rejected the 1960s and 1970s belief in social intervention and problem solving. What is striking is that, while Congress struggled to safeguard programmes, there was little concerted resistance to this changed perspective; social engineering appeared dead. Where the Reagan administration did not succeed – its critics maintained it did not really try – was in cutting the core middle class entitlement programmes of social security, Medicare, and military and civil service pensions. The less well defended, means tested programmes therefore bore the brunt of domestic cutbacks. As Glazer reminds us, the Reagan administration 'believed people could manage by themselves and had no need of sophisticated federal government interventions'.[31] Domestic policy initiatives, in that sense, were seen as a redundant category in Reagan's agenda for economic growth and a reduced government presence. A purposive strategy of 'negative government' as Heclo termed it, is thus a fitting epitaph for the Reagan years.

Notes

1. J. L. Palmer, 'Introduction', in J. L. Palmer (ed.), *Perspectives on the Reagan Years* (Washington DC: Urban Institute Press, 1986) p. 1.
2. See G. Peele, *Revival and Reaction* (Oxford: Clarendon Press, 1984); and Chapter 2 of this volume, 'The Agenda of the New Right'.
3. M. Turner, 'The Reagan White House, the Cabinet and the Bureaucracy', in J. Lees and M. Turner (eds.), *Reagan's First Four Years: A New Beginning* (Manchester: Manchester University Press, 1988).
4. M. Turner, ibid.; for a different perspective see W. Niskanen, *Reaganomics* (New York: Oxford University Press, 1988).
5. H. Heclo, 'One Executive Branch or Many', in A. King (ed.), *Both Ends of the Avenue* (Washington DC: American Enterprise Institute, 1983) p. 46.
6. H. Heclo, 'Reaganism and the Search for a Public Philosophy', in J. L. Palmer (ed.), *Perspectives on the Reagan Years* (Washington DC: Urban Institute Press, 1986) p. 49.
7. R. K. Weaver, 'Controlling Entitlements', in J. E. Chubb and P. E. Peterson (eds), *The New Direction in American Politics* (Washington DC: The Brookings Institution, 1985) p. 310.
8. J. L. Palmer and I. V. Sawhill (eds), *The Reagan Record* (Cambridge, Mass.: Ballinger Publishing Co., 1984) p. 13.
9. D. L. Bawden and J. L. Palmer, 'Social Policy', in Palmer and Sawhill, ibid., p. 214.
10. H. Heclo, in Palmer, *Perspectives on the Reagan Years*, p. 50.
11. See: F. I. Greenstein (ed.), *The Reagan Presidency: An Early Assessment* (Baltimore, Maryland: Johns Hopkins University Press, 1983) pp. 58–9.
12. N. Glazer, *The Limits of Social Policy* (Cambridge, Mass.: Harvard University Press, 1988) pp. 43–4.
13. J. Krieger, 'Social Policy in the Age of Reagan and Thatcher', *The Socialist Register*, 1987, p. 190.
14. J. A. Pechman (ed.), *Setting National Priorities: The 1983 Budget* (Washington DC: The Brookings Institution, 1982).
15. P. Domenici, 'Programs to aid the poor slashed, right? No, wrong', *Chicago Sun-Times*, 13 November 1988.
16. *The New Consensus on Family and Welfare* (Washington DC: American Enterprise Institute for Public Policy Research, 1987) p. xiii.
17. J. L. Palmer and I. V. Sawhill (eds) *The Reagan Record* (Cambridge, Mass.: Ballinger Publishing Co., 1984) p. 22.
18. D. L. Bawden and J. L. Palmer, 'Social Policy', in Palmer and Sawhill, ibid., p. 213.
19. R. Reagan, *Inaugural Address*, Washington DC, 20 January 1981.
20. R. B. Hawkins, Jr (ed.), *American Federalism: A New Partnership for the Republic* (San Francisco, Cal.: Institute for Contemporary Studies, 1982); Neal R. Peirce, 'New Panels to Move Quickly to help Reagan "Unbend" the Federal System', *National Journal*, 2 May 1981, pp. 785–8.

21.   T. H. White, *America in Search of Itself: The Making of the President 1956–1980* (New York: Harper & Row, 1982) p. 7.
22.   G. E. Peterson, 'Federalism and the States', in Palmer and Sawhill, *The Reagan Record*, p. 219.
23.   D. Tate, 'New Federalism No Panacea For State, Local Governments', *Congressional Quarterly Weekly Report*, Vol. 39, 17, 25 April 1981, p. 709.
24.   D. R. Beam, 'New Federalism, Old Realities: The Reagan Administration and Intergovernmental Reform', in L. M. Salamon and M. S. Lund (eds), *The Reagan Presidency and the Governing of America* (Washington DC: Urban Institute Press, 1984) p. 441.
25.   G. E. Peterson, in Palmer and Sawhill, *The Reagan Record*, p. 258.
26.   Congress of the United States, *Work-Related Programs for Welfare Recipients*, Congressional Budget Office, April 1987, p. xii.
27.   C. Murray, *Losing Ground: American Social Policy 1950–1980* (New York: Basic Books, 1984); C. Murray, 'Have the Poor Been "Losing Ground"?', *Political Science Quarterly*, Vol 100, 3, Fall, 1985; L. Mead, *Beyond Entitlement* (New York: Free Press, 1985); *The New Consensus on Family and Welfare*, 1987, ibid.
28.   Housing and Urban Development (HUD), *The President's National Urban Policy Report 1982* (Washington DC: Government Printing Office, 1982) p. 13.
29.   Ibid., p. 57.
30.   A. Downs, 'The Future of Industrial Cities', in P. E. Peterson (ed.), *The New Urban Reality* (Washington DC: The Brookings Institution, 1985) p. 290.
31.   N. Glazer, *The Limits of Social Policy*, p. 56.

9 The Reagan Presidency and Foreign Policy

Raymond A. Moore

REAGAN'S APPROACH TO FOREIGN POLICY

Ronald Reagan, like his predecessor Jimmy Carter, came to the presidency with little, if any, foreign policy experience, and with strong convictions about what was wrong with United States foreign policy. Reagan was convinced that the US had grown weak under Carter, in spite of the fact that Carter himself had undertaken a defence buildup in his last two years. The new President was determined not only that the US should undertake a $1.5 trillion defence buildup over a five-year period to correct the imbalance with the USSR, but also that it would deal firmly with the 'the Evil Empire' and resist every Soviet effort to expand its influence. The supposed loss of *élan* and patriotism at home was to be replaced by a reborn pride in the US as a great and good nation which would provide renewed leadership in meeting the challenge of Communist ideology and Soviet expansionism.

Ronald Reagan exhibited a simplistic view of the world during his presidency which did not serve him well in a period of complexities and nuances. His previous careers as movie actor and governor of California provided him with no direct experience in world affairs, and except for Richard Allen, Reagan's first National Security Advisor, Reagan's early White House staff appointments did not fill this experience gap in foreign policy. Reagan's first Secretary of State was Alexander Haig, a man of long experience in international relations who wanted to be the 'vicar' of American foreign policy but who was unable to overcome his rivals in turf battles at the White House and in the Defense Department. The result was great confusion in the management of foreign policy, especially in Regan's first year.

HAIG THE VICAR

General Haig's appointment appeared to promise a State Department-centered foreign policy. He had not only been Supreme Allied Commander in Europe (SACEUR) and a deputy to Kissinger at the National Security Council under Nixon but had been instrumental in making the difficult transition from Nixon to Ford. His background and experience seemed to augur well for the conduct of foreign policy under a president who knew little of international affairs, but who generously delegated powers to trusted subordinates. Moreover, the role of the National Security Advisor was much reduced, and Allen, the first of six NSC advisors, had to report to Edwin Meese, not directly to the president as had been the arrangement under Nixon and Carter.

Haig's sensible efforts to stake out his role as chief advisor and spokesman on foreign policy soon ran aground when both his ego and a pragmatic approach to policy brought him into conflict with James Baker and Edwin Meese of the White House Troika. The situation worsened when Haig declared himself 'in control' of the White House after President Reagan was shot just seventy days into the new administration. Not only was he wrong about constitutional succession, but his panic reaction alienated Reagan's White House advisors and Caspar Weinberger at the Defense Department. As Larry Speakes observes, 'From then on, other members of the Reagan team would be viewing him with suspicion, and within fifteen months their hazing would drive him out of the White House'.[1]

Haig's short tenure was an unhappy one and a major disappointment considering his outstanding credentials and broad based outlook on international affairs. During his watch, Haig oversaw US efforts to support Great Britain against Argentina in the Falklands War, gave his tacit approval for the Israelis to invade Lebanon and outlined a hard-line policy toward the Sandinistas.[2] A series of disagreements, however, with Weinberger, Baker, Meese, Allen and finally Deaver eventually forced a resignation which was accepted by Reagan.[3]

THE COMING OF GEORGE SHULTZ

The first nine months of Reagan's term were marked by constant turmoil in managing foreign and national security policy. Richard V.

Allen resigned under pressure in the first year and was replaced by William Clark who moved across from being Under Secretary of State into the White House. Clark, a close friend of the President, was short on foreign policy experience, but long on loyalty to Reagan. He was misplaced both at State and the NSC and soon moved to the Interior Department. The early imbroglios over foreign policy did not ease until George Shultz was appointed as Haig's successor. Shultz was a man of great experience in government, having previously served in President Nixon's Cabinet. His appointment was widely applauded and he remained in this post until the end of Reagan's administration. His relations with Secretary of Defense Caspar Weinberger, a former colleague under Nixon and at the Bechtel Corporation, were often difficult when foreign policy and military considerations clashed. Shultz also managed an uneasy relationship with William Casey of the CIA and National Security Advisors Robert McFarlane and John Poindexter. Despite occasional threats of resignation, which were never accepted by the President, he managed to come out of the Iran–Contra scandal relatively unscarred after he and Weinberger united to oppose the arms for hostages deal and the subsequent relaying of funds to the Contras. Although some observers felt that, as a matter of principle, Shultz should have resigned over the Iran–Contra affair, he hung on and emerged from the Reagan era as one of the shining lights of the administration. Under his guidance US foreign policy took on some semblance of order, even though there was heavy competition from the Defense Department, the Central Intelligence Agency, the National Security Council and the White House staff for control of that policy.

OUTLINES OF POLICY

According to Shultz,'the Reagan Administration reasserted America's leadership as an engaged, global force for prosperity, security and democratic change'.[4] Domestically, the US sought to improve its export competitiveness, resist protectionism and bring the growing budget deficit under control. Abroad, it tried to promote the growth of international trade through an open trading system and encouraged other countries, especially Japan, South Korea, and the European Community nations to reduce barriers to trade. Foreign countries would be encouraged to emulate the US free market economy.

On security matters, the administration sought to strengthen NATO through increased consultation. It also sought to stem the flow of sensitive technology to the Soviet bloc and pressed Moscow for equitable, balanced and verifiable arms control agreements. The State Department set out to play a leadership role in resolving disputes between Iran and Iraq, Israel and the Arab states, Angola and South Africa. Another goal was to maintain the free flow of oil in the Gulf area. To counter the threat posed by the Soviet arms build-up, especially in strategic nuclear weapons, the administration proposed a three-pronged approach:

(1) Modernization of US strategic forces;
(2) Pursuit of mutual verifiable reductions in nuclear arms;
(3) Search for a safer, more stable and morally preferable way to deter war by greater reliance on defenses. This was to be accomplished through the Strategic Defense Initiative (SDI), commonly known as Star Wars.

On the ideological front, the US gave support to democratic institution building wherever possible. In Latin America such support helped in the transition to democracy of many countries. By 1988, 26 of 33 countries were presumed to be democratic or moving in that direction and it was claimed that 90 per cent of the population were living under freely elected governments, a growth of 30 per cent since 1976. In Asia, democracy was nurtured in the Philippines by the support of Corazon Aquino against Ferdinand Marcos while in South Korea free elections were encouraged. In South Africa, the administration brought pressure on the government to ease apartheid and increase black participation in politics. It also contined to protest human rights violations in such countries as Vietnam, Cuba, Afghanistan and Cambodia, and although it is clear that the human rights policy was not carried out with the same fervour as in the Carter administration it was a keystone of foreign policy.[5]

As part of the administration's ideological struggle against Communism, the so-called Reagan Doctrine evolved as a rationalization to aid 'freedom fighters' in their struggles against Communist controlled regimes. In Nicaragua, Afghanistan and Angola opposition movements were supported with money, guns and supplies in an effort to overthrow or undercut Marxist governments. President Reagan took great pride in these efforts to take the offensive against entrenched Communist governments, at one time even comparing the contra 'freedom fighters' to American revolutionaries fighting against King George III.

Far more than its predecessor, the Reagan administration was willing to use force to back up US policies. Overcoming the Vietnam Syndrome against using US power overtly, the Reagan administration was not averse to using force to oust Cubans in Grenada or to attack Gaddafi in Libya, send marines to Lebanon and naval forces to the Persian Gulf. Even though such actions were small scale and, in the case of Grenada and Libya against minor league foes, the very use of military forces was a major change from the days of Jimmy Carter who had proclaimed a 'new world that calls for a new American foreign policy', a new world—wide mosaic of global, regional and bilateral relations 'with interdependence the new international reality, controlled by neither the US or the USSR, where mutual cooperation would be not just a convenience but a necessity'.[6]

REAGAN'S IMAGE ABROAD

Although Ronald Reagan was very popular at home and finished his second term with 60 per cent approval ratings, he was less popular abroad. Reagan began his first term by intensifying ideological warfare against the Soviet Union. As a result, relations between the two countries became so hostile that many observers criticised Reagan for being overly confrontational. To the Soviet leaders, Reagan appeared as a dangerous crusader, particularly compared to the more business-like approach of Nixon and Kissinger. Relations between the two superpowers deteriorated so badly that in 1983, George Arbatov, the leading Soviet expert on America, accused Reagan of behaving like Hitler.

Although in 1981 Reagan lifted the grain embargo originally imposed by Carter and communicated by personal letter to Leonid Brezhnev, he avoided proposed summit meetings during Brezhnev's tenure, which ended in 1982. Reagan failed to attend the funerals of Brezhnev, his successors Yuri Andropov and Konstantin Chernenko, and did not meet with any Soviet leaders until the summit meeting in Geneva with Mikhail Gorbachev in November, 1985. Until Gorbachev's ascendancy, the Reagan administration frequently felt that there was no one in charge of the Soviet Union. With Gorbachev's rise, a new relationship between Soviet and US leaders was established and Reagan found a worthy competitor for the title of the

Great Communicator. In Geneva Reagan and Gorbachev established what appeared to be a good working relationship, although subsequent events dashed early hopes for comprehensive arms control agreements.

With Western European leaders, Reagan's relations were often uneasy at best. Many perceived him to be 'ill equipped for the responsibility that he bears, a kind of cowboy figure, bellicose, ignorant, with a simplistic view of the world pieced together from journals of right-wing opinion and old Hollywood movies'.[7] He established a good rapport with Britain's Mrs Thatcher, and with West Germany's Helmut Kohl, but many others found themselves at odds with him over his Soviet policy, trade and the Nicaraguan situation.

Early administration policy toward China went very poorly until 'a combination of domestic pressures, alliance insistence, and diplomatic realism compelled the administration to pull back from early policy changes'. As Deng Xiaoping encouraged private initiative in China, however, President Reagan became increasingly sympathetic to a man whom he believed agreed with his supply-side economic views.[8] Reagan's standing with such leaders as Menachem Begin of Israel, President Zia of Pakistan, Edward Seaga of Jamaica and Jose Lopez Portillo of Mexico, was considerably better than that of Jimmy Carter. American influence in the Middle East, though, declined under Reagan's tenure and such allies as King Hussein of Jordan and Hosni Mubarak of Egypt experienced increased difficulties in dealing with the White House. The enunciation of the Reagan Doctrine brought Reagan great influence and prestige with the insurgency leaders, but most governments regarded these efforts with profound skepticism. The decrease in ideological diplomacy in Reagan's second term, coupled with a new and successful effort toward US-Soviet arms control agreements, gave many world leaders hope that the United States would exercise more responsible world leadership.

THE REAGAN AND GORBACHEV SUMMITS

After the 1984 election and the rise to power of Mikhail Gorbachev, the scene was set for the first summit meeting of the Reagan presidency. This was held in Geneva in November 1985. While the meetings yielded little in the military sphere, they did establish direct relations between the two leaders and their foreign policy advisors, including Shultz and the new Soviet Foreign Minister Eduard Shevardnadze who had replaced Andrei Gromyko. The doors were also opened to further summits and after Reagan and Gorbachev had spent fifteen hours face to face, the hard edge of the president's anti-communist rhetoric began to soften. As Dallin and Lapidus shrewdly observe, ' . . . both leaders wanted their encounter to be a success: each needed the other's tacit cooperation for his own political purposes'.[9]

The Geneva Summit was soon followed by an exchange of New Year's greetings by the two leaders on American and Soviet television networks and by a series of arms control proposals by the Soviets which were largely rejected by the US. The next summit at Reykjavik, Iceland in October, 1986 was sudden and ill-prepared and included on the agenda such subjects as arms reduction, human rights, regional conflicts, and bilateral relations. The date of Reagan's departure was set, as were many of the president's appointments, after Mrs Reagan consulted with a West Coast astrologer. Donald Regan, President Reagan's second Chief of Staff, described the incident as follows: 'Mrs. Reagan also consulted with her Friend as to the best day for the Presidential departure, and the astrologer informed us that Thursday, October 9, was the most auspicious date. We wrote it into the schedule'.[10]

Reykjavik turned out to be full of surprises with both Reagan and Gorbachev coming up with radical proposals. These ranged from the Soviet proposal for a 'zero option' (i.e. no intermediate range missiles in Europe), which Reagan liked because it eliminated a whole class of nuclear weapons in one geographic area, to Reagan's proposal for five years of SDI research, testing and development linked to a simultaneous 50 percent reduction in strategic nuclear weapons and the elimination of all strategic nuclear weapons by 1996.

These breathtaking proposals came to naught when the Soviet balked at the deployment of SDI. Reagan quickly counter-proposed that all ballistic missiles be eliminated by 1996 while testing of SDI would go forward under the rules of the ABM Treaty. Gorbachev then offered to eliminate all strategic forces, but made this contingent upon a ten-year extension of the ABM Treaty and a ban on developing and testing SDI beyond the laboratory. Reagan could not accept this and the summit collapsed soon afterwards. Instead of truly earthshaking breakthroughs, therefore, came great disappointment and mutual recrimination. Nevertheless, the groundwork laid in Geneva and Reykjavik prepared the way for subsequent achievements in Washington and Moscow. Reagan himself saw it this way, 'Far from being a defeat, Reykjavik was a milepost, a turning point in disarmament negotiations. It will lead to eventual agreements. It is not the end, but a furthering of the process'.[11]

At the next summit meeting in Washington in December 1987, Reagan and Gorbachev were able to accomplish two very significant things: sign an Intermediate-Range Nuclear Forces Treaty (INF) and lay the foundations for a strategic arms reductions agreement (START). The INF treaty provided for the elimination of an entire class of missiles within three years after the treaty took effect. Agreement was also reached on the most comprehensive verification procedures in the history of arms control and an unprecedented exchange of information on the numbers, locations and technical specifications of all INF missiles and launchers. Site inspections were authorized to confirm the validity of data and to witness the destruction of missiles. Altogether the Soviets agreed to destroy systems capable of carrying over 1500 nuclear warheads, the US agreed to eliminate about 400 warheads.

INF was an important first step in reducing US and USSR arsenals of nuclear weapons. It also prepared the way for further negotiations on strategic weapons with the nominal goal being a 50 per cent reduction. A start toward this was made when agreement was reached on subceilings for ICBM and SLBM warheads and Reagan and Gorbachev each decided to go forward with their own research, and development and even deployment and testing of new systems within the ABM treaty of 1972.

After the meetings, considerable infighting took place in the White House before an agreed position was reached regarding SDI, the ABM treaty and strategic arms talks. The resignation of Caspar Weinberger and the appointment of Frank Carlucci as his successor, plus Howard Baker's presence as Reagan's Chief of Staff in place of Donald Regan, eased the tensions and helped pave the way for a Moscow Summit in June 1988. The Senate passed the INF treaty after a spirited debate and prepared the way for a cordial atmosphere. Strobe Talbott reported that the START treaty was about 90 per cent complete, but the remaining 10 per cent proved so troublesome that no final agreement was reached either at the Moscow Summit or before Reagan left office.[12]

THE MOSCOW SUMMIT

The Moscow Summit between Reagan and Gorbachev saw the final ratification of the INF Treaty and modest progress on START. It encouraged strategic arms negotiators at Geneva to keep working on such difficult issues as verifiable limits on sea and air-launched cruise missiles, mutual restrictions on deployments of mobile missiles and the linkages between START and SDI. The Summit discussions also covered prior notification of missile tests, a verification protocol to make possible future ratification of the 1974 peaceful nuclear explosions treaty and an agreement to permit experiments at nuclear sites to facilitate verification of nuclear explosions. In addition, human rights and Jewish emigration, freedom of religious practice in the Soviet Union, trade issues and regional conflicts in Angola, the Middle East, Central America, Cambodia and Vietnam were on the agenda.

All things considered the Moscow conference ended on a positive note. While START was not finished, it was well under way and further progress was promised before Reagan's term was out. The stage at least was set for George Bush to continue the work begun by his former chief. Indeed, Soviet–American relations had come a long way from the early days of 1981 and there was every indication that, as a result of Reagan's four second term summits, a new administration could look forward to a new openness in superpower relations and the realistic possibility of a meaningful reduction in strategic nuclear weapons. As Cold War historian John Lewis Gaddis observed. 'This administration has . . . confounded its critics by raising, more seriously than any of its predecessors, the possibility of a nuclear-free world'.[13]

In early December 1988, Mikhail Gorbachev paid his last visit to Ronald Reagan while in the United States to address the United Nations General Assembly. This so-called 'mini-summit' lasted only two hours, but it permitted Gorbachev to say a sentimental farewell to Reagan and renew his relationship with president–elect George Bush. As Gorbachev himself observed, the most important thing that happened in those two hours was the establishment of continuity.

The 1988 mini-summit occurred after the Soviet leader had delivered a dramatic speech at the UN which included praise for that organization, appeals for the de-ideologization of relations among states, support for democracy and human liberty, rejection of class warfare and economic and cultural isolation, foreswearing the use of force and the announcement of a unilateral cut of 10 per cent of Soviet armed forces. This sensational proposal included a 500,000 troop reduction over the next two years, the withdrawal of six tank divisions from East Germany, Czechoslovakia and Hungary and their disbandment by 1991, and cuts in Soviet European forces of 5000 tanks, 8500 artillery systems and 800 combat aircraft. Needless to say, these unilateral cuts were welcomed by Reagan, Bush and Shultz, although Shultz warned that a serious asymmetry would still exist between Nato and Warsaw Pact forces even after these reductions were made.

In the midst of what was a triumphant visit, a major earthquake hit politically troubled Armenia and Gorbachev quickly cancelled his plans to visit Castro and flew home to lead efforts to confront the devastation in his homeland. He left behind an aura of goodwill and the promise of a further improvement in relations with the US and with Reagan's successor. He also received from Reagan and Bush their blessings for his far−reaching reforms in the political and economic life of the Soviet Union. Whether his initiatives stemmed from domestic needs or a new openness or a combination of both, there is little doubt that they added a welcome lift to the final days of Ronald Reagan in the White House.

ECONOMIC SUMMITS 1981–8

President Reagan attended eight economic summits from the Ottawa meeting of 1981 to the Toronto meeting of 1988. These meetings, between heads of states, foreign and economic ministers and representatives from the European Community, gave the President a forum to preach his free market philosophy, an endeavor in which he found a firm ally in Prime Minister Thatcher.

At Ottawa, Reagan outlined a US policy which promoted 'sustainable, market-oriented noninflationary growth by reducing government spending, changing tax codes to promote saving and investment and targeting stable and moderate money growth'.[14] He also warned against excessive dependence on Soviet energy resources. A year later at Versailles, the US joined with other participants to work for world-wide monetary stability and stronger support for the International Monetary Fund surveillance process. At Williamsburg in 1983, the US committed itself to a joint strategy for coping with international debt and promulgated a plan for arms control that firmly tied Japan to the Western alliance. In 1984 in London, Reagan's policies of sustainable growth and prudent monetary policies were strongly endorsed, as was a US proposal for renewed East West talks on nuclear arms control. The US position in these talks was endorsed at the next summit in Bonn. The following year, 1986, in Tokyo, members agreed to form a 'Group of Seven' finance ministers and included agriculture on the agenda for the first time. The Reagan case-by-case approach to debt problems, as outlined in the fall of 1985, was accepted. Strong statements were issued against Libyan terrorism and for a convention on nuclear accidents.

In 1987, the summit partners met in Venice and drew up strategies for reducing global imbalances, with emphasis on the need for appropriate growth patterns in industrialized countries and on the shared responsibility of newly industrialized countries to preserve free world trade. Creditor nations were also urged to ease debt burdens through favorable rescheduling terms.

The last of the economic summits which Reagan attended, in 1988, met across the border in Canada and saw 'the Gipper' as the center of attention as he prepared to ride off into the sunset. He pressed for the end of farm subsidies by 2000 and pointed to the US–Canadian trade agreement as a model for free trade. Reagan's agenda also called for coordination among the seven summit nations for economic growth, aid for the Philippines, and a crackdown on banks that laundered illicit drug profits. But with Reagan essentially a lame-duck, none of the participants was inclined to make commitments on difficult issues such as currency values and the prospects of inflation. A recent improvement in the US trade deficit figure gave the leaders enough breathing space to dodge the issues until after Reagan left office. Nevertheless, the summiteers accepted a James Baker proposal for a new statistical index to monitor international price movements of commodities, gold included. All major industrial countries were urged to speed up efforts to overhaul regulatory policies and tax codes that slow economic growth. Finally, Reagan pushed hard for a worldwide pledge to deny refueling to any hijacked planes.

Reagan rang down his reign in Toronto when he had moved to the center on such issues as arms control, relations with the Soviet Union and stabilizing the dollar's value. His long advocacy of free markets, economic deregulation and a hard line on terrorism had weathered the storm of eight years well. While vague compromise language papered over numerous long-lasting disagreements, Reagan emerged from his last 'roundup' with not only generous toasts, but also with some genuine satisfaction that things had gone his way during his two terms. Except for the trade and budget deficits he came out of the eight economic summits looking better than might have been expected, considering the lower performance expectations that his economic partners held. If he did not have the mental agility and work ethic of Margaret Thatcher, he was considerably more genial, and had James Baker along as a strong right hand.

Subsequent to the Toronto Summit, 96 signatories to the General Agreement on Tariffs and Trade, GATT, met in Montreal in December 1988, but because of major disagreements between Washington and the European Community over agricultural measures, the meeting broke up after a week of negotiations. The dispute stemmed from the longstanding refusal of the Europeans to accept American demands that the Community phase out export subsidies and price controls. Both sides threatened to retaliate against each other if a future agreement could not be made.

ACCOMPLISHMENTS

In assessing the accomplisments of the Reagan administration in foreign policy, a promising place to begin is with the large buildup of US defences in the first term that redressed the balance of military power with the Soviets and allowed the US to bargain from a position of strength in the second term. The reopening of a constructive dialogue with the Russians, followed by four summits, the INF Treaty, progress on strategic arms limitation talks and mutual on-site inspections of military bases, exercises and facilities are not small achievements, even if the coming of Gorbachev and domestic Soviet needs played important roles in bringing these to fruition.

Reagan not only upgraded the US military and improved its morale, but restored the CIA, by providing additional funds and giving William Casey considerable access to the White House, to a prominent place in US foreign policy. Furthermore, Reagan displayed a willingness not only to flex US muscles, but also to use them in Grenada, Libya, the Middle East, the Persian Gulf and against terrorists.

Reagan's support for Britain's Falkland War, for the insurrection against Marcos in the Philippines which brought Aquino to power, and for free trade against protectionist forces within the US must all be regarded as positive achievements of his administration. He also backed a comprehensive ban on chemical weapons, the eradication of narcotic crops, new and broader immigration laws for the US and international efforts to control ocean and atmospheric pollution.

Under Reagan the US continued its support for NATO, for the peace process in the Middle East, for South American countries such as Mexico, Brazil, Argentina and El Salvador and for Asian countries such as South Korea and Pakistan, and for Australia. It negotiated a free trade treaty with Canada which could serve as a model elsewhere. The administration kept the Sandinistas in Nicaragua on the defensive throughout Reagan's two terms, a result which, in some quarters, might be considered a considerable accomplishment.

In addition to George Shultz at State, the administration could boast of able players in the persons of Paul Nitze, Kenneth Adelman and Richard Perle on arms negotiations, Richard Burt and John Whitehead at State, Frank Carlucci and Colin Powell at NSC, and James Baker and Richard Darman at Treasury. As the late-blooming 'vicar' of American foreign policy, George Shultz stands out as an experienced, moderate and responsible leader, perhaps not a Dean Acheson or Henry Kissinger – the best of post-World War II Secretaries of State – but a sensible and pragmatic voice among the many 'true believers' striding the corridors of power in this most conservative of recent administrations.

Perhaps Reagan's most important contribution was restoring America's faith in itself after the malaise of Watergate, the Vietnam War, the Iran hostage crisis and the faltering economy of the late 1970s. His appeals for patriotism, national defense and American leadership all contributed to a renewed *élan*. The Great Communicator became the Great Salesman for a stronger America – an America willing to bargain from a position of strength – an America willing to exert force if thought necessary – an America in an economic recovery willing to preach the virtues of free markets and competition to all who would listen. Reagan believed fervently in his own message and was able to convice many at home and abroad that America indeed had come back to a position of global leadership.

SHORTFALLS OF POLICY

If Jimmy Carter conducted his foreign policy with more than a hint of naive idealism, then Ronald Reagan overcompensated in the opposite direction. He launched his foreign policy with a belligerent 'realpolitik' that led to such simplifications as calling the Soviet Union an 'Evil Empire', and his refusal to meet Soviet leaders in the first term. His decision on tax cuts while initiating a vast US arms buildup, helped to create a massive budget deficit, which in turn contributed to an immense trade deficit. Reagan dragged his feet on meaningful arms negotiations in the first term and turned down the very promising compromise reached by Paul Nitze and Yuli Kvitsinsky in their famous 'walk in the woods'.[15] Subsequently, his preparations for the Reykjavik summit were hasty, while his sudden willingness to make radical agreements with Gorbachev led European allies to question the integrity of the US security guarantee. Reagan's infatuation with the Strategic Defense Initiative began early and lasted until the end of his term of office, long after it became clear that there were many complications, both political and technical, with making SDI operable and deployable.[16]

What David Stockman called Reagan's 'awesome stubbornness', applied not only to Star Wars but also to the prolonged positioning of the Marines in Lebanon in an exposed and vulnerable situation and the unrelenting political and military pressure put on the Sandinista regime in Nicaragua.[17] In spite of long, costly, and at times illegal support of the Contras, the efforts wound down to near zero by the end of the second term. Reagan's denial of support for the Arias peace plan for Central America undercut the best hope of an early settlement in that troubled region.

Reagan's second term also saw two of the biggest scandals as well as some of the biggest triumphs. One scandal was the Iran–Contra Affair which is dealt with elsewhere in this book. Suffice it to say that the affair not only revealed the existence of a covert policy which contradicted a publicly stated policy of the administration – no deals for hostages – but also showed that an inattentive president allowed the NSC to become an operational, instead of a coordinating, body which indulged in shady and illegal acts. The Tower Commission observed in its conclusions on the 'Failure of Responsibility':

> The President did not seem to be aware of the way in which the operation was implemented and the full consequences of U.S. participation. . . . He did not force his policy to undergo the most critical review of which the NSC participants and the process were capable. At no time did he insist upon accountability and performance review. Had he chosen to drive the NSC system, the outcome could well have been different.[18]

Closely associated with this failure was the dubious behavior of the CIA and its controversial director, William J. Casey. Casey, who was a long-time intimate of the President, enjoyed frequent and easy access to the White House and generous appropriations from Congress. The CIA prospered under Casey, but it also ran wild with questionable covert operations, and Casey himself was the likely *eminence grise* behind the Iran–Contra caper. Reagan's loose administrative style allowed the CIA to wander off the reservation more than once.[19]

The other major scandal revolved around arms procurement policy in the Pentagon. Considering the amount of money spent on military equipment and supplies through the 1980s, it is little wonder that in Reagan's last year massive irregularities were uncovered in the defence procurement system. The investigation centered on the relationship among Defense Department procurement officials, contractors who did business with them and consultants who worked as intermediaries between the Pentagon and the contractors. Dozens of people in the Pentagon, mainly in the Navy and Marine Corps, were investigated and as many as 85 contracts worth billions of dollars were involved.[20]

As previously mentioned, Reagan's management of foreign affairs was spotty at best with early problems at State and later problems at NSC. Even his White House Staff contributed to some of the shortfalls. As former Speaker of the House Tip O'Neill has observed:

Just before I stepped down as Speaker, the Iran–Contra Affair became public. In my view, nothing like this could have happened if Reagan's first term staff – including Jim Baker, William Clark and Mike Deaver – had still been around. Nobody at the White House or the National Security Council could have gotten away with acting behind the scenes, because one of them would have caught it. These men were master image-makers who would never have permitted a situation to develop that made the President look so bad.

But Don Regan is another story. When you have a president who likes to delegate, assisted by a White House chief of staff who likes to amass power, it's a formula for disaster.[21]

Finally, it must be noted that the Reagan administration's problem with its appointees getting into trouble with the law – the so-called sleaze factor – contributed to a general atmosphere of laxness and permissiveness. This caused a blurred image both at home and abroad in the administration's crusade against Communism, terrorism and drugs. When high-ranking members of the White House staff, the Cabinet, the NSC and the Pentagon leave service under fire, it weakens the reputation of the President and the moral force of his policies.

ASSESSMENT

According to Larry Speakes,

> During the 1980 campaign, Ronald Reagan made a decision that he would live to regret. He told voters he would downgrade the position of national security advisor. It was a pledge he set out to keep but all he succeeded in doing was to allow two of his foreign policy directors, Bud McFarlane and John Poindexter, to get out of control'.[22]

Speakes further notes that not only did the President downgrade the office of the NSC advisor, but he also made poor choices. Richard Allen, William Clark, McFarlane and Poindexter all lacked the personality and stature to be of much help to the President in the conduct of foreign policy. They averaged less than a year and a half on the job. Moreover, they were unable effectively to mediate between Shultz and Weinberger who were constantly at odds over policy on superpower relations and arms control, South Africa, the Middle East and Central America. This situation proved not only disturbing to US allies, but also to the press at home. It never really changed until Reagan appointed Frank Carlucci as National Security Advisor in January 1987. Carlucci was an old Washington hand who moved in to clean up the NSC after the Iran–Contra débâcle. He proved to be an effective appointment, but moved on to replace Caspar Weinberger at Defense in November 1987. Reagan and his Chief of Staff Howard Baker then followed previous practice by promoting the number two man, Lieutenant General Colin Powell, to take Carlucci's place. Many, including Speakes, believed that Reagan, in appointing Powell, had not learned from his previous mistakes in promoting military men to the post. In this instance, however, the military man turned out to be a competent, low profile professional who had the respect of both Carlucci and Shultz.

Reagan's experience with the NSC was a very costly one and the poor quality of his initial appointments plus his own loose oversight of the NSC allowed it to become operational under McFarlane and Poindexter and thereby become the agent for the biggest foreign policy disaster of his administration. The performances of Carlucci and Powell at the end of Reagan's second term, however, allowed the President to leave office with a semblance of order in the NSC and, indeed, in US foreign policy. Carlucci at Defense proved to be more flexible on the budget, choice of weapons systems and arms negotiations. He also got along better with Shultz than did his predecessor. Shultz, in turn, stayed the course until the end and played a strong role in directing the Department's negotiations over the Angola, South Africa, Cuba and Namibia problem, the Soviet withdrawal from Afghanistan and the successful conclusion of the Intermediate Range Nuclear Forces Treaty. Even the Iran–Iraq cease-fire seemed to reflect favorably on the presence of US military forces in the Persion Gulf.

Shultz's denial of a visa for Yasir Arafat to attend a UN General Assembly meeting December 1988 after the PLO had moderated its stand on recognition of Israel and on terrorism, was of dubious legality and a sharp rebuke to Arab moderates seeking a solution to the Palestine question. Two weeks after Reagan and Shultz acted against Arafat, the UN met in special session in Geneva to hear Arafat speak. In his speech and in subsequent press conferences, he fulfilled Shultz's three conditions for US contact with the PLO. These conditions were that the PLO clearly accept UN Security council Resolutions 242 and 338, recognize Israel's right to exist in peace and security and renounce terrorism. On 14 December, in the late winter of Reagan's final term, the Secretary of State, the President and the President-elect all issued statements that the US pre-conditions to talk had been met and that the US government would proceed to open discussions with the PLO through the US Ambassador in Tunisia. This historic breakthrough came after the PLO had moderated its stand and the Swedish government and American Jewish moderates had acted as go-betweens with the State Department. Shultz and Reagan accomplished a major achievement and George Bush was given a fresh opportunity to break the Middle East logjam.

Thus only the Central America quagmire seemed beyond improvement. A new base rights agreement was signed with the Philippines, the US space program got back on track, the Olympics went off with no major hitches and both South and North Korea began talking seriously about reunification. The US Canadian free trade agreement survived the US and Canadian elections of 1988. China and the USSR began emulating US free market policies, and Europe was moving toward economic unification by 1992. While the Reaganauts claimed credit for these promising developments, they failed to come to grips with the 'Twin Towers' deficits in foreign trade and the domestic budget, and with the problems of Third World debt and the deteriorating environment of the planet as evidenced by growing concerns about the ozone layer and the greenhouse effect.

A head start, however, had been made for President Bush to pick up negotiations on strategic arms reduction talks, to continue research and limited deployments on SDI and to strengthen conventional forces and modernize US strategic forces. Further, frequent contacts with the Soviets were underway on a wide range of subjects from trade and cultural exchanges to global environment concerns and control of regional conflicts. Although the Reagan administration began with a massive buildup, denunciations of the Soviet Union, a reluctance to negotiate on arms and a tendency for unilateralism, a mellowing of policy occurred in the second term. This resulted from the pressure of public opinion, a US position of strength, persistent diplomacy and a Soviet willingness to deal. Perhaps Nancy Reagan's concern for her husband's place in history and her thwarted ambition for the President to receive a Nobel Peace Prize, or George Shultz's ascendancy as a real 'Vicar' of foreign policy, or the fortuitous convergence of US–USSR national interests under those two great communicators, Reagan and Gorbachev, made it possible for Ronald Reagan to leave office, as a likeable and well-intentioned, if inattentive and often uninformed, president. He even proved willing to accept Soviet inspectors witnessing the destruction of US missiles under the INF Treaty and to give a farewell speech to the UN praising its record as an honest broker in world politics and judging it worthy of receiving the Nobel Peace award for its peacekeeping forces.

By 1988, Ronald Reagan had come a long way from 1980 in his understanding of the modern world. He still supported his favorite 'freedom fighters', refused to face squarely the consequences of the Twin Towers and held a misplaced belief that Star Wars would and could solve US strategic defense problems with the Soviets. Nevertheless, he left office with the knowledge that he still retained the support of the US public and enjoyed a late and remarkable string of foreign policy successes which earned the labels 'peace epidemic' and 'global Spring'.[23] After 8 November, 1988, Ronald Reagan also had the satisfaction of knowing that his two-term Vice-President, George Bush, had been elected to take his place and continue, at least in broad outlines, the main direction of the foreign policies he had forged as the only two-term president since Dwight Eisenhower.

Reagan's first term was a time when the old 'cold warrior' engaged in ideological warfare with the Soviets, prepared a buildup of US forces and set the stage for a second term of performance in negotiation by the administration's pragmatists. Reagan was a very fortunate president who was able to take advantage of forces and trends outside his control and use them for his benefit. While some presidents are gifted in their conduct of foreign affairs, Reagan was lucky. This was especially so in the autumn of his second term. However, Reagan lost opportunities to deal with the budget and trade deficits, world debt problems, American competitiveness and strategic nuclear arms.

Indeed, 'For every great Reagan success, there is a terrible failure'.[24] This is a good assessment of the conduct of foreign policy during the watch of the fortieth president.

Notes

1. L. Speakes, with R. Pack, *Speaking Out: Inside the Reagan White House* (New York: Charles Scribner's Sons, 1988) p. xii.
2. See A. Haig, *Caveat* (New York: Macmillan Publishing Company, 1984).
3. See M. Deaver, *Behind the Scenes* (New York: William Morrow and Company, 1988), pp. 171–2 for details of his resignation.
4. Secretary of State George Shultz, *Fundamentals of U.S. Foreign Policy* (US Department of State, Bureau of Public Affairs, Washington DC, 1988) p. 1.
5. See M. G. Abernathy, D. M. Hill and P. Williams (eds), *The Carter Years* (New York: St. Martin's Press, 1984), ch. 4, 'The Carter Presidency and Foreign Policy'.
6. President Jimmy Carter, 'A Foreign Policy Based on America's Essential Character', Notre Dame University, South Bend, Indiana, 22 May, 1977, *Department of State Bulletin*, June 13, 1977, p. 622.
7. D. Watt, 'As a European Saw It', *Foreign Affairs: America and the World, 1983*, Vol. 62, 1984, pp. 521–32.
8. C. W. Maynes, 'Lost Opportunities', *Foreign Affairs*, Vol. 64, 1986, pp. 413–34.
9. A. Dallin and G. W. Lapidus, 'Reagan and the Russians: American Policy Toward the Soviet Union', Chapter 7 in K. A. Oye, R. J. Leber

and D. Rothchild (eds), *Eagle Resurgent? The Reagan Era in American Foreign Policy* (Boston: Little Brown and Company, 1987) p. 235.

10.   D. Regan, *For the Record: From Wall Street to Washington* (New York: Harcourt Brace Jovanovich, 1988) p. 344. See pp. 3–4 for further details.

11.   Quoted in ibid., p. 355.

12.   S. Talbott, *Time*, 30 May, 1988, p. 21, and *The Master of the Game: Paul Nitze and the Nuclear Peace* (New York: Knopf, 1988).

13.   J. L. Gaddis, *The Washington Post National Weekly*, 31 October–6 November, 1988, p. 35.

14.   H. Culley, editor, *GIST*, Bureau of Public Affairs, US Department of State, September, 1988.

15.   See L. I. Barrett, *Gambling with History* (New York: Penguin, 1984) pp. 314–15 and S. Talbott, *Deadly Gambits* (New York: Knopf, 1984) pp. 116–51.

16.   *The New York Times*, 7 October, 1988, p. 1.

17.   D. Stockman, *The Triumph of Politics* (New York: Avon Books, 1987), cited by I. M. Destler in C. O. Jones (ed.), *The Reagan Legacy* (New York: Chatham House, 1988), ch. 8, pp. 241–61.

18.   *The Tower Commission Report* (New York: Bantam and Times Books, 1987) pp. 79–80.

19.   See R. Woodward, *Veil: The Secret Wars of the CIA 1981–1987* (New York: Simon & Schuster, 1987).

20.   *The New York Times*, 17 July, 1988, p. 1.

21.   Tip O'Neill with W. Novak, *Man of the House* (New York: Random House, 1987) pp. 372–3, to F. M. 23.

22.   Speakes, *Speaking Out*, p. 264. See Chapter 16, pp. 264–77.

23.   S. Hoffman, 'Lessons of a Peace Epidemic', *New York Times*, 6 September, 1988, p. 27 and M. M. Kondracke, 'The World The Candidates Forgot', *The New Republic*, 21 November 1988, pp. 24–7.

24.   J. Hagstrom, *Beyond Reagan: The New Landscape of American Politics* (New York: Norton, 1988) p. 13.

10 The Reagan Administration and Defence Policy

Phil Williams

INTRODUCTION

Of all areas of public policy, that of defence was perhaps the most important for the Reagan administration. The President came to office in 1981 determined to regenerate American power after a decade marked by external defeat and internal disarray. During the 1970s, the United States had lost a war, the presidency had been tarnished, and the Carter administration had talked of malaise. The new administration saw these problems as temporary and attributed them to what was characterised as a 'decade of neglect'. The implication was that any decline in American power was the product not of long-term secular trends in the international system, nor of changes in the instruments of influence in international politics, but simply of the failure of the Nixon, Ford and Carter administrations to devote sufficient resources to the maintenance of American military strength. Concomitantly, reversing the decade of neglect became a leitmotif of the new administration. The Reagan administration defined its main tasks as regenerating American power, re-establishing national confidence and vitality, and placing the United States in a position to negotiate from strength rather than weakness. The main purpose of this chapter is to consider the extent to which the Reagan administration succeeded in these tasks.

The success of a policy, of course, depends partly on the ability and skill of those responsible for its development. Consequently, the chapter looks initially at Reagan's main appointments for defence policy making. It then examines the pattern of defence expenditure during the Reagan years. Although the Reagan administration differentiated itself from its predecessor, there were also strong strands of continuity. Consequently, the chapter explores the issue of continuity and change before turning to two of the most salient issues of US national security in the 1980s – land-based missile vulnerability

199

and President Reagan's Strategic Defence Initiative. In addition, the Reagan approach to arms control is analysed and the extent to which the administration was successful in its use of force is considered. The final section offers an overall appraisal of the Reagan administration's defence policy.

POLICY-MAKING

The Reagan administration's defence policy was determined in large part by the choice of key policy-makers. With the appointment of Caspar Weinberger as Secretary of Defence, President Reagan had someone who not only shared his ideological antipathy towards Moscow but was determined to restore American military strength. Furthermore, Weinberger believed that military advice had not been given sufficient attention by previous administrations. Accordingly he became a strong advocate of many military positions, especially in relation to the possible use of force. Even so serious differences sometimes emerged between Weinberger and the Chiefs of Staff. General David Jones, Chairman of the JCS until 1982, for example, was a strong critic of the nuclear strategy enunciated during the first two years of the Reagan administration. There was also a belief amongst the military that their views on arms control were ignored. For the most part, however, the armed services were sympathetic to a Secretary of Defence who presided over a massive increase in military spending.

A Secretary of Defence can define his role in ways which combine the characteristics of manager, strategic innovator, and political advocate. Weinberger saw his task in narrow and very simple terms as being to regenerate American military strength by obtaining the highest possible level of funding from Congress. Accordingly, he focused most of his attention on mobilising support for increases in the defence budget – something that evoked considerable support in the early 1980s but gradually encountered more resistance.

Weinberger relied heavily upon key civilian aides, appointing his long-term friend and aide Frank Carlucci (who was to succeed Weinberger as Secretary in 1987) as Deputy Secretary of Defence. Carlucci was given responsibility to oversee the management problems, freeing Weinberger to play his role as political advocate in the budgetary battles. The other most notable civilian appointment was that of Richard Perle. A former aid to Senator Jackson and one of the most effective critics of *détente* in the 1970s, Perle was particularly knowledgeable on strategy and arms control and became very influential with Weinberger. As a result, he had an impact that was unusual for an Assistant Secretary of Defence. Perle was a vigorous opponent of arms control with the Soviet Union favouring instead a 'squeeze' strategy which combined an intensified arms race with restrictions on technology transfer to the Soviet bloc. The purpose of this was to place increasing pressure on the Soviet system in an attempt to disrupt and ultimately to destroy it.

The public rationale for the defence build-up, however, was based on the need to restore parity rather than the desire to achieve superiority. The Reagan administration entered office with massive support for increases in defence spending. In January 1980, 74 per cent of those polled wanted increases in defence spending and a tougher security policy, and this sentiment had further crystallised by the time Reagan entered office.[1] The urgings of the Committee on the Present Danger as well as Reagan's campaign had sensitised the American public to the need for urgent action to restore American power and security. Although Jimmy Carter had taken steps in this direction, especially in 1979 and 1980 the Reagan administration presented increased defence spending as something it was initiating after a period of decline and neglect.

THE DEFENCE BUDGET

By skilful use of what was widely interpreted as a mandate for making America strong again, the Reagan administration initiated

> what was to become the largest and speediest build-up of defence budget authority in American peacetime history. From 1980 to 1985 budget authority as a whole grew by nearly 53 per cent in real terms. The main beneficiary of this growth was procurement, which more than doubled in real terms, with research, development test and evaluation (RDT & E) not far behind, increasing by more than 80 per cent. As was to be expected, outlays grew less rapidly; overall they increased by just under 35 per cent.[2]

Almost equally striking was that the number and cost of 'black programmes' (i.e. those programmes in which the technologies were so sensitive that the details were not even disclosed to Congress) increased significantly.

There were problems with maintaining the public and congressional consensus in favour of increased defence spending however. Part of the difficulty was the lack of an overall strategic design for making most effective use of the increased funding. Indeed, 'as procurement was decentralized and greater authority granted to the four armed services, the defence budget became the sum of individual interests, limited only by the need to keep the budget deficit from exceeding all bounds'.[3] A second difficulty was that the Pentagon budget appeared to be badly managed. During the mid-1980s there were numerous reports of waste and graft in defence procurement. Disclosures of the exorbitant costs of spare parts led many critics to conclude that the administration and the military services were being profligate with the resources provided by Congress. When this was combined with the belief that the administration had been fairly successful in re-establishing American pre-eminence and with growing concern about the overall budget deficit, it was not surprising that the consensus in favour of higher defence budgets evaporated. In 1985 Congress passed the Balanced Budget and Emergency Deficit Control Act (Gramm–Rudman—Hollings). Thereafter the Reagan administration had a series of acrimonious battles with Congress over the defence budget. From fiscal year 1982 through to fiscal year 1985 Congress had cut the budget request by an average of 6 per cent, while still allowing very healthy annual increases. In fiscal years 1986 and 1987 the cuts were over 11 per cent, and there was a decline in overall budget authority of around 12 per cent from fiscal 1985 through fiscal 1989. Because of the budgetary system, however, and especially the fact that 40 per cent of budget outlays in any one year come from authorizations made in previous years, defence outlays continued to increase until fiscal year 1988.[4]

Although it presided over the largest peacetime military build-up in history, the Reagan administration did not succeed in breaking the traditional pattern of feast and famine in the budget cycle. Nor did it consider the choices and issues that would have to be faced as the boom years in defence spending were replaced by a period of austerity. Indeed,

> Weinberger continued to insist on maintaining force structure, pushing the current modernization programme (although at a slower pace) and preparing for the early production of such costly

new systems as the advanced technology (Stealth) bomber. . . . At
no point did he appear to have asked how he could reconcile the
congressional pressure for a reductions in defense spending with
his own, understandable, desire for strong defense. As a result, the
irresistible force simply by-passed and ignored the immovable
object.[5]

Although the uncompromising approach adopted by Weinberger
may have staved off even deeper cuts by Congress in the short term,
the longer-term effect was to confront the Bush administration with
extremely difficult choices about defence priorities. The down-turn in
defence spending in the latter half of the 1980s also meant that the
Reagan administration did not succeed in differentiating itself from
its predecessor nearly as much as it would have liked.

CONTINUITY AND CHANGE

The contrast between the Carter and Reagan administrations was
greatest at the declaratory level. The Reagan administration pursued
policies and programmes initiated by Carter, but provided a very
different rhetorical overlay. Whereas the Carter administration often
appeared weak and indecisive on national security policy, the Reagan
administration was strong and decisive, thereby ignoring elements of
continuity. This is not to ignore the substantive differences between
the two administrations. Particularly important were the changes of
emphasis in the pattern of defence spending, with the US Navy
improving its share of the budgetary allocation. This was not surprising. The one area where the notion of a decade of neglect was
appropriate was US naval power. In the late 1960s and the early
1970s the funds that would normally have been used for the refurbish-
ment of the Navy were channelled into the Vietnam War. Subsequently, the congressional desire for a 'peace dividend' led to cuts in
the defence budget and a further postponement of naval modernisation. The Carter administration was less sympathetic to its plight than
the Navy might have expected with the President not only cancelling
a new aircraft-carrier but restricting the naval role to defensive sea
control.

The Reagan administration was much more favourably disposed
towards the Navy. It committed itself to the goal of a 600-ship Navy
and planned to increase the number of Carrier battle groups from 12

to 15. At the same time, the Navy was encouraged to develop new concepts which were enshrined in what became known as the Maritime Strategy. This strategy went through several permutations. Initially the emphasis was on 'horizontal escalation' – in the event of a Soviet–American conflict the United States would not restrict its operations to the initial theatre of operations, but would extend hostilities to those areas where the Soviet Union was vulnerable or exposed. This was justified in terms of strengthening deterrence, but was attacked by critics as increasing the likelihood of uncontrollable escalation. Although never formally abandoned, the concept of horizontal escalation became a more muted theme in the Maritime Strategy. Other elements in this strategy included early and aggressive forward movement, the deployment of hunter killer submarines into the Barents Sea to threaten the Soviet SSBN bastion, attacks on the Soviet naval base and other targets on the Kola Peninsula, and the destruction of Soviet SSBNs in the conventional phase of hostilities in Europe.[6] It was argued that the destruction of Soviet nuclear assets would force the Soviet leadership to sue for peace. Critics regarded this idea as rather disingenuous, contending that the Martime Strategy was not only dangerous, expensive, prone to escalation and lacking in political sensitivity, but diverted resources from other areas where they might have greater effect.

A second area where the Reagan administration made well publicised changes was in relation to the Air Force. Jimmy Carter, in a decision which had undermined his credibility on national security issues, had cancelled the B-1 Bomber. There were two reasons for this. One was the greater cost-effectiveness of equipping B-52s with Air Launched Cruise Missiles (ALCMs), the other was the continuing development of a new manned bomber based on 'stealth' technology that made it virtually undetectable by enemy radar. In spite of the ALCM programme, Reagan restored the B-1 bomber while also continuing with the development of the Stealth bomber or B-2 as it became known.

The administration's strategic modernisation programme was unveiled on 2 October, 1981, when, in addition to its decision about the B-1, it announced that it would be deploying more Trident submarines, would be developing the M-X missile and was taking further measures to enhance the survivability of command control and communications systems. Although these were relatively minor modifications to Carter programmes, the administration also made changes in its plans for nuclear war–fighting. Whereas the Carter administration had adopted a countervailing strategy designed to ensure that the Soviet leadership would not conclude that it could win a nuclear war, the Reagan administration went further, and in the Consolidated Defence Guidance drawn up in 1982 enunciated a concept of prevailing in a protracted nuclear war. Although Secretary of Defence Weinberger denied that the United States was confident it could win a nuclear war, planning was predicated on the assumption that nuclear war might be lengthy and that the United States should be in a position not only to terminate hostilities on favourable terms, but to ensure that in the postwar world it would not be vulnerable to Soviet coercion.

There was an important gap, however, between the rhetoric and the reality. The Reagan administration had problems in producing and deploying the weapons systems that would provide the necessary underpinnings for the prevailing strategy. As a result of environmental pressures, President Reagan rescinded Carter's decision to deploy 200 M-X missiles on an underground rail track with a multiple point firing system (MPS). The issue of M-X deployment was to prove a controversial issue for the remainder of the Reagan administration, and one which was passed on to his successor. Indeed, it was ironic that a President who championed strategic modernisation should end up with a smaller M-X capability than that projected by Jimmy Carter.

THE VULNERABILITY ISSUE

Questions about the vulnerability of the land-based component of American strategic forces can be traced back to the 1950s and the analyses of Albert Wohlstetter. Although the American deployment of the Minuteman force based in hardened silos temporarily eased concerns over what Wohlstetter had called the 'delicate balance of terror', these anxieties re-emerged in the late 1960s when Secretary of Defence Laird emphasised the threat posed to US land-based missiles by the Soviet SS-9 missiles. The SALT One Agreement combined with the US decision to place Multiple Independently-targeted Re-entry Vehicles on its missiles provided another respite. As Soviet strategic modernisation proceeded very rapidly in the 1970s, however, so concerns over the threat to American land-based missiles increased. The large Soviet missile the SS-18 was able to carry 10 or more warheads, and became a source of great concern to

Paul Nitze who until 1974 was a member of the SALT delegation and subsequently played a pivotal role in the Committee on the Present Danger. The CPD highlighted the threat even more and castigated the Carter administration's inadequate response. The 'planner's nightmare' was that the Soviet Union would be able to launch a first strike attack and deter the United States from retaliation by keeping enough forces in reserve for a second salvo. It was also argued that this strategic edge would enable Moscow to coerce Washington in a superpower crisis. In fact, the first strike scenario presumed a degree of confidence on the part of Soviet military planners about the accuracy of their missiles that was most unlikely. If the threat was exaggerated, however, it was also a powerful weapon with which conservatives could beat the Carter administration.

Carter's M-X decision was partly a response to this pressure and partly a move designed to mobilise support for SALT II. Yet the size of the M-X, its role as a major counter-force system, and the environmental consequences for Utah and Nevada or the MPS being made, made the Carter plan highly controversial. Indeed, Reagan inherited a deployment scheme 'requiring enormous amounts of financial and natural resources and portending massive environmental and social disruption'.[7] The President himself was strongly in favour of M-X deployment, but during the election campaign had criticised MPS as inadequate.

It was against this background that the Reagan administration began to re-assess the basing options for M-X deployment. In March 1981 the Townes Committee was appointed to examine the M-X issue. The panel reported in July, and cast doubt on the survivability of the M-X under the projected MPS deployment, as had a study released by the Office of Technology Assessment in March 1981. Facing the opposition of key Republican Senators, Jake Garn of Utah and Paul Laxalt of Nevada, Reagan formally abandoned the Carter scheme and intensified the search for alternatives which were strategically survivable and politically acceptable. This decision was announced on 2 October. The President also revealed that the number of missiles would be cut from 200 to 100, and that, as an interim measure, 40 M-X missiles would be deployed in existing Minuteman and Titan silos, which would be further hardened to offer greater protection. This decision

was more clearly calculated to release funds for continued development of the project than to close the so-called window of vulnerability, his administration's avowed objective. Congress, throughout the year, had made it clear that no more money could be spent unless a basing mode decision was made. Evidently, Reagan never had a proposed basing plan feasible enough to compete with the abandoned Carter plan which he claimed to have rejected for strategic reasons.[8]

Rather than signalling the end of the administration's concern with M-X, therefore, the October announcement highlighted a continuing preoccupation. The new deployment scheme did not run afoul of the environmentalist groups, but was not effective in alleviating concerns about the window of vulnerability: 'selling interim silo basing to Congress after more than five years of debate about missile vulnerability was an impossible task'.[9] Indeed, critics argued that a vulnerable M-X was the worst of all worlds – as well as posing a first strike threat to the Soviet Union, it also offered a tempting target. The result was the development of a coalition in Congress hostile to interim basing, and the administration's increasing involvement in what critics described as a 'basing mode of the month club'.[10]

The Townes Committee had suggested that deployment of the M-X on continuous patrol aircraft was one answer to the vulnerability problem, but also considered the possibility of closely based spacing – what was to become known as dense-pack. The first of these ideas initially won support in the Reagan administration but was not popular in the air force or with Congress.[11] Consequently, in 1982, a revamped Townes Committee was appointed to assess the dense-pack system, which relied for survivability on the fact that incoming Soviet missiles would destroy each other – a phenomenon known as fratricide. Although the Commission provided some support for this concept, there was not much enthusiasm for it. Nevertheless, Reagan announced the dense-pack basing mode in a televised speech on 22 November, 1982 – a speech in which the M-X was christened 'Peacekeeper'. The new scheme had little credibility. Its wisdom was not universally accepted even among the Joint Chiefs of Staff. Furthermore, the debate took place against a background of increasing popular support for a nuclear freeze and concerns over increases in defence spending. It was not surprising, therefore, that on 7 December, the House of Representatives rejected the dense-pack scheme by 248 votes to 176. Although Congress refused to provide funds for testing and production of the M-X, it did allocate funds for further research and development, while directing the Administration to reassess its modernisation and arms control policies and to report back after 1 March, 1983.

In response, the Reagan administration on 3 January, 1983 appointed an independent commission to review the modernisation programme and the future of land-based missiles. The Commission, chaired by former National Security Adviser Brent Scowcroft, was a bipartisan group of well-respected figures in the national security policy field, including James Woolsey, an attorney with considerable experience of defence policy in both the executive and the congress. The Senior Counselors to the Commission included Henry Kissinger and former Secretaries of Defence, Laird, Schlesinger, Rumsfeld and Brown. This was one sign that the Reagan administration, somewhat belatedly, had realised the importance of establishing a broadly based consensus on the M-X. Accordingly, the Commission used the next several months for extensive consultation not only with technical experts but with members of congress. The Commission explicitly attempted to replace what one member was to describe as the 'political chaos of the previous two years on strategic and arms control questions' with a coherent assessment and set of recommendations that not only integrated modernisation and arms control considerations but was capable of winning bipartisan support and restoring domestic consensus.[12]

The Scowcroft Report reiterated the importance of the strategic triad, the ICBMs bombers and SLBMs and defined away the 'window of vulnerability' in relation to land-based missiles by contending that the different components of US strategic forces should be assessed collectively and not in isolation. As it stated: 'Our bombers and ICBMs are more survivable together against Soviet attack than either would be alone . . . '.[13] By acknowledging that co-ordinated and effective surprise was a matter of considerable complexity for an attacker, the Commission was implicitly acknowledging that the requirements of survivability were less stringent than had hitherto been assumed.

The Commission also argued that it was impossible to replicate the survivability that Minuteman had enjoyed during the 1960s and much of the 1970s and that the focus on the M-X was too narrow: 'By trying to solve all ICBM tasks with a single weapon and a single basing mode in the face of the trends in technology, we have made the problem of modernising the ICBM force so complex as to be virtually insoluble'.[14] The solution was a three-pronged approach: the design of a single warhead small missile which would be less attractive as a target and less threatening to Soviet missiles; a more serious search for arms control agreements in which the emphasis should be placed on warhead rather than launcher limits; and the deployment of M-X in existing silos to remove the Soviet advantage in ICBM capability, to ensure that the United States could place Soviet hard targets at risk, and to encourage Moscow to move towards a more stable and controlled approach. Although the deployment mode of the small ICBM was not specified, the Commission was particularly interested in hardened mobile launchers. Indeed, there seems to have been a clear preference among at least some members of the Commission for moving away from multiple warheads and back to single warhead missiles as a means of enhancing strategic stability.

The new missile was presented as an addition rather than an alternative to M-X, however. This was partly because the M-X was the only existing ICBM modernisation programme and partly for political reasons.

> The importance of putting together a solution that the Administration and other M-X supporters could endorse, the importance of not asking our allies to deploy intermediate-range land-based systems while we would be canceling our own analogous strategic system on land, and the importance of having some bargaining leverage with the Soviets in the ongoing START talks, all militated against unilateral cancellation.[15]

The new package was unveiled on 11 April, 1983 and endorsed by the President on 19 April. The immediate problem, however, was still M-X funding especially in the House of Representatives. The Democrats had made a gain of 26 seats in the mid-term elections and the House was more liberal than it had been the previous December when M-X had run into serious difficulties. Woolsey though was able to elicit the support of Representatives Les Aspin, Albert Gore and Thomas Foley, and with their help the administration was able to get a positive vote on M-X. The pro-M-X coalition, however, remained fragile and in order to generate more support the administration amended its arms control policy in the direction desired by key members of Congress. Although this provided short-term success, the issue remained highly controversial. In 1984 M-X survived only by the casting vote of Vice-President Bush after the Senate had tied 48–48. Congress authorised funding for production of the first 21 missiles, but mandated that the money could not be spent until the new Congress voted to release the funds some time after 1 March, 1985.

In 1985 therefore, the administration had once again to engage in extensive lobbying on behalf of M-X. The White House Report on the M-X issued 4 March 1985 emphasised the continued Soviet build-up of strategic forces and reiterated the need for 100 missiles, arguing that a reduction in this number would give the wrong signals to the Soviet Union as new arms control talks were beginning. Although this argument helped the administration to obtain a positive vote for the first 21 missiles, Congress subsequently limited to 50 the number of missiles that could be placed in existing silos and made authorisation of the remaining M-X dependent upon congressional support for a new basing mode.

In response, the Pentagon devised several other options, before the President, in December 1986, approved proposals for a rail garrisoned M-X. The initial plan was to have 25 trains with each one carrying two missiles. The trains would remain at air force bases, but in a period of tension or crisis would be dispersed along the domestic rail system. Although rail garrison was almost as controversial as other deployment schemes for M-X, by 1988 the first 50 missiles based in silos had become operational. A new twist was added when Secretary of Defence Carlucci not only authorised development of a rail-based launching system but argued that all 100 Peacekeepers should be rail mobile.

The Scowcroft compromise, therefore, had provided only a temporary respite in the M-X saga. The Commission had argued that the M-X and the small ICBM or Midgetman were complementary. Increasingly, however, they were regarded as alternatives. The proponents of nuclear warfighting strategies contended that the Peacekeeper was far more cost-effective than the small ICBM – a point that became increasingly important in a period of budgetary stringency – while those in Congress who were more concerned over strategic stability emphasised the greater survivability of the Midgetman, especially under a possible arms control regime based on deep cuts in strategic warheads. The final Reagan defence budget gave Midgetman a very low priority but the Bush administration would have to make the final decisions as to the balance between the two missiles. President Reagan, who had come to office determined to close the 'window of vulnerability' had left office without obtaining a sustainable consensus on modernisation of the ICBM force. It was partly because of the difficulties with mobilising support for a new generation of ICBMs, however, that Ronald Reagan had placed an unprecedented emphasis on defence against strategic nuclear forces.

THE STRATEGIC DEFENCE INITIATIVE

Rarely has a single speech had as much impact on the United States defence posture as President Reagan's speech of 23 March 1983 announcing his Strategic Defence Initiative. In the speech the President called upon the scientific community to provide the capability to render nuclear weapons 'impotent and obsolete'. He announced that to facilitate this he was

> directing a comprehensive and intensive effort to define a long-term research and development program to begin to achieve our ultimate goal of eliminating the threat posed by strategic nuclear missiles. This could pave the way for arms control measures to eliminate the weapons themselves. We seek neither military superiority nor political advantage. Our only purpose – one all people share – is to search for ways to reduce the danger of nuclear war'.[16]

Reagan offered both a vision of the future and a statement of dissatisfaction with the mutual vulnerability of the Soviet and American homelands (Mutual Assured Destruction). His initiative was designed to replace it by Mutual Assured Survivability, with particular emphasis on the survivability of the United States.

The origins of SDI can be understood in terms of technological opportunity, the conservative agenda for regenerating American power, the President's own sense of vision, the problems attendant upon strategic modernisation and what one observer had described as 'the crisis in domestic support for Reagan's arms policy'.[17] It was this combination of factors which determined both the timing and the content of the March 1983 speech.

The initiative was based very much on the President's convictions and preferences as well as his own sense of vision. 'Even before assuming the Presidency, he had expressed strong interest in trying to defend the nation from enemy missiles and had shown a curiosity about the powers of high technology'.[18] Influenced by a visit he had made to the North American Air Defence Headquarters, (NORAD)

Reagan had considered making a major issue out of the lack of population protection in the 1980s campaign. His ideas were subsequently crystallised by discussions with the physicist, Edward Teller who believed that new and more exotic technologies such as the X-ray laser would provide a capacity for intercepting ICBMs and, to a lesser extent, by General Daniel Graham, former head of the Defence Intelligence Agency and director of the High Frontier Group which campaigned for strategic defences based on space-based kinetic kill systems. Although Teller and Graham were part of a Heritage Foundation group, their disagreements over the most appropriate means to achieve effective defences led to a split. Nevertheless, they both contributed not only a sense of vision to the President but the belief that the technologies of strategic defence were within reach. Although research on the technologies of ballistic missile defence had continued through the 1970s (despite the Anti-Ballistic Missile Treaty of 1972) it was not 'technological push' from this work but the arguments of Teller and Graham that led Reagan to conclude that there were new and exciting technological opportunities for strategic defence.

The desire to develop and grasp these opportunities was all the greater because of the administration's sense of frustration with continued vulnerability. For a President who was deeply concerned about the Soviet threat, dependence on Soviet restraint – even when that restraint was induced by American threats of retaliation – was uncomfortable. Furthermore, 'with the call for revitalising American strength and an increasingly aggressive attitude towards foreign policy, it seemed . . . defeatist to accept vulnerability in the super-power relationship – even if the Soviet Union found itself in precisely the same situation'.[19] In this sense, ballistic missile defence was a natural extension of the right-wing political agenda. It had been advocated strenuously for some years by Senator Malcolm Wallop of Wyoming and had been mentioned in the Republican Party's 1980 platform.

The SDI speech was also a response to domestic political pressures. These stemmed partly from the nuclear freeze movement, partly from the slump in Reagan's popularity resulting from the apparent failure of supply-side economics, and partly from differences with Congress over spending priorities. The difficulties that the administration faced in obtaining domestic support for a new generation of land-based ICBMs added another important dimension to the Reagan administration's deliberations in early 1983.

The critical meeting within the administration took place on 11 February, 1983, and was engineer in part by Deputy National Security Adviser, Robert McFarlane and Navy Chief of Staff, Admiral Watkins, who had collaborated in drafting a briefing paper on 'freedom from fear'.[20] At this meeting the possibility of giving new momentum to research on ballistic missile defence was discussed with the Joint Chiefs of Staff. It appears, however, that the JCS had something more modest in mind than extensive population defence and while they triggered the President to move in a particular direction they did not shape the formulation of SDI.[21] Reagan's speech of 23 March was a top down initiative rather than something which had bubbled up from the bureaucracy.

Prior to the speech there was some opposition from within the bureaucracy, with Richard Perle succeeding in confining the President's proposal to defence against ballistic missiles. Furthermore, McFarlane and others were warning about the dangers of oversell. In view of the political circumstances of early 1983, however, oversell appeared very attractive. SDI would not only allow the administration to seize the moral high ground against the freeze proponents and the Catholic bishop's pastoral letter on war and peace, but would help to mobilise what had been a dissipating support in Congress for the defence budget. Furthermore, it would give the administration a renewed strength of purpose: 'A program to point the way to the future, to electrify the nation and to raise before it a vision' would help Reagan to regain the political leadership at home.[22] SDI would also strengthen the administration's position in its dealings with the Soviet Union.

For all this, the initiative was greeted with considerable scepticism not a little derision by many members of the strategic community. Indeed, the 23 March Speech was only the first step in what was to become one of the most controversial elements in the Reagan administration's defence policy. Part of the problem arose from confusion over the precise purpose of SDI, and its relationship to the idea of deterrence based upon retaliatory capabilities. It also came at an inopportune time for Western European governments concerned with deploying cruise and Pershing missiles in the face of public opposition. By suggesting that nuclear deterrence was immoral, Reagan provided tacit support for the protest movement in Western Europe.

In the aftermath of the 23 March speech the administration appointed several panels to study the strategic and technological dimensions of strategic defences. The Defensive Technologies Study Team – known as the Fletcher Committee – examined the technological problems associated with strategic defence and concluded that the challenges were great but not insurmountable.[23] The other committee, the Future Security Strategy Study, focused rather less on long-term goals and more on near-term possibilities, arguing that partial systems should be deployed to buttress retaliatory deterrence – strategic defences could have considerable utility even if they were not leak-proof. In particular they could deny the Soviet Union its strategic objectives and thereby contribute to deterrence.[24]

From the outset, therefore, modest and ambitious schemes for strategic defence were vying for acceptance. This contributed to the confusion of the policy debate, as it was not clear whether strategic defence was intended to replace deterrence – as the President seemed to envisage – or to supplement it – which seemed to be the preference in other parts of the executive branch. In spite of these uncertainties, the deliberations and reports of the two committees as well as an unreleased inter-agency study known as the Miller Panel – resulted in a 26 billion dollar research programme over five years to test the feasibility of the idea. It was widely accepted that a programme of research and development on strategic defence was a prudent hedge against Soviet advances in this area. Because of the way the programme had been introduced, however, and the visionary nature of the President's objectives – it precipitated a far-reaching debate about the future of American strategy. Although it was not based on a solid technological foundation, the debate raised fundamental issues about the future direction of American nuclear strategy.

The critics were sceptical not only about the feasibility of the President's proprosal, but also over its desirability. While doubting that the kind of leak-proof system envisioned by President Reagan could ever be built, they also argued that SDI would intensify the arms race, undermine crisis stability, and exacerbate Soviet–American tensions. Considerable emphasis was placed on possible Soviet counter-measures, which would be cheaper than the costs of defence itself. Other critics argued that even if SDI did not come to fruition it would result in an anti-satellite capability, which could also have some destabilising effects. The programme also raised serious concerns in Western Europe and generated fears that it presaged the return to a 'Fortress America' policy and the abandonment by the United States of its NATO allies. Against this some argued that the

American nuclear guarantee to Western Europe would be more credible if the United States was able to minimise damage to its homeland.

In large part, the arguments revolved around the merits of a superpower relationship based upon mutual assured destruction as opposed to one based on mutual assured survivability. The supporters of SDI contended that a phased transition was possible in which the United States and the Soviet Union would both move to defence dominant strategies. On several occasions the President even suggested that the United States would share SDI technology with the Soviet Union in order to achieve a managed transition to a defence dominant world. This did not appear very credible, however, in an administration committed to tightening restrictions on technology transfer to the Soviet bloc.

While the Reagan administration wanted to engineer a defensive transition through new arms control arrangements, its attitude towards existing arms control was ambivalent. The ABM Treaty of 1972 was particularly important obstacle in the way of SDI, especially as it banned the testing or deployment of space based defences or components thereof. Consequently, the administration enunciated a more permissive interpretation of the Treaty, arguing that the development and testing of exotic systems (i.e. those based on new physical principles) was permitted even if these systems were not ground based. This was challenged by members of Congress including most notably, Senator Sam Nunn, Chairman of the Armed Services Committee. Nunn argued the case for a restrictive interpretation of the ABM Treaty, contending that the administration's re-interpretation was unacceptable and that if pushed it would create 'a constitutional crisis of profound dimensions'.[25]

The programme was also subject to considerable attrition with Congress restricting funding for SDI. It was not surprising, therefore, when in the Autumn of 1988 the Pentagon made clear that the initial deployments would not take place until the late 1990s and would be predominantly ground based and more modestly priced than had earlier been suggested. Another idea that was being actively considered was what Sam Nunn had christened Accidental Launch Prevention System – or ALPS – a relatively thin ground-based strategic defence which could be deployed at minimum cost. Although the programme was still alive when the Reagan administration left office, therefore, the terms of reference had become much more constricted. The vision had been replaced by schemes that were carefully circumscribed and unlikely to move to the defence dominant world that Ronald Reagan had envisaged.

If SDI had become an important political issue in relations between the executive and congress it had also become an important element in arms control negotiations. Its effect, however, was paradoxical in that it encouraged the Soviet Union to negotiate more seriously and to make concessions yet made it all the more difficult to obtain agreement at least at the strategic level.

THE ARMS CONTROL DIMENSION

The Reagan administration included many critics of both *détente* and the SALT process in the 1970s, but at the outset was discriminately hostile to arms control. The President himself had stated that SALT II was a fundamentally flawed treaty, and along with many of his advisers, started from the premise that the Soviet Union could not be trusted to observe arms agreements. In addition it was believed that arms control considerations during the 1970s had inhibited the regeneration of American military power, and that this must not be allowed to happen again. Consequently, arms control would have a much lower priority than strategic modernisation. Insofar as the administration was prepared to negotiate with the Soviet Union, it was to be negotiation from strength. In these circumstances, it was hardly surprising that the arms control policy-making process during the early years was somewhat chaotic, or that meetings to discuss arms control were not taken seriously.[26] The policy-making process was characterised by endemic bureaucratic infighting with Richard Perle at DOD and Richard Burt at the State Department playing the key roles.

One of the first issues on the agenda was what to do about SALT II. This became a highly divisive issue in which the State Department and the Joint Chiefs of Staff who 'preferred the relative certainties of parity to the uncertainties of a major new cycle of competition' argued that the United States should continue to observe the terms of the unratified agreement.[27] They were arrayed against Weinberger and Perle, supported by the White House Staff and the CIA, who claimed that the Soviet Union was systematically violating a range of arms control agreements including both SALT II and the ABM treaty of 1972.[28]

Those who wanted to observe SALT II had some early successes, and in May 1982 Reagan announced that he would refrain from measures which would undercut existing agreements.[29] This stemmed less from a revised assessment than from expediency: the SALT II limits would not inhibit American modernisation until the mid-1980s, while they constrained Soviet options before then. Even so the issue remained controversial, and in June 1985 Reagan acknowledged that there would be 'proportionate response to Soviet breaches of the agreement'.[30] The issue of Soviet non-compliance became increasingly important in the next few months, and concerns about the Kranoyarsk radar, and the Soviet deployment of the SS-25 mobile missile, prepared the way for the decision of April 1986 to abandon the SALT II limits. Yet once again there was an element of expediency about the decision as by 1986 the SALT II limits had begun to constrict the American modernisation programme. Partly because of this, the Joint Chiefs, who had played a major part in the initial decision to comply, became more neutral. When President Reagan, on 27 May 1986, announced that in view of Soviet non-compliance, the US was no longer willing to observe the SALT II limits, this 'reflected a late success for the American critics and opponents of arms control'.[31] The irony is that by then the superpowers were negotiating far more seriously about new arms control proposals.

During the early 1980s the administration's lack of enthusiasm for arms control was reciprocated by a Soviet desire to use the talks on Intermediate Nuclear Forces in Europe as a way of preventing NATO from implementing the December 1979 decision to deploy cruise and Pershing II missiles in Western Europe. Both superpowers in fact seemed to be using arms control simply as an extension of the arms competition by other means. Each side included jokers in its proposals that it knew to be unacceptable to the adversary. The Reagan administration, for example, enunciated the zero option – which would give up the deployment of cruise and Pershing in exchange for a Soviet willingness to dismantle the SS-20 missiles. The logic was that Soviet rejection of zero would help to legitimise the NATO deployment in the face of protest from the peace movements of Western Europe. Similarly at the strategic level, President Reagan, in his Eureka speech of 9 May, 1982, unveiled a proposal for strategic arms reductions which was clearly intended to dismantle a large proportion of the Soviet land-based ICBM force, while offering little in return. Although pressure from Congress and the nuclear freeze movement led to greater flexibility in the US negotiating position at START, the United States remained unwilling to offer more than very limited concessions.

At both levels, progress was slow. In July 1982, however, Yuli Kvitsinsky and Paul Nitze, the Soviet and American chief representatives in the INF talks mapped out a possible agreement as a result of informal discussions which became known as the 'walk in the woods'. Both Washington and Moscow rejected the deal and in November 1983, with the first American missiles arriving in Europe, the Soviet Union walked out of the negotiations. The arms control process had reached an impasse.

Several candidates contributed not only to a resumption of talks, but to a more serious effort to reach agreement. The re-election of the Reagan administration intensified Soviet concerns about SDI. Although there were many critics in the United States who dismissed SDI as a chimera, for the Soviet Union it evoked traditional fears about American technological prowess. When this was coupled with the obvious failure of the Soviet attempt to derail the INF deployment, and the emergence of a new Soviet leadership concerned with domestic restructuring and therefore anxious for a relaxation of international tensions the way was open for a more constructive arms control agenda.

The Reagan administration, however, continued to be divided about the merits of arms control. The conservative ideologues or 'squeezers' – like Weinberger and Perle – wanted to eschew arms control in favour of an intensified arms race. The State Department, however, partly in the belief that US resources were not unlimited and partly in the recognition of the Soviet willingess to make sacrifices in order to retain strategic parity, was sceptical of such an approach. The 'dealers' were anxious to move towards an arms control agreement with Moscow.[32]

In January 1985, the dealers began to have an increasingly important impact on US arms control policy. After talks in Geneva between Shultz and Gromyko, the superpowers agreed to resume the arms control dialogue in three separate but related baskets, space weapons, strategic forces, and theatre or INF systems. Serious difficulties remained, especially concerning the linkage between cuts in strategic forces and possible restrictions on space weapons. President Reagan was unwilling to accept restrictions on his vision of strategic defence. This was to be both a bargaining asset and a stumbling-block to agreement. In the end, however, the Soviet

Union may have decided that SDI would have less political support in the United States if progress was made towards agreement in other areas. Accordingly the linkage between an INF agreement and limits on SDI was eventually dropped by Moscow. Reagan never decided unequivocally in favour of the dealers. Nevertheless, during his second term the ideological shibboleths of the first administration were abandoned in favour of a more pragmatic approach. To some extent this was the result of the President's reappraisal of the Soviet Union in the aftermath of his meeting with the new Soviet leader Mikhail Gorbachev, at Geneva in November 1985. Although substantive progress at the Summit was limited, the two leaders established a genuine sense of rapport and committed themselves to continuing their dialogue and improving US Soviet relations.

In January 1986 Gorbachev outlined a plan for the elimination of all nuclear weapons by the year 2000, and suggested that, as a first stage, the US and Soviet Union should reduce their theatre nuclear forces to zero – a statement which suggested that the Soviets might retreat from their insistence on keeping enough SS-20s to counter French and British strategic nuclear forces. Although there was some movement in the first half of 1986, however, progress remained slow.

It was against this background that the Reykjavik Summit occurred. Not intended as a full-blown summit, the Reykjavik meeting nevertheless produced arms control discussions that were more ambitious than anything previously contemplated. In spite of confusion about which proposals were serious and which for propaganda effect, the talks were far-reaching. There was some discussion about the elimination of nuclear weapons by 1996 and it was not clear whether this referred only to ballistic missiles – as the US subsequently claimed – or to all strategic nuclear forces. In the end the Summit broke down over SDI and its relationship to the ABM Treaty. While both leaders accepted the need to reaffirm the ABM Treaty, they differed about what activities it proscribed. Gorbachev, taking a view that was shared by some critics of SDI in the US, argued that only laboratory research and testing was permitted, whereas Reagan wanted to be able to research, develop and test strategic defences outside the laboratory so that after ten years the United States would be able to deploy a defensive shield.

The reactions to Reykjavik ranged from disappointment that agreement had not been reached to a feeling of relief that the United States had not agreed to measures which could be damaging to its own security and that of its West European allies. After a period in which the superpowers mulled over opportunities lost and dangers avoided, a breakthrough was made when Gorbachev proposed detaching the INF package from the other elements. Initially, it was not clear that the United States would take advantage of Gorbachev's concessions. Reagan, as a result of the political difficulties caused by the disclosure of the Iran–Contra affair, however, had additional incentives to reach agreement. For an increasingly beleaguered administration a successful Summit and a major arms control agreement looked extremely attractive. Political expediency was buttressed by conviction: the removal of nuclear missiles from Europe was in line with the philosophy of a President who really was interested in the abolition of nuclear weapons. In this sense the INF Treaty was not very different in purpose from research on SDI.

The INF Treaty signed at the Washington Summit in December 1987, removed all ground-launched missiles from Europe with ranges between 500 kilometres and 5500 kilometres. This agreement was not entirely welcome in Europe, where there were those who feared that the removal of cruise and Pershing would undermine extended deterrence and the NATO strategy of flexible response.

The problems of alliance management were accompanied by the need for a certain amount of domestic management as the INF came before the Senate for approval. While there were a few hard-right Senators who were implacably opposed to the Treaty, however, the debate revealed once again that hard-line presidents have greater flexibility than their moderate or conciliatory counterparts. The outcome of the Senate vote was never really in doubt and in May 1988, when President Reagan was meeting Mr. Gorbachev in Moscow, the Treaty was approved by 93 votes to 5.

In spite of expectations that the INF Treaty would increase the momentum of arms control negotiations and that a START agreement would be signed before Reagan left office, this did not occur. Although the dealers had emerged triumphant in Washington there were continuing differences of opinion, and the arms control policy-making system remained disorderly. In addition to these procedural difficulties, substantive problems remained. Differences over issues such as the inclusion or exclusion of sea-launched cruise missiles, as well as the continued problem of the linkage between a START agreement and the ABM Treaty made it difficult to translate the broad agreement that there should be a 50 per cent cut (which because of the counting rules was more like a 30 per cent cut) in strategic forces into a detailed formula. The result was that Reagan

left office without agreement on strategic armaments. Yet in view of
the first term this is perhaps less surprising than the fact that
agreement was reached on INF.

THE USE OF FORCE

The Reagan administration was intent on re-establishing American
credibility and moving beyond the Vietnam syndrome which, it was
argued, had inhibited the protection of American interests in the
Third World during the latter half of the 1970s. Yet the use of force
was to prove a controversial issue in the administration, with a hard
line being taken by Secretary of State Shultz, and Secretary of
Defence Weinberger advocating restraint. In November 1984, Weinberger made a speech laying out the conditions which had to be met
before the United States should resort to military force. Acknowledging that the tests could not be applied mechanically, Weinberger
nevertheless contended that 'applying these tests to the evidence will
make it clear that while there are situations in which US troops are
required, there are even more situations in which US combat forces
should *not* be used'.[33] In his view Washington should not commit
forces to combat unless vital interests of the US or its allies were at
stake, unless it was prepared to commit sufficient forces to achieve
victory, and unless there were clear political and military objectives.
Furthermore, 'the US government should have some reasonable
assurance of the support of the American people and their elected
representatives in Congress'.[34] Even then force should only be used
as a last resort and in the understanding that there would be
continuous reassessment and adjustment in US combat capabilities
whenever possible. In a statement that was clearly aimed at Shultz's
argument that without the willingness to use force US diplomacy
would become ineffective, Weinberger reiterated the need for caution:

> The world consists of an endless succession of hot spots in which
> some US forces could play, or could at least be imagined to play, a
> useful role. The belief that the mere presence of US troops in
> Lebanon or central America or Africa or elsewhere could be useful
> in some way is not sufficient for our government to ask our troops
> to risk their lives.[35]

In advancing these arguments Weinberger reflected the views of the military leadership and the continued resentment at the experience in Vietnam. In a sense, therefore, the Reagan administration did not really succeed in going beyond the Vietnam syndrome.

The experience in Lebanon underlined the difficulties the United States faced in using force in the Third World. In many ways the involvement of the marines as a peacekeeping force in Lebanon violated all the criteria that Weinberger was subsequently to establish. US forces initially became involved in Lebanon in August 1982 to provide free passage for the withdrawal of the Palestine Liberation Organization from Beirut. Once this was accomplished the marines withdrew but were to return as part of a reconstituted multinational force on 27 September, 1982. Congress was anxious about this commitment from the outset and became especially concerned in the Spring and Summer of 1983 as the marines themselves began to come under attack. On 29 September, however, a compromise was reached whereby the President could keep US forces in Lebanon for 18 months. On 23 October, this compromise fell apart when a terrorist attack on the marine compound in Beirut killed 241 men and provoked congressional and public demands for withdrawal. In February 1984 US forces were withdrawn.

The withdrawal of the marines avoided a major confrontation with Congress over the War Powers Act, but also marked a recognition that there had been serious flaws in US policy. The administration had become involved partly because it viewed events in the Lebanon as part of the global struggle with the Soviet Union; it attempted to remain involved after the bombing because of a concern with credibility that, publicly at least, seemed to unite Shultz and Weinberger. The administration also failed to understand Lebanese realities and to recognise that its attempt to be a neutral arbiter while supporting the Gemayel government were doomed to failure in a country where the state had disintegrated into warring factions and there was no legitimate government. The assumption that the marines were being deployed into a 'relatively benign environment' was mistaken.[36] While the marines were certainly not the most appropriate force for a defensive peacekeeping role, their vulnerability was exacerbated by restrictive rules of engagement.

If Lebanon underlined the limits on American influence in the Middle East, the military intervention in Grenada, at one level at least was more successful. The intervention was prompted by increasing concerns over growing Cuban influence in Grenada, and the building of an air-field on the island, which it was contended was part of a Cuban design for Caribbean domination. When the Grenadan Prime Minister, Maurice Bishop was overthrown and killed in October 1983, the administration had both pretext and opportunity to intervene. The initial rationale was the need to safeguard the lives of 1100 American citizens especially students, on the island, and to restore order. Underlying this though was the concern about Cuban activity. Although there was some resistance from Cubans on the island, the US task force secured control fairly rapidly. Limitations on press coverage meant that the performance of the military was not examined at the outset as carefully as it might have been although subsequent reports that a hospital had been hit cast some doubt on the efficiency of the operations. Senator Sam Nunn was highly critical of the inability of the army and navy to co-ordinate their operations effectively. In spite of these questions marks, however, the intervention was quick, decisive and popular in the United States.

If Grenada was, in part at least, a target of convenience, the same could be said of Libya. US Libyan relations had been strained during the late 1970s but became even more acrimonious when the Reagan administration's emphasis on combating terrorism, and restoring American status encountered the strident anti-Americanism of Colonel Gaddafi. There were early clashes between Libyan and American airplanes over the Gulf of Sidra in August 1981 and the administration subsequently gave Gaddafi a degree of attention that outweighed his importance. Indeed, one columnist writing in April 1986 observed that the Reagan administration's belief that the answer to international terrorism was to do something about Gaddafi represented 'another disastrous triumph of the American image making machine – the star system applied to international politics'.[37] Yet Gaddafi was a far more attractive target than either Syria or Iran both of which had a larger role in fomenting international terrorism. Retaliation against Syria carried dangers of confrontation with the Soviet Union, while Iran's geopolitical position gave the administration an interest in improved relations.

Gaddafi had none of these advantages and in the first three months of 1986 the Reagan administration authorised a series of naval exercises off the coast of Libya. In March there were clashes between Libyan and US forces as a result of which the United States attacked a Libyan missile launch site at Sirte. At the same time the administration was attempting to persuade its European allies to take stronger economic and political sanctions against Libya. With the allies reluctant to do this, the United States decided that more drastic action was necessary and on 15 April – shortly after the European Community had voted to impose sanctions on Libya – F-111s based in Britain joined carrier-based aircraft in attacks on Tripoli and Benghazi. According to the administration, the raid was a retaliatory measure in response to Gaddafi's support for recent terrorist activities against American service-men based in Europe. It also appeared, however, that an attempt had been made to kill Gaddafi. At the very least, it was hoped that the raid would act as a warning against further terrorist activity and would make clear that the United States was not prepared to act with forbearance. Although the action evoked considerable criticism in Europe – which was intensified by the fact that the French embassy and residential buildings had been hit – it had much greater support in the United States. Members of Congress approved the action although there were some concerns that consultation had not met the requirements of the War Powers legislation.

More controversial, however, was American naval involvement in the Gulf during the Iran–Iraq War. The Gulf had long been a focus of Western security concerns, and in the 1980s these concerns were exacerbated by the hostilities between Iran and Iraq. The war was less of an impediment to the flow of oil than had been anticipated, but in September 1986 Iran began to attack oil tankers trading with Kuwait. In response Kuwait asked the Soviet Union to reflag several of its tankers. This raised longstanding American concerns about Soviet influence in the Gulf and the United States agreed to a more extensive reflagging operation. The dangers in this exercise – and in the American naval presence in the Gulf – became obvious in May 1987 when an Iraqi plane attacked an American frigate, the *USS Stark* with the loss of 37 US sailors. In the subsequent weeks opposition to the reflagging exercise crystallised on Capitol Hill but a House vote to block the reflagging for 90 days was not supported by the Senate which failed to defeat a Republican filibuster. The American presence, however, remained controversial, especially when the *USS Vincennes*, operating under more permissive rules of engagement as a result of the *Stark* incident, shot down an Iranian Airbus full of civilians. Although the ending of the Gulf War shortly afterwards was held up by the Reagan administration as justification of its policy, the episode had shown American military forces in a rather poor light – and added to concerns over efficiency.

In addition to the overt use of military force the Reagan administration also engaged in a series of more covert and indirect activities.

These were particularly important in Central America where the administration became preoccupied by the threat from the Sandinistas in Nicaragua. The Nicaraguan government, it was argued was a proxy for Cuba and the Soviet Union and deeply engaged in regional subversion and insurgency. Invoking a regional variant of the old domino theory the administration argued that such actions could spread north to Mexico and south to Panama – in both cases threatening vital American security interests. Yet the administration was constrained from direct military intervention by the lack of support from the Joint Chiefs of Staff and from Congress. Accordingly, it was forced to follow a rather more moderate policy than at least some of its members wanted, providing military aid to the Contras in their continued struggle against the Ortega government. Even the aid was controversial, however, and in 1982 Congress passed the Boland Amendment to the defence appropriations bill prohibiting the use of funds by the CIA or DOD to provide military support intended to overthrow the government of Nicaragua. Since the administration had not stated this as its aim this was not a total prohibition and limited funding was provided by Congress. In 1984 Congress passed a more comprehensive Boland Amendment prohibiting all funds for military or paramilitary operations in Nicaragua. Even so, the administration succeeded in obtaining funding for humanitarian aid to the Contras, and Congress, concerned that it might be held responsible for the failure of the administration's policy, backtracked from the second Boland Amendment. Yet Nicaragua remained a controversial issue. In early 1984 the mining of Nicaraguan ports and harbours generated considerable friction in executive–congressional relations, partly because the Senate Committee on Intelligence had not been informed of the action. As a result of both domestic and international pressures the administration was compelled to desist from its blockade. It continued with its covert actions against Nicaragua, and the National Security Council staff became involved in raising private funds to support the Contras. This effort to circumvent congressional restrictions on military aid was to culminate in the Iran Contra affair.

Throughout the Reagan years, therefore, the executive branch was seriously constrained by Congress in its attempts to overthrow Ortega. This did not prevent the administration from enunciating what became known as the Reagan Doctrine which committed the United States to assist revoluntionary forces fighting against Marxist–Leninist governments in the Third World. In an effort to reverse the

Soviet gains of the 1970s the old Republican notion of liberation or rollback in Eastern Europe was resuscitated and applied to the Third World. Yet there remained an important gap between the rhetoric and the implementation of the doctrine. Although assistance was provided to the forces of UNITA in Angola and to the Mujahideen in Afghanistan, as well as to the Contras, it fell far short of what the administration would have liked. Nevertheless, by 1988 the administration was claiming some success with the Soviet decision to withdraw from Afghanistan. While US assistance to the rebel forces – and especially the supply of Stinger missiles – was a factor, however, the Soviet decision to leave Afghanistan reflected a more fundamental reappraisal of Soviet policy by Mikhail Gorbachev. Furthermore, it was clear that the United States was still reluctant to intervene directly in the Third World. By the late 1980s in fact both the Soviet Union and the United States had, in effect, acknowledged, that the Third World was resistant to superpower control. In this area, as in so many others, the Reagan administration had reluctantly acknowledged the limits of American power.

CONCLUSION

Assessing the Reagan administration's defence policy is a formidable undertaking, partly because there is considerable disagreement about the impact of the administration's defence policy. On the one hand, it is possible to argue that it was eminently successful. Not only did the President restore American pride and prestige, but the defence policy provided the necessary support for a foreign policy towards the Soviet Union which was initially somewhat bellicose but which gradually became much more conciliatory. This, of course, was encouraged by the reform of Soviet domestic politics initiated by Mr Gorbachev. Yet the Reagan administration ascribed the new flexibility in Soviet policies to its own stance of negotiating from strength. This enabled it to respond positively to some of the overtures and help to establish what was effectively a renewed *détente* albeit by another name.

An alternative view of the defence policy is that it fell far short of the rhetoric. The gap between organisation and achievement was a large one, even if it was covered by the President's plans not only as a great illuminator but also as a great eliminator. If the 1970s was a decade of neglect – and this is an over-simplistic characterisation – the 1980s was a decade of profligacy and waste in defence spending. The defence budget was increased at a remarkable rate for the first five or six years of the Reagan era, but the increases in American military strength were certainly not commensurate with the budgetary increases. Indeed, some critics contended that the Reagan administration had gone on a defence binge, and had simply thrown money at problems without any sense of coherent strategic design.[38] The overall effect was to create a bloated defence establishment in which inefficiencies were magnified and in which there was enormous duplication, waste and corruption. In June 1988 it was disclosed that a two-year investigation had unearthed rampant bribery in defence procurement, with DOD employees providing information to defence contractors that gave them unfair advantage in competitive bidding for contracts.

A large part of the responsibility for the inefficiencies and other shortcomings of the defence acquisition process must be placed on Caspar Weinberger. Indeed, Weinberger's inability to formulate a coherent strategic rationale for the allocation of resources within defence, ensured that in spite of the largest military build-up in history, the Reagan administration did not bequeath to its successor a robust basis for continued growth in defence spending. Many of its decisions simply postponed difficult choices and magnified the traditional pattern of feast and famine in American defence spending.

The second point is that there were many tensions, ambiguities and paradoxes in Reagan's defence policy, some of which were never confronted fully let alone resolved. After the Scowcroft Report, for example, there were two competing rationales for strategic nuclear modernisation – one based on the primacy of warfighting considerations, the other more preoccupied with stability and more explicitly related to arms control. The irony is that although the administration's preference was for the M-X, the small and highly mobile Midgetman with far fewer warheads looked much more attractive under the kind of ceilings that seemed likely to emerge from START.

Another area of confusion was SDI, where the programme was bedevilled by lack of agreement over its ultimate purpose and scope and by uncertainty about what would happen after the Reagan presidency. Although SDI and deep cuts in strategic offensive forces were in a sense mutually reinforcing, it was not clear by 1988 whether the Reagan administration had come to accept nuclear deterrence or still wanted to move to defence dominance. Similarly the relationship between American strategic modernisation programmes on the one hand and the vision of a nuclear free world on the other was problematic to say the least. There was also a large gap between what the administration wanted and what it achieved. The desire for superiority was tempered by the difficulty of achieving it, concepts of primacy were moderated by the attractions of stability, grandiose aspirations were stifled by continued domestic constraints, and the language of confrontation was succeeded by superpower summitry and a new *détente*. The Reagan administration may have wanted revolutionary changes in US defence policy, but did not succeed in bringing about a revolution in either doctrines or programmes.

Yet at one level, US defence policy from 1981 to 1988 seemed to have been eminently successful. The rhetoric of the Reagan defence policy made the American public believe that the difficulties stemming from the decade of neglect had been overcome. Yet not only did the Reagan administration exaggerate the neglect of the 1970s but it also exaggerated the capacity of the United States in the 1980s to transcend the long-term constraints and limits on American power that had been evident during the 1970s. While this brought popularity and short-term acclamation, it should not obscure the fact that the Reagan administration presided over a decade of strategic confusion, managerial incompetence and a short-lived resurgence rather than a sustainable long-term defence programme.

Notes

1. D. Yankelovich and L. Kaagan, 'Assertive America', in W. Hyland (ed.), *The Reagan Foreign Policy*, A Foreign Affairs Reader (New York: Meridian for Council on Foreign Relations, 1987) p. 11.
2. W. W. Kaufmann, 'A Defense Agenda for Fiscal Years 1990–1994', in J. Steinbruner, *Restructuring American Foreign Policy* (Washington DC: Brookings Institution, 1987) p. 57.
3. H. Haftendorn, 'Toward a Reconstruction of American Strength: A New Era in the Claim to Global Leadership?'. in H. Haftendorn and J. Schissler (eds), *The Reagan Administration: A Reconstruction of American Strength* (Berlin: de Gruyter, 1988) p. 8.
4. The details on the budget are taken from Kaufmann, 'A Defense Agenda for Fiscal Years 1990–1994'.
5. Ibid., pp. 61–2.
6. The Maritime Strategy was given its definitive statement by Admiral Watkins, the Chief of Naval Operations, in a Special Supplement to the United States Naval Institute Proceedings of January 1986.

7. L. H. Holland and R. A. Hoover, *The M-X Decision: A New Direction in U.S. Weapons Procurement Policy* (Boulder: Westview Press, 1985) p. 95. The subsequent discussion rests heavily on this study.
8. Ibid., pp. 179–80.
9. Ibid., p. 219.
10. Ibid., p. 215.
11. R. J. Woolsey, 'The Politics of Vulnerability', *Foreign Affairs*, Vol. 62, No. 4, Spring 1984, pp. 805–19 at p. 810.
12. Ibid., p. 812.
13. *Report of the President's Commission on Strategic Forces* (Washington DC: Government Printing Office, April 1983), p. 8.
14. Ibid., p. 14.
15. Woolsey, 'The Politics of Vulnerability', p. 815.
16. The relevant part of the 23 March statement is reproduced in F. Long, D. Hafner and J. Boutwell (eds), *Weapons in Space* (New York: Norton, 1986) pp. 351–3.
17. K. Zimmerman, 'Decision in March: The Genesis of the "Star Wars" Speech and the Strategic Defense Initiative (SDI)', in Haftendorn and Schissler (eds), *The Reagan Administration*. See p. 149.
18. W. J. Broad, 'Reagan's "Star Wars" Bid: Many Ideas Converging', *New York Times*, 4 March 1985.
19. Zimmerman, 'Decision in March', p. 146.
20. Ibid., p. 153.
21. Ibid., p. 154.
22. Ibid., p. 157.
23. See D. L. Hafner, 'Assessing the President's Vision: the Fletcher, Miller and Hoffman Panels', in Long, Hafner and Boutwell (eds), *Weapons in Space*, p. 95.
24. Ibid.
25. Quoted in J. Newhouse, *The Nuclear Age* (London: Michael Joseph, 1989).
26. For a useful and succinct account of arms control in the first Reagan Administration see S. Talbott, *U.S.–Soviet Nuclear Arms Control: Where We Are and How We Got There*, Rand/UCLA Occasional Paper OPS–001 (Santa Monica: Rand Corporation, January 1985).
27. Newhouse, *The Nuclear Age*, p. 340.
28. Ibid., p. 342.
29. M. Staack, 'Farewell to SALT II', in Haftendorn and Schissler (eds), *The Reagan Administration*, pp. 199–200.
30. Ibid., p. 202.
31. Ibid., p. 212.
32. On this distinction see A. L. Horelick and E. L. Warner III, 'US Soviet Arms Control: The Next Phase', in *US Soviet Relations: The Next Phase* (Ithaca: Cornell University Press, 1986) pp. 225–56.
33. See C. Weinberger, 'U.S. Defense Strategy', in Hyland (ed.), *The Reagan Foreign Policy*, pp. 190–1.
34. Ibid., p. 191.
35. Ibid., p. 194.

36.   The Long Commission quoted in B. W. Jentleson, 'The Lebanon War and the Soviet-American Competition: Scope and Limits of Superpower Influence', in S. L. Speigel, M. A. Heller and J. Goldberg (eds), *The Soviet American Competition in the Middle East* (Lexington, Mass.: D. C. Heath, 1988).
37.   William Pfaff quoted in T. Zimmerman, 'The American Bombing of Libya: A Success for Coercive Diplomacy', *Survival*, Vol. 29, No. 3, May/June 1987, p. 197–8.
38.   R. Stubbing, 'The Defense Program: Buildup or Binge', *Foreign Affairs*, Vol. 63, No. 4, Spring 1985, pp. 848–72.

Part IV
The Legacy

11 The Reagan Legacy

Dilys M. Hill and Phil Williams

President Reagan in his final State of the Union address of January 1988 presented himself as a president who:

> at a critical moment in world history reclaimed and restored the American dream. Seven years ago, America was weak and freedom everywhere was under siege; today, America is strong and democracy everywhere is on the move.

In effect, Reagan was claiming that the modern presidency possessed real power and was genuinely relevant to people's lives and choices. That such a claim could be made – and believed – after the doubts and crises of the 1970s is both remarkable and of major political significance. The revitalisation of the presidency is crucial to the effective functioning of the American political system. As James Barber put it, if people are sceptical about the substantive power and relevancy of the presidency then the presidential system descends into symbolism. In these circumstances, the rampant pluralism inherent in American democracy becomes almost completely dominant. Barber stressed that: 'Take away the President's power and we the people may turn him into an entertainer, who, however seriously he may take himself, need not furrow our brows with real-world calculations'.[1] By revitalising the presidency Reagan avoided, or at least postponed such an eventuality.

The revitalised presidency, however, did not bring the radical recasting of American politics that Reagan had sought – the hoped-for revolution was incomplete. There was also the irony that the restoration of the presidency – which despite Irangate was undoubtedly one of Reagan's most considerable achievements – was accomplished largely through symbolic actions. The use of force, for example, in Grenada and Libya symbolised both a revitalised presidency and a regenerated United States.

In neither of these cases did American military forces face large-scale resistance. The Lebanon episode, which was rather less successful, was also a more typical example of the difficulties attendant upon the use of force and the continued question marks over domestic support for sustained military deployments. Nevertheless, it was one of Reagan's strongest attributes that, in addition to his successes, he was able to transcend the setbacks and failures of his policies. Reagan's strategy was to place himself above the detail, avoiding culpability while claiming credit for successes. The 'teflon' presidency survived both policy reversals and political gaffes and the real reckoning on the Iran–Contra affair was postponed beyond Reagan's incumbency. One of the major achievements of the Reagan administration must be the contribution which it made to the renewal of trust in American national government. The President's charisma – combining as it did Reagan's relaxed style, good humour, decisiveness and faith in the eternal verities with an ability to communicate a strong sense of pride in the nation – was the dominant factor in this process.[2]

Reagan was able to succeed in revitalising the presidency and regenerating the nation partly because he avoided the public pessimism and introspection engaged in by Jimmy Carter, and partly because of the skill displayed by top officials in what was sometimes termed 'spin control'. Yet Reagan's own role in this was of great importance. The President himself was masterly at limiting the damage to his presidency from policy failures and setbacks. He did this partly through his ability to change direction – even at the last minute – and then claim credit for being farsighted. His strategy was to 'declare victory' even when circumstances did not warrant it. The contrast with the Carter Administration was instructive. Because of poor public presentation of policy even Carter's victories were heralded as defeats, with the result that setbacks became self-perpetuating. The Reagan administration did the opposite and its initial successes created a mythology of effectiveness that helped give the President a political momentum that lasted until the mid-term elections of 1986.

Reagan's initial success in changing the terms of political debate, in advancing supply-side economics with the massive tax cuts of 1981, in demanding domestic expenditure cuts and an expanded defence budget, led commentators to praise his legislative leadership and to give him claims to being one of the twentieth century's great presidents. But the successes of 1981 were not repeated. Although Congress continued to support him, if on occasion rather grudgingly, in foreign and defence matters, it resisted the scale of domestic policy retrenchments and rejected measures to curtail school bussing, to allow prayer in schools and to limit federal support for abortion. In the second term, Reagan still achieved some of his major objectives, winning congressional support for the expansion of the M-X programme and for 'non-military' aid to Nicaraguan Contras. And, though the deficit continued to mount alarmingly, Reagan succeeded in what was defined as the major domestic policy objective of his second term, that of tax reform. As a result, David Mervin has concluded that Reagan's claim to have brought about non-incremental change and to have altered 'the terms of the debate' is a substantial one and places him alongside Truman, Eisenhower and Johnson as an effective and competent president.[3]

One area where this seems to be borne out is the shape of the judiciary. Reagan tried to influence the course of policy by his appointments to the Supreme Court and to the federal bench. He elevated the conservative William Rehnquist to Chief Justice, and appointed three right-wingers, Sandra Day O'Connor, the first woman Supreme Court Justice, Antonin Scalia and Anthony Kennedy, to the Court. But it is with the federal bench that Reagan's appointments were most influential. Reagan appointed close to half the judges in the lower federal courts in his two terms, and this will almost certainly have a significant long-term impact.[4] Indeed, the recasting of the federal judiciary on conservative lines may be one of the most long-lasting elements in the Reagan legacy.

In certain respects, however, the legacy of the two-term President was less positive and clear cut than all this suggests. The Reagan administration left behind not only a great deal of unfinished business and a series of incomplete programmes, but also an economic base that combined a number of positive trends and some highly disturbing features. In both domestic and foreign policy the Reagan administration had presented itself as revolutionary, yet it had succeeded only in bringing about incomplete revolutions, the ultimate success of which was uncertain to say the least.

The restoration of American pride and the regeneration of American power were major achievements of the Reagan administration. Yet both achievements had a certain fragility about them. Reagan had restored American military strength, but had not fully overcome the Vietnam syndrome, had failed to create a consensus in favour of continuing the high levels of military expenditure and had not really found an answer to the growing trend towards the vulnerability of land-based missiles. The Strategic Defence Initiative had begun with a sense of vision that was novel and exciting, but had become mired in disputes over the interpretation of the ABM Treaty and the appropriate level of funding, as well as uncertainty over the ultimate purpose of the deployment of strategic defences. At the end of 1988, there was a feeling that the notion of astrodome defence had been such a personal vision of President Reagan that it would not survive his departure from office. The programme was so ambitious and long term that even a two-term president, wholly committed to its implementation could do little more than start the process. Reagan had initiated a revolution in strategic concepts, but the revolution in physics that was required to transform concepts into reality remained elusive. Elsewhere, the Reagan legacy was equally ambitious. Reagan – along with Gorbachev – had changed the agenda of arms control so that the idea of deep cuts in strategic forces had become a focus of serious negotiation between the superpowers. Yet even here the INF Agreement had not been followed by a START Accord, and it was uncertain how much further the new agenda would be taken.

If Reagan was in some respects a revolutionary politician he also had an acute sense of the limits of the possible. The result was that some of his achievements arose not because he stuck to his initial principles and precepts but because he was willing to deviate from them, and take advantage of new opportunities as they appeared. The administration, however, was particularly good at rationalising its policies in ways which enabled it to avoid the appearance of inconsistency. The improvement of relations with the Soviet Union, for example, was justified with claims that it marked a success for negotiating from strength. Although this may have contributed to the Gorbachev reappraisal of Soviet foreign policy, the major impetus for this had actually come from domestic considerations, and in particular the need for a radical restructuring of the Soviet economy. Nevertheless, the Reagan claim was a useful and important legitimising device in American domestic politics, defusing opposition to a shift in policy that was anathema to many of Reagan's most hard-line supporters. The irony was that the more flexible policies of the second term – which ranged from the INF agreement with the Soviet Union to the readiness to trade arms for hostages in Iran – reflected the fact that the administration was, if only gradually and reluctantly, coming to terms with the limits of American power. The difficulty for the administration was a lack of congruence between the familiar rhetoric and the emerging policy realities. Yet the fact that Reagan had been so successful in reaffirming his hard-line credentials and in creating a new confidence ensured that the more moderate approach was accepted with little more than token challenge – and this from his erstwhile supporters on the right. They, of course, recognised that the revolution in foreign policy and national security was being abandoned in favour of policies that the President had once claimed to despise.

The other area where the Reagan administration failed to bring about a revolution was in electoral politics. The paradox about the Reagan presidency is that, even after two Reagan landslides, there was little evidence that millions of voters had shifted their identification and voting from the Democrats to the Republicans. At the beginning of the Reagan presidency it was believed that his personal appeal was so strong as to win him congressional and public support for his policies, even in areas where these were unpopular. In fact the public opinion polls at that time were saying something rather different: Reagan's rhetoric and aims were strongly in line with the national mood. Reagan did not lead public opinion, he portrayed it. And this convergence was not uniform or lasting. By 1984 it was clear that at national level it was middle-class confidence about the seeming victory over inflation which Reagan had achieved which ensured his reelection. But the overall electoral mood of 1984 shows a very different picture: it was the Democrats who came out of the elections controlling most city and county governments, state legislatures, two-thirds of the governorships, the House of Representatives (and were in 1986 to regain control of the Senate).

Reagan's second term saw a continuation of this paradoxical situation in which his personal popularity was high yet there was a lack of enthusiasm and support for his programmes. The polls consistently showed that, in opposition to Reagan's position, support for domestic social spending, including health care, education, aid to minorities and to cities, actually increased during his presidency. Similarly, public opinion continued to reject Reagan's policies on social issues such as abortion and state aid to private schools.[5]

It is clear, therefore, that the Reagan legacy in domestic matters is a mixed one. In spite of major changes in the basic approach to policy and the dramatic shift in taxation brought by the 1981 success in Congress, the Reagan presidency did not culminate in a realignment of public opinion nor an electoral shift, and the Republican party did not capture either the national Congress or make substantial gains in state legislatures.

Part of the reason for this was that the Reagan administration's management of the economy was far from being an unqualified success. This is not to deny that, on certain indicators, the performance of the American economy during the Reagan presidency was rather impressive. Over the years 1979 to 1988 there was an average 2.3 per cent annual growth rate in GDP, higher than that in Britain and the European Community, though lower than that in Japan. At the same time, however, America's population grew at 1.1 per cent a year compared with almost no growth in Europe, and the resulting growth per head was less than elsewhere. Inflation was below 5 per cent in 1988 and unemployment had fallen to around the 5 per cent level. Against this must be set a number of adverse factors: the major beneficiaries were those in the top half of the income distribution; the numbers in poverty increased sharply; private and public sector investment was low. The lesson of Reaganomics was a consumer boom, set against a background of low savings and payments deficits fuelled by the high interest rates used by the Federal Reserve in 1980–85 to stem the rise in the dollar. In the period of the Reagan presidency, the United States moved from being the world's largest net creditor to that of largest net debtor. Fears over the long-term impact of the trade deficit, with the undercurrent of a repeat of the Wall Street slide of 'Black Monday' in October 1987, appeared to have lessened at the end of 1988, but question marks remained over the value of the dollar and over consumer spending.

The economic legacy of President Reagan presented his successor with major problems, most notably that of the budget and trade deficits. In November 1988 the General Accounting Office (the independent, non-partisan and normally conservative federal agency) issued a series of reports which implicitly criticised the policy of the outgoing administration in what were seen as unprecedented terms. The reports said that the Bush administration would have to address many domestic problems neglected by the Reagan administration, rethink military commitments, strengthen Federal regulation of banks and stockbrokers, and provide new Federal incentives for private investment in low-rent housing (estimating that some 3 million people were homeless and that the numbers were rising). The reports also called for regulation of industries and activities deregulated under Reagan, particularly in transport, savings and loans institutions (nearly one-third of which were verging on insolvency) and hazardous waste disposal. It was also acknowledged that the costs of these necessary actions would be 'staggering'.[6] In view of all this, it is hardly surprising that some commentators were very critical in their assessments of the Reagan era, with one journalist describing the eight years of the Reagan administration as being 'as empty and vacuous and idle and purblind as the man who led it.'[7]

Yet such censure did little to diminish President Reagan's sustained belief in the effectiveness of his leadership and of his administrations. This was evident both in the words cited at the opening of this chapter and in the way in which Reagan laid blame for failures elsewhere. Reagan blamed 'special interests' and 'flawed' congressional budget procedures for the budget deficit rather than his own policies. Although this willingness to attribute responsibility for failure elsewhere was crass opportunism, it was also one of the strengths of the administration in that it helped Reagan to restore the American people's faith in themselves and in the presidency.

It is another irony that President Reagan benefited from the public mood almost as much as he formed it. Reagan provided reassurance after a prolonged period of national crisis and in return found that both press and public were relatively tolerant of his mistakes. Indeed, it became apparent during the Iran–Contra scandal that there was little desire on the part of the American public to see another weakening of the presidency. Consequently, there was a reluctance, even in Congress, to push the issue to a point where it might negate the gains in national confidence that had been achieved during Reagan's first six years in office. The country was in no mood for impeachment over Iran–Contra and the slow and complicated pace of the investigation, and the cessation of overt hostilities in the Iran–Iraq war, appeared to mitigate the feelings of his responsibility, however deniable in details, in Irangate. Although the administration's last two years in office were its most difficult years, therefore, they did not negate the gains that had been made in restoring the faith of the American public in the presidency.

The real legacy of the Reagan administration was mixed: an incomplete revolution in terms of policy given the failure of the new right to achieve its social agenda, the continued existence of the basic New Deal welfare state, and the failure of the 'New Federalism' proposals. But the legacy in terms of American confidence was very real. Although the depth, permanence and resilience of this new-found confidence remain uncertain, it is indisputable that 'Reagan restored a sense of normality after the social traumas of the 1960s, the economic chaos of the 1970s and the foreign policy disasters of both decades'.[8] This was a remarkable achievement – and if at least some of it was based on illusion, it was nevertheless as welcome as it was necessary.

Notes

1. J. D. Barber, *The Presidential Character*, 2nd edition (Englewood Cliffs, New Jersey: Prentice-Hall, 1977) p. v.
2. J. Citrin and D. P. Green, 'Presidential Leadership and the Resurgence of Trust in Government', *British Journal of Political Science*, Vol. 16(4), October 1986, pp. 431–53.
3. D. Mervin, 'The Competence of Ronald Reagan', *Parliamentary Affairs*, 1987, pp. 203–217.
4. D. M. O'Brien, 'The Reagan Judges: His Most Enduring Legacy?', in C. O. Jones (ed.), *The Reagan Legacy: Promise and Performance* (Chatham, New Jersey: Chatham House Publishers, 1988) p. 84.
5. S. M. Lipset, 'The Reagan Factor', *New Society*, 10 October 1986, pp. 17–19.
6. R. Pear, '*Reagan is Leaving* Many Costly Domestic Problems, the G.A.O. Tells Bush', *New York Times*, 22 November 1988.
7. S. Hoggart, *Observer*, 15 January 1989.
8. J. Cassidy, 'Revolutionary Flop but a Great Survivor', *Sunday Times*, 15 January 1989.

Index